CSS Web Design FOR DUMMIES®

by Richard Mansfield

WILEY

Wiley Publishing, Inc.

CSS Web Design For Dummies®

Published by
Wiley Publishing, Inc.
111 River Street
Hoboken, NJ 07030-5774

www.wiley.com

Copyright © 2005 by Wiley Publishing, Inc., Indianapolis, Indiana

Published by Wiley Publishing, Inc., Indianapolis, Indiana

Published simultaneously in Canada

For general information on our other products and services, please contact our Customer Care Department within the U.S. at 800-762-2974, outside the U.S. at 317-572-3993, or fax 317-572-4002.

For technical support, please visit www.wiley.com/techsupport.

Wiley also publishes its books in a variety of electronic formats. Some content that appears in print may not be available in electronic books.

Library of Congress Control Number: 2005920081

ISBN: 978-0-7645-8425-1

Manufactured in the United States of America

10 9 8 7 6 5 4

1O/QS/QT/QV/IN

WILEY

About the Author

Richard Mansfield was the editor of *COMPUTE!* Magazine from 1981 to 1987. During that time, he wrote hundreds of magazine articles and two columns. From 1987 to 1991, he was editorial director and partner at Signal Research. He began writing books full-time in 1991 and has written 36 computer books since 1982. Of those, four became bestsellers: *Machine Language for Beginners* (COMPUTE! Books), *The Second Book of Machine Language* (COMPUTE! Books), *The Visual Guide to Visual Basic* (Ventana), and *The Visual Basic Power Toolkit* (Ventana, coauthored by Evangelos Petroutsos). His books combined have sold more than 500,000 copies worldwide and have been translated into 12 languages.

Richard's recent titles include *Office 2003 Application Development All-in-One Desk Reference For Dummies, Visual Basic .NET All-in-One Desk Reference For Dummies, Visual Basic .NET Weekend Crash Course, Visual Basic .NET Database Programming For Dummies, Visual Basic 6 Database Programming For Dummies* (all published by Wiley), *Hacker Attack* (Sybex), and *The Wi-Fi Experience: Everyone's Guide to 802.11b Wireless Networking* (Pearson Education, coauthored by Harold Davis).

Dedication

This book is dedicated to David Lee Roach.

Author's Acknowledgments

I want to thank acquisitions editor Katie Feltman for her thoughtful and helpful advice. I've worked with Katie before, and she knows her stuff. I was also lucky to have two strong editors improve this book. Project editor Linda Morris asks the right questions, makes lots of good suggestions, and overall stands in as a representative of the reader. She requests clarification when necessary, and ensures that the reader will find consistent, useful information. She deserves credit for her taste and the high quality of her editing.

The technical editor, Vanessa Williams, reviewed the entire manuscript for technical quality. For that I thank her. I'm happy to report that she found few flaws in the programming code, but I'm certainly glad to have an opportunity to fix the few flaws she did spot. Vanessa also suggested alternative CSS techniques and additional resources, deepening the technical information available in the book.

To these, and all the other good people at Wiley who contributed to the book, my thanks for the time and care they took to ensure quality every step along the way to publication.

Publisher's Acknowledgments

We're proud of this book; please send us your comments through our online registration form located at www.dummies.com/register/.

Some of the people who helped bring this book to market include the following:

Acquisitions, Editorial, and Media Development

Project Editor: Linda Morris

Acquisitions Editor: Katie Feltman

Copy Editor: Linda Morris

Technical Editor: Vanessa Williams

Editorial Manager: Carol Sheehan

Media Development Manager:
Laura VanWinkle

Media Development Supervisor:
Richard Graves

Editorial Assistant: Amanda Foxworth

Cartoons: Rich Tennant
(www.the5thwave.com)

Composition Services

Project Coordinator: Adrienne Martinez

Layout and Graphics: Carl Byers, Andrea Dahl, Lauren Goddard, Joyce Haughey, Stephanie D. Jumper, Melanee Prendergast

Proofreaders: Leeann Harney, Jessica Kramer

Indexer: TECHBOOKS Production Services

Publishing and Editorial for Technology Dummies

Richard Swadley, Vice President and Executive Group Publisher

Andy Cummings, Vice President and Publisher

Mary Bednarek, Executive Acquisitions Director

Mary C. Corder, Editorial Director

Publishing for Consumer Dummies

Diane Graves Steele, Vice President and Publisher

Joyce Pepple, Acquisitions Director

Composition Services

Gerry Fahey, Vice President of Production Services

Debbie Stailey, Director of Composition Services

Contents at a Glance

Table of Contents

Introduction

*W*elcome to the world of Cascading Style Sheets (CSS). With CSS, you can design gorgeous and highly effective Web sites. CSS offers power and flexibility to Web site developers and designers. This book shows you how to use CSS to make your Web pages come alive.

Marketing experts like to say that the box helps sell the jewelry. CSS does several useful things, but one of the most important is to help you design much more attractive packages to hold your Web page contents.

Creating Compelling Designs

CSS allows you to separate presentation from content when building a Web site. Put another way, HTML itself is rather limited in what it can effectively display. It's fine for holding or describing *content* (such as a paragraph of text), but the appearance of raw HTML Web pages isn't very stylish (to put it kindly).

With HTML, you often can't find an easy way — or any way at all — to display the content so that it looks really good when someone views it in a browser. Using CSS techniques, you can often make your site much more attractive, and at the same time, enforce style rules that help unify the entire site's appearance across all its pages.

In this book, you find out how to wrap your online content in appealing visual designs using CSS, including special dramatic effects such as animated transitions between images or entire pages. Style sheets can provide striking, well-designed containers into which relatively plain HTML content is poured.

The best Web pages aren't merely efficient, logical, and stable — they also *look really cool*. The end result of employing CSS is a more attractive Web site with a more coherent, effective overall design.

Separating Content from Style

CSS also improves efficiency by allowing you to separate content from the styles that control the content's appearance. You can describe your CSS styles in the header section of a Web page — thereby moving them up and out of the HTML code. Or you can even put your CSS style rules in entirely separate files. A Web page's HTML resides in one file. It merely includes a link specifying the location of the independent CSS file that contains the style rules (how a Heading 1 headline or paragraph elements are supposed to look, where they're positioned, how big they are, what texture underlies them, and so on).

If you're a designer working on a Web page with a programmer, it's more efficient for you to separate your code from the programmer's HTML or script code. A designer can work on an external CSS style sheet, rather than wading through the programmer's HTML files and trying to manage style attributes embedded within the HTML code. The HTML programmer will appreciate this, and so will you, the CSS designer. No more stepping on each other's toes.

Of course, many Web sites are designed by a single person wearing many hats: HTML, script, and CSS can all be written by one talented individual. This book doesn't neglect that audience. Most of the CSS examples in this book are contained within HTML pages, demonstrating how the entire page works in harmony. You can just load the book's examples into your browser and see the delightful results immediately. An entire chapter is even devoted to scripting, so that you can get your feet wet with interactive dynamic CSS effects as well.

Benefiting from the Cascade

CSS offers various kinds of benefits. For example, a single style sheet can *cascade* its effects through all the pages in a Web site. One side of effect of this is that if you decide to change your site's default body font from Arial to Times New Roman, you need make that change only once within the style sheet, rather than hunting down all the attributes throughout the entire set of HTML code files that make up your site. Another benefit of using CSS is that the style sheet only needs to be downloaded once to the user's computer. Thereafter, it's called up from a local cache, resulting in smaller HTML pages. Your Web pages load faster into the user's browser — still a major consideration for the 60 percent or so of online Americans who still don't have broadband high-speed Internet connections.

If you've already worked with CSS, this book will sharpen your skills and show you lots of new techniques. You'll take your Web design to the next level. If you're new to CSS, you're in the right place: You'll find just what you need here to build unified, attractive, inviting Web sites.

This book shows you, the CSS designer, how best to exploit, expand, administer, and write code for Web pages. The book covers all the essentials of CSS, with many step-by-step examples showing how to manage the various elements of CSS, including:

- ✔ How to design Web pages without using tables
- ✔ Understanding CSS inheritance
- ✔ Best coding techniques
- ✔ Page elements (spacing, fonts, colors, and so on)
- ✔ Practical ways to integrate CSS into new or existing Web sites
- ✔ Syntax rules, properties, and values
- ✔ How CSS works together with HTML and scripting
- ✔ Embedded and external style sheets
- ✔ Advanced visual effects such as transitions
- ✔ Selectors and declarations
- ✔ The latest CSS3 features

The End of the Browser Wars

CSS has been available for several years, but, like DHTML (dynamic HTML for Web page animation effects), CSS languished because of the browser wars. Basically, Netscape's Navigator and Microsoft's Internet Explorer attempted to enforce different, proprietary standards. Now that Netscape is all but dead in the marketplace and standards have become relatively stable because of the dominance of Internet Explorer, CSS has become a major technology for the creation and design of first-rate Web sites. Some incompatibility issues still exist, but this book deals with them only occasionally. Why? Because often you need not write complex, workaround code to take into account an audience so small that, practically speaking, many Web pages simply ignore them.

That said, I realize that some designers are forced to deal with browser compatibility issues, so I do explore the topic in some depth in Chapter 17. You see how to detect which browser and version the user has and how to take appropriate steps to deal with it in your Web page code. I also tell you where to find the best compatibility charts online; how to see what your page looks like and test its behavior in non-compliant browsers; and how to automatically redirect a browser to a different Web page or Web site if that browser can't deal with your CSS code.

A few years ago, people were moving from Netscape to Internet Explorer, but a large percent of your Web site's audience was still using Netscape. You had to write CSS (and HTML and scripting) that worked effectively in both browsers.

That's simply no longer true. The migration is over; Netscape is merely a ghost wandering the halls of the computer history museums.

Most CSS books waste lots of space on compatibility issues. I've decided to greatly reduce coverage of that topic for precisely the same reason that today's newspapers infrequently devote space to the Gulf War of 1991. That war's over. Same with Netscape and the other, minor browsers like Opera that have a small user base. History and popular opinion has elected Internet Explorer (IE) as the standard — who are we to argue? One exception is Mozilla Firefox, which is coming out of left field and could eventually challenge Internet Explorer's dominance in the browser arena.

Firefox is an "open source" — in other words, "no charge" — piece of software. Of course, Internet Explorer is also sometimes described as free. True, it comes "free" with Windows, but as we all know, that's not precisely the same as *no charge*. You do buy Windows, and its browser is a feature of Windows that you get bundled into the operating system.

Another meaning of *open source* is that the code, the programming underlying the Firefox browser, is available to anyone. Lots of good programmers are writing interesting plug-ins and modifications that you can add to Firefox to give it new features.

Firefox is fast, sleek, and overall pretty stable. In fact, it's not under constant attack by hackers, as is IE. There are two reasons for this: not too many people are using Firefox (yet), so the payoff of using it to spread viruses is rather poor. Second, virus authors are frequently in sympathy with the ideals of the open source software community, and, shall we say, less inclined to appreciate Microsoft.

So, watch out, IE. Firefox, or something similar, could eventually gain market share and, possibly, eventually become the browser standard. But for now, more than 95 percent of browser users are looking at your Web page through IE, so you can generally ignore the problems that arise when you try to make your CSS code work with all possible browsers and all possible versions of those browsers. IE is likely to continue to dominate for at least the next few years.

Just relax and assume that your Web page visitors are either using IE, or are accustomed to the penalties for sticking with a fringe browser. But if you must face the compatibility issue, take a look at Chapter 17.

Who Should Read This Book

This book is designed to satisfy a broad audience, including both Web programmers and designers. The book shows how to exploit CSS by developing solutions to common Internet coding and Web-page design problems.

Programmers discover how to more effectively control browser elements in order to build Web clients that are as interactive and efficient as traditional Windows applications. Designers see how to create attractive, coherent Web sites. Beginners will find the book to be an effective tutorial introduction to CSS; experienced users will find it a useful, up-to-date reference.

For designers, would-be designers, programmers, and developers alike

The book is written for a broad audience: designers, would-be designers, programmers, developers, and even small office staff or individuals who want their Web pages to come alive. In other words, the book is valuable to everyone who wants to design more effective Web pages and do the work more efficiently.

The book shows how to exploit validators to ferret out errors in your code, and how to solve design problems using utilities, features, hidden shortcuts, and other CSS techniques.

The book is also for would-be designers who want to get involved in creating, customizing, or improving Web page design, but just don't know how to get started. Whether you want to sell cars, create a good-looking blog, or are interested in creating a great visual impression, you'll find what you need in this book. The book is filled with useful advice about design (what looks good, what looks bad, and what looks just plain boring). And you get plenty of practical, real-world CSS examples, including

- ✔ Following best design practices
- ✔ Managing text effectively
- ✔ Using the *rule of thirds* for effective overall page design
- ✔ Creating dynamic, animated effects such as fades and moving shadows

Making do in a shaky economy

No matter what they tell us from the bully pulpit, *we* know how shaky the economy is, don't we? The primary trend in nearly all industries today is toward making do with less: fewer workers, less time to complete tasks, and stretching resources as much as possible. This trend demands improved productivity. Some offices respond by letting some of the staff go and heaping additional work on the remaining employees. In many cases, a more successful long-term tactic is to improve the general efficiency of the staff, downsized or not.

CSS is loaded with features to improve productivity for Web page design and maintenance, *if* the designer knows how to exploit them. *CSS Web Design For Dummies* is the handbook that takes the reader from idea to finished site.

I hope that all my work exploring CSS benefits you, showing you many useful shortcuts and guiding you over the rough spots. I won't pull any punches: I confess when I had to wrestle with CSS or other code for several hours to accomplish something. But after I've put in the time getting it work, I can almost always show *you* how to do it in a few minutes. The example code is here in this book, ready to do what you need done.

Plain, Clear English

Also, unlike some other books about CSS (which must remain nameless — they know who they are!), this book is written in plain, clear English. Novices find many sophisticated tasks made easy: The book is filled with step-by-step examples that beginners can follow, even if they've never written a line of CSS or HTML, or designed a single Web page. And if you're an experienced CSS designer, better still. You'll find out how to accomplish sophisticated tasks quickly. You also discover how to harness the machinery built into CSS. You also find out how to leverage your current skills to prepare for the future of CSS programming: moving beyond CSS2 to CSS3.

How to Use This Book

This book concentrates on the currently accepted version of Cascading Style Sheets: CSS2. The next version, CSS3, is not scheduled to become official (translation: fully adopted by Internet Explorer) for several years. However, the CSS committees continue to meet, exchange e-mail, and accept suggestions from the likes of us. They also plan to roll out "modules" — parts of the CSS3 recommendation will appear occasionally for the next few years. If you want to experiment with some of the new stuff, download Mozilla Firefox and try some of the CSS3 code examples in Chapter 15. They won't work in Internet Explorer, as yet.

This book obviously can't cover every feature in HTML, scripting, and still do a good job with CSS itself. Yet these technologies intimately interact in the better, more dynamic, and engaging Web sites. CSS adds beauty and coherence to a site. HTML contains the content and organizes it into a tree structure. Scripting offers sophisticated interaction with the user, dramatic animated effects, and other benefits.

As you try the many step-by-step examples in this book, you'll become familiar with the most useful features of CSS and find many shortcuts and time-saving tricks — some that can take years to discover on your own. (Believe me, some of them have taken me years to stumble upon.) You also see how to exploit HTML and scripting in the context of CSS design. As you'll discover, it's fascinating to make these technologies stand together and kick high in the air as one, as if they were a single organism. Kinda like the Rockettes.

Many people think that HTML is impossibly difficult and that scripting (programming in the classic meaning of the term) is even more difficult. They don't have to be.

In fact, you find solutions in this book that you can simply copy. Just copy and paste a few lines of code, for example, to be able to automatically change your CSS styles *while the user is viewing your page in the browser.* In other words, you can, for instance, resize a paragraph if the user clicks on it. The paragraph's font-size style can *change* in response to events like a click. Or, you can set up a timer that makes things happen after a period of delay, or on regular intervals. This sort of thing amplifies your CSS designs and is worth adding to your bag of designer tricks.

This book tells you if a particular wheel has already been invented. It also shows you how to save time by using or modifying existing Web pages to fit your needs, instead of building new solutions from scratch. But if you're doing something totally original (congratulations!), this book also gives you step-by-step recipes for tackling all the CSS tasks from the ground up.

Foolish Assumptions

In writing this book, I had to make a few assumptions about you, dear reader. I assume that you know how to use a computer, its mouse, and other parts.

I also assume that you don't know much, if anything, about CSS programming. Perhaps most importantly, I assume that you don't want lots of theory or extraneous details. You just want to get Web design jobs done, not sit around listening to airy theory about complex selector inheritance and such. When a job can be done in CSS, I show you how. When you need to reach out to the more advanced scripts or HTML techniques, I show you that, too. Whatever it takes, the job gets done.

You *do* end up understanding all about inheritance and selectors and how they work. It's just that you don't have to sit through a lecture on the abstract philosophy underlying CSS behaviors. You'd fall asleep, believe me. Instead, you get practical advice, and all the necessary information you need to make progress toward your goals.

How This Book Is Organized

The overall goal of *CSS Web Design For Dummies* is to provide an enjoyable and understandable guide for the CSS designer. This book is accessible to people with little or no CSS experience.

The book is divided five parts. But just because the book is organized doesn't mean you have to be. You don't have to read the book in sequence from Chapter 1 to the end, just as you don't have to read a cookbook in sequence.

In fact, if you want to see what's coming up in CSS3, just go to Chapter 15 right away.

If you want to find out how to create well-designed Web pages without resorting to the traditional HTML tables to hang your elements on, just flip over to Chapter 12, which explains how to build pages using only CSS positioning features. You're not expected to know what's in Parts I or II to get results in Part III. Similarly, within each chapter, you can often scan the headings and jump right to the section covering the task that you want to accomplish. No need to read each chapter from start to finish. I've been careful to make all the examples and CSS code as self-contained as possible. Each of them works, too. They've been thoroughly tested.

All of the source code for all the examples in this book is downloadable from this book's Web site at www.dummies.com/go/csswebdesign.

The following sections give you a brief description of the book's five main parts.

Part 1: The ABCs of CSS

This first Part introduces CSS, explaining its purposes and fundamental nature. You see how common tasks are accomplished and find out all about the elements of CSS design. You also discover how CSS improves on HTML and find out how to build practical style sheets for real-world Web site solutions. You figure out how to think beyond HTML — putting together Web pages that have style and grace — all because of the added power that CSS gives a designer. Topics in this part include starting from scratch, migrating from HTML to CSS, understanding the meaning of the *cascade,* and getting your feet wet with the major building blocks of CSS behavior: selectors and inheritance. You also consider what kind of editor (if any) you might want to use to assist you in building CSS styles.

Part II: Looking Good with CSS

Part II begins with some practical exploration of the details of CSS design: how you position the pages various zones, conditional formatting, relative positioning, absolute and fixed elements, and stacking flow. You go on to see all about handling text: a refresher course for designers who need to brush up on classic fonts, weights, special effects, and good text design principles in general. This section also serves as a course in text display techniques for those new to the subject. All the essentials are covered, from simple concepts such as font size, to advanced subjects like the uses of the various font families (and why you should avoid some of them like the plagues that they are). This book also covers the kinds of *values* you can provide to CSS properties, like color and position. You explore the units of length and measurement, color values, percentages, and related positioning and sizing specs. Part II concludes with a chapter where you play around with some great designer secrets: kerning, leading, custom backgrounds, adding textures, and using graphics applications to improve the quality of some of your page elements. In general, you find out how to achieve striking, compelling design and how to manage something equally important: avoiding vulgarity in your designs.

Part III: Adding Artistry: Design and Composition with CSS

Part III picks up and expands the topics that concluded Part II: how to make beautiful Web pages using CSS. You consider the elements of good page composition, the secrets of Web design gurus, and the issues involving symmetry. (Is severely symmetrical layout *ever* a good idea, outside of debutante-ball and wedding invitations?) You also find out how to take a new look at your overall design, abstracting the shapes so that you're not reading any text or viewing any photos. Instead, you're looking at the black, white, and gray rectangles (and hopefully other shapes) that compose your page.

In this Part, you go on to manipulate margins, padding, borders, lines, and frames. These elements allow you to build effective zones within your page, cuing the viewer about the nature of each zone and collecting related information inside separate zones. For example, a caption and the photo it describes can be considered a logical zone, so you might want to frame them, or use a line beneath them, or add some margins around them.

This Part also explores the best way to display tables and lists and how to get rid of tables that are not displayed. (Traditionally, tables have been used as hooks on which to hang the other elements of a Web page, allowing designers to position things. Now, you can get that job done better with pure CSS.)

Part III concludes with some cool transition effects. You see how to gently fade in some text or graphics. (You've seen the effect on the better-designed Web pages: One element gradually grows dim as a second element underneath it becomes visible.) You also discover other special effects like those seen in movies and TV. Do you want to add some of these animations and transitions to your own pages? You can.

Part IV: Advanced CSS Techniques

Part IV focuses on various sophisticated techniques for those of you who have mastered the CSS basics, beginning with an exploration of the ways that CSS styles cascade, the tree structure, and inheritance in general. You also discover the latest cutting-edge selectors, pseudo-elements (they're not as *pseudo* as they might seem), and how CSS3 will redefine the way CSS behaves.

You find out how to employ *scripting,* which for many designers is their first exposure to true computer programming. True, any time you communicate with a computer (CSS included), you're using a computer language and, in a technical sense, programming. But scripting is hard-core programming. You can tell the Web page to do pretty much *anything* you want it to do with scripts. You learn about dynamic code (changing CSS properties and styles while your page is in the user's browser), timers, animation techniques, toggling, and other cool effects possible only via scripts.

You need not go on to *become* a script programmer, however, to put these effects into your Web pages. You can just copy and paste — monkey see, monkey do fashion — and the scripts do their jobs just as well as if you knew what you were doing. Part IV concludes with how to fix ailing CSS and HTML code. Called *validating, parsing,* or more accurately, *debugging,* you find out the best way to track down and repair Web pages that misbehave and don't do what you want them to do.

Part V: The Part of Tens

This is the smallest Part in the book, but it's moist and succulent. It includes various tips, tricks, techniques, and topics that I wanted to include in the book but didn't quite find a perfect place for elsewhere.

Sure, it's a grab-bag — I'm not hiding that fact — but you might find the just tip you've been looking for here. The topics include a utility that you can use to understand complex CSS selectors (it translates complicated CSS code into ordinary English); how to avoid common CSS coding errors; a browser-independent way to center headlines, text, or graphics; fixing script problems; some of the best CSS online resources, including a site that offers excellent, understandable tutorials on the more baffling aspects of advanced CSS coding; an explanation of why you should consider using Visual Studio as a CSS editor; an online site that specializes in ways to use CSS to build columns into your pages; and more. Each tip was chosen for its succulence.

Conventions Used in This Book

This book is filled with examples that serve as recipes to help you cook up finished CSS Web pages. Some of these examples are in the form of numbered steps. Each step starts off with a boldface sentence or two telling you what you should do. Directly after the bold step, you may see a sentence or two, not in boldface, telling you what happens as a result of the bold action — a menu opens, a dialog box pops up, a wizard appears, you win the lottery, whatever.

I've tried to make the examples as general as possible, but at the same time make them specific, too. Sounds impossible, doesn't it? Sometimes it was; in other cases, it wasn't easy. The idea is to give you a specific example that you can follow while also giving you a template: an understandable, useful technique that you can apply directly to your own Web pages. In other words, I want to illustrate a technique, but in a way that employs real-world, useful CSS.

Special symbols

Note that a special symbol shows you how to navigate menus. For example, when you see "Choose File⇨Save As," you should select the File menu, and then select the Save As submenu.

When I display programming code, you see it in a typeface that looks like this:

```
<style>

#pfirst {

font-size: 8px;
width: 400px;

}

</style>
```

Parts of the code that are important to the topic under discussion are in boldface, like the font-size property in this code. When I mention some programming code within a regular paragraph of text, I use a special typeface, like this: width: 400px;. That way, you can easily distinguish programming code from ordinary text.

Avoid typos: find all the code online

Every line of code that you see in this book is also available for downloading from the Dummies Web site at

```
www.dummies.com/go/csswebdesign
```

Take advantage of this handy electronic version of the code by downloading it from the Web site so that you can then just copy and paste source code instead of typing it in by hand. It saves you lots of time and of course avoids those pesky typos.

What you need to get started

To use this book to the fullest, you need only one thing: a PC running Windows. To test and modify the CSS and HTML Web page code that illustrates this book's various examples, you merely need Windows Notepad and Internet Explorer. Both come with Windows, so you're home-free. I mainly use Internet Explorer to demonstrate and test the CSS-driven Web page examples throughout the book. Some examples — notably those that use dynamic filters and transitions in Chapters 13 and 16 — work only in Internet Explorer. However, I also briefly employ Mozilla Firefox, which is free for the downloading and doesn't cause any side-effects when run on the same computer as Internet Explorer. Go ahead and install Firefox if you want to try it out.

Icons used in this book

Notice the lovely, eye-catching little icons in the margins of this book. They're next to certain paragraphs to emphasize that special information appears. Here is what the icons mean:

The Tip icon points you to shortcuts and insights that save you time and trouble. This is the icon I use most of the time.

A Warning icon aims to steer you away from danger. It's used only once or twice because CSS has yet to be *proven* to cause suicide in lab rats.

A Technical Stuff icon highlights nerdy technical discussions that you can skip if you want to. I've used it sparingly — I'm not too fond of unnecessary technical stuff.

Part I
The ABCs of CSS

The 5th Wave   By Rich Tennant

In this part . . .

Using CSS to create effective, gorgeous Web page designs doesn't have to be a tough job. If you've been working with CSS but remain a bit baffled by it, or if you're trying it for the first time, you've chosen the right book.

Been confused by blizzards of new concepts: selectors, inheritance, specificity, tree diagrams, embedded rules, and plagues of locusts? Been turned off by books that make almost everything seem hard to understand? Part I of this book drops you gently into the world of CSS and ensures that you have a good, solid understanding of what CSS is, how it works, and all the great things you can do with it.

CSS offers the Web designer a variety of techniques that are highly effective and, in most cases, very easy to understand and use. I tell you which techniques aren't useful and should be avoided. I also demonstrate how to use the majority, which *are* useful.

Chapter 1

CSS Fulfills a Promise

• •

• •

*U*nderneath all Web pages is good old HTML, the markup language that controls things such as font sizes and color of text, where an image goes, and info about other elements of the page. HTML is sometimes called *plain* HTML, to distinguish it from Web pages built with more sophisticated techniques such as style sheets. And *plain* is sure a good word for HTML.

Without help, HTML often produces truly boring pages. Just as unpleasant as the lackluster pages it produces is the jumble of HTML code that results from trying to describe an entire Web page using HTML alone. Style sheets to the rescue.

Improving HTML

CSS (Cascading Style Sheets) was a technology recommended by the World Wide Web Consortium (W3C) in 1996. An easy way to understand the purpose of CSS is to view it as an addition to HTML that helps simplify and improve Web page design. In fact, some CSS effects are not possible via HTML alone.

Another advantage of CSS is that it allows you to specify a style once, but the browser can apply that style many times in a document. For example, if you want some of the pictures displayed in your Web site to have a thin, blue frame around them, you can define this frame as a style in your CSS. Then, instead of having to repeat an HTML definition of the thin and blue frame — each and every time you want that particular frame — you can merely insert the CSS style as an attribute for each graphic element that you want framed.

Put another way, you use CSS to define general rules about how the elements in your Web pages behave and how they look — where they're located, their size, their opacity, and so on. Then you can merely refer to the rule's name whenever you want to enforce it within your HTML page.

Here's a CSS rule that defines a couple of qualities you decide to apply to your largest headlines, H1:

```
<style>
H1 { font-size:16pt color:blue;}
</style>
```

With this CSS rule in effect, any HTML code containing an H1 element is automatically rendered in 16-point type and colored blue:

```
<html>
    <body>
        <h1>this headline is blue and 16 pt.</h1>
    </body>
</html>
```

CSS rules can be defined in a separate .css file or embedded within the HTML file. Here's the CSS headline style rule embedded within the header of an HTML file:

```
<html>
    <head>
        <style>
h1 { font-size:16pt color:blue;}
        </style>
    </head>
    <body>
        <h1>this headline is blue and 16 pt.</h1>
    </body>
</html>
```

Notice the `<style>` element. You can define your CSS styles inside this element. (You can also have multiple `<style>` elements on a page if you wish.)

For efficiency, nearly all the CSS code for the examples in this book is put right in the HTML document, within a `<style>` element, as in the preceding code. This makes saving the entire example — CSS plus HTML — as an .htm file easier. Just double-click the file in Windows Explorer to automatically load the example into Internet Explorer to see it work. However, in your own work, you're likely to put CSS in its own separate file, and then use the `<link>` element in the HTML document to import the CSS. You can put CSS styles in three places: an external file (with .css as the file extension); in the HTML file within the header section inside a `<style>` element; or even inside an HTML element, using the `style=` attribute. More on these issues in Chapter 3.

Getting Efficient with CSS

Defining a style in one location as CSS does has several advantages. First, it eliminates redundancy: You don't have to keep specifying its font size and color each time you use the <h1> tag in your document, for example. That makes Web page code easier to read and to modify later. If you're familiar with computer programming, think of a simple CSS style rule as something like a programming language *constant*: You specify, for example, the local tax rate by making up a name such as LocalTax, and then assigning a value to it like this: Constant LocalTax = .07. Thereafter, throughout your program, you don't need to repeatedly specify the .07. You merely use the constant's name LocalTax.

Similarly, after you've defined a CSS headline style, you can thereafter merely use the class name for that style, no matter how lengthy and complex that style might be. In this example, you use no class name, so every H1 headline is rendered with this style:

```
        <style>
h1 { font-size:16pt color:blue;}
        </style>
```

A second advantage of gathering all style definitions into a single location is that you can more easily make global changes. What if you decided to change all the H1 headlines to red instead of blue? If you didn't use a style sheet, you would have to search for all H1 elements throughout the entire Web site's HTML files and modify each of those elements in turn.

But if you had the foresight to use a style sheet, you need only change the *single* definition of the style for H1 in the style sheet itself. The specs are automatically applied throughout the HTML. In other words, just make this change from blue to red in the style sheet:

```
H1 { font-size:16pt color:red;}
```

All the headlines between the <h1> and </h1> tags throughout the entire Web site are now displayed as red text.

Changing Web design for the better

HTML originally was designed to work something like an outline, specifying the *structure* of a document, without too much attention paid to the actual *visual style*, or design, of the document. An outline merely organizes ideas hierarchically: A, B, C, and so on are the major ideas. Within those categories, you have subdivisions such as 1, 2, 3, 4 and even lower divisions such as a, b, c, d and so on. The equivalent outline structure in HTML is described with various headline levels such as H1, H2, H3, and so on.

HTML was supposed to simply define content: This is body text, this is a headline, this is a table, and so on. But Web designers naturally wanted to offer ever more compelling, visually attractive Web pages. After all, the Internet more often competes with lively television ads than with dry, highly structured, academic journals. HTML began to grow willy-nilly by adding many special formatting elements and attributes such as italics and color. This inflation of tags made creating, reading, and modifying HTML increasingly cumbersome. Separating the content (structure) from the page's design and layout became necessary. Enter CSS. When you use CSS, the HTML is left to primarily handle the structure and the CSS file contains the styles defining how the HTML elements look.

Also, CSS also offers the Web page designer features unavailable in plain HTML. And as you'll see throughout this book, CSS gives a designer much greater control over the appearance of a Web page.

Being ready for anything

Of course, you'll never have *absolute* control over Web pages if you create sites for the Internet. There will never be a truly stable, single, predictable display for Web pages. Why? Because, like some celebrities, a Web page never knows where it's going to end up from minute to minute. It has to be prepared to be on display in all kinds of situations.

A Web page might be shown on a Pocket PC PDA screen — with very few pixels and in black and white. Or it might be shown on the huge Diamond Vision display in Hong Kong, which is longer than a Boeing 747, or even the Jumbotron screen in Toronto's Skydome, which measures 110 feet wide by 33 feet tall.

Not only do you have to consider huge differences in size, but also in *aspect ratio* (shape). Many computer monitors are still the traditional square shape, but increasingly Internet users are switching to widescreen monitors — wider than they are high, like a movie screen — to better display HDTV and DVDs. For Internet users, widescreen just means you see more horizontal information per page. Web pages designed with absolute (unchanging) positioning leave several inches of empty white space along the right side of a widescreen monitor. What would Vincent do?

How would van Gogh have dealt with the problem of designing a picture of a vase of sunflowers that might be shown on a widescreen Jumbotron, but also on a little square monitor?

The basic solution to this problem is to specify size and position in *relative* rather than absolute terms. For example, instead of saying, "The sunflower is 2 inches high and is located 12 inches from the left side," (an *absolute* specification), you say, "The sunflower is 6 percent large and 35 percent from the left side" (*a relative specification*). Other ways of specifying sizes relatively include *pixels* (which are the smallest units of information that a given monitor can display, so they vary from monitor to monitor) or such general terms as *x-large* or *large*.

Alert readers might be asking at this point, "Six percent of what?" The percentage is calculated based on the *containing block*. It can be the browser window (`<body>`), but it can also be such blocks as a `<div>` within the `<body>`. In this example, the containing block is the total size of the browser, but you can also specify percentage for other, smaller, containers within the browser window. More on this issue in Chapter 4.

Relative specs translate well into various sizes of displays. A sunflower 6 percent large would be displayed with about 48 pixels on an 800x600 computer monitor, but displayed 18 feet wide on a Jumbotron that's 300 feet wide.

In other words — when you specify *relative* measurements or positions — your graphics or text are automatically *scaled* as necessary to fit whatever size display is being used at the time.

Of course, if you're building pages for an *intranet* site, you might well know that everyone in your office network is required to use the same size screen, the same browser, the same operating system, and allowed no family photos in their cubicle. If that's the case, why are you working for a fascist organization? Just kidding. In those situations where uniformity is enforced across the entire company, you *can* provide absolute specifications, but such situations are relatively rare.

To play devil's advocate here, I would advise that you not worry yourself *too* much about how your Web pages look on various devices. I realize that most books on CSS — and certainly the theorists and committees that wrestle with CSS standards — are very troubled by "browser independence." They want CSS styles to not only be scalable (stretch or shrink to fit various screen sizes), but to also display your page designs, colors, and other effects *the same way on different browsers and even all the old versions of all those browsers*.

One big problem with this theory is that when you try to put browser- and device-independence into practice, you're often forced to accept the lowest common denominator. In my view, you should design Web pages for Internet Explorer (IE) version 6 running on a typical 17" monitor. Why? Here are the reasons:

✔ More than 95 percent of the people visiting your Web site use IE 6.

✔ You can take advantage of lots of cool effects that work only in IE or IE 6.

> ✔ Your job is much easier if you're designing for a predictable, stable canvas.
>
> ✔ A design that works equally well on a PDA screen and a computer monitor is rare indeed, and many more users access your Web pages with a desktop computer than a PDA.

True, several years ago, Internet users were divided between Netscape and IE, so you had to take Netscape and its peculiarities into account. No more. At least for now, the browser wars are over, and Netscape is merely a small, marginal player these days.

Designers Want to Design

It's not surprising that designers, not to mention marketing people, want to build attractive Web pages. Color, transition effects, and even various kinds of animation and other special effects are all desirable attributes and, designers say, necessary goals in a competitive world.

Designers have worked for years with feature-rich image manipulation tools such as Photoshop and powerful page design tools such as PageMaker. In the early years of the World Wide Web, designers saw no reason why they shouldn't be able to manipulate Web pages with the same freedom. True, animation adds considerable complexity, and there's always the possibility of future multi-platform conflicts for Web design, requiring that you sometimes design for more than one platform.

But regardless of the daunting obstacles, the goal remains to make Web sites as compelling, entertaining, and beautiful as possible. CSS is clearly a step in the right direction. Designing for a predictable target platform such as Internet Explorer 6 makes design far easier, and the results far more attractive.

With CSS, a designer can accomplish many things that are either difficult or impossible using ordinary HTML. For example, just a few of the tasks you can accomplish via CSS are:

✔ Customizing text indention

✔ Creating fades, dissolves, and other transitions between pages

✔ Gaining additional control over formatting, such as adding frames around blocks of text

✔ Precisely positioning or tiling background graphics

✔ Being highly specific about point size and other measurement units such inches when describing the size and position of graphics or text

Understanding the digital effect

Those of us who work within the digital domain are just beginning to realize what a profound difference digitization makes. A digital camera memorizes a mathematical pattern of pixels. With film, you can manipulate the picture only grossly — with techniques such as over exposure, solarization, scratching it with a knife, cutting and pasting, or superimposing two negatives. These and other *analog* effects are extremely crude compared to digital effects. Digital manipulation can be as complete, as subtle, and as refined as reality itself. You've doubtless seen those short animations where one object transforms into another — a boy into a girl, an ostrich into a Buick, and so on. This illustrates the total manipulability of digital information. Given that you can easily control *every pixel* in a digital photo, you can transform anything into anything else. What's more, you have the ability to modify an image infinitely.

It's no longer a world of compromises, with less-than-special effects like Claymation, stop-frame, scale models, and so on. These have become quaint historical techniques.

It is no longer a matter of whether you do something on screen: It's just a matter of how much it costs and how long it takes. New cartoons like *The Polar Express* and *Finding Nemo*

demonstrate that digital effects are increasingly easy to achieve.

Artists are now getting control over the auditory (music) and visual realms (movies and photos) that publishers got over the typographic realm when Guttenberg invented moveable type. No longer must things be done clumsily by hand, like monks lettering and designing pages of the Bible, one Bible at time. Instead, with digital effects, you can, for example, effectively add a shadow to a visual element by merely selecting the object and then clicking a button to add a semi-transparent shadow. What makes all this so easy is that *every tiny dot* in the photo is represented as a set of numbers. And numbers, unlike film negatives, can be endlessly and precisely manipulated in *any way*. Adding a shadow is a matter of figuring out the mathematical function that adjusts pixels to make them look shadowed. This, and countless other visual functions, has been worked out by the people who developed Photoshop and other graphics applications. (One approach is to have the computer analyze a real shadow to see its mathematical gradient and other qualities.) So, if you have a particular background effect in mind for your Web page, you can achieve it — if you have the experience and skill to go about digital manipulation.

✔ Managing margins effectively

✔ Manipulating with great precision character and word spacing, in addition to kerning (adjusting the spacing between lines of text), leading (space between lines), and justification

✔ Providing unique navigation tools for the user

✔ Specifying the z-axis (what is "on top") for layers of text and graphics

Where CSS Fits with the Tools You Already Use

You can write a style sheet using any plain text editor, such as Notepad. However, you can also use specialized CSS editors that offer shortcuts to the creation of a style sheet. With editors like Microsoft's Visual Studio or TopStyle Pro from Magia Internet Studio, you can, for example, choose a text color from a palette, drag and drop a graphic from a toolbox, or select a font size from a list. Then the editor automatically translates your choices (generally made by dragging and dropping or clicking with the mouse) into the text descriptions that make up a style sheet. For such activities as moving page elements around to find the most attractive layout, mouse dragging can be a real time-saver.

If you open a CSS file, and you've been using Microsoft's Visual Studio on your computer, by default, the CSS is displayed in Visual Studio, as shown in Figure 1-1.

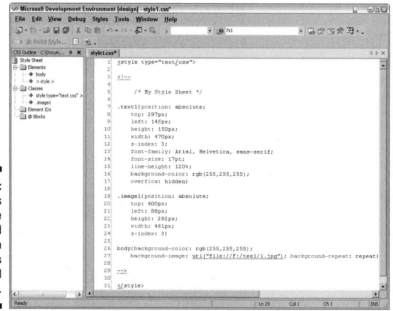

Figure 1-1: CSS files can be managed within Microsoft's Visual Studio.

Many Web programmers use Visual Studio and its ASP.NET features to create richly interactive Web sites. But artists and designers can also use Visual Studio to create CSS files. As you see in Figure 1-1, this style sheet specifies a text box, an image, and a background image. On the left is an abstract view (an "outline") of the style sheet; on the right is the actual, editable code. If you want to add some more style definitions, nothing could be simpler. You *don't have to write the code yourself*. Just click the Build Style button and the Style Builder dialog box opens, as shown in Figure 1-2:

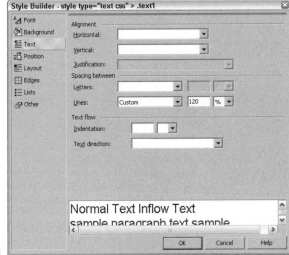

Figure 1-2: Create new styles the easy way, with Style Builder, a feature of Visual Studio.

Click any of the categories on the left — such as Background, Position, or Lists — and you see a new dialog box with additional options.

To start from scratch and create a brand-new style sheet, choose File➪ New➪File and double-click the Style Sheet icon.

To create a new style by associating it with an existing HTML element such as <h2>, choose Styles➪Add Style Rule. The Add Style Rule dialog box opens, as shown in Figure 1-3:

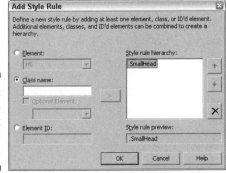

Figure 1-3: Use this dialog box to introduce new styles.

Remember that when you add CSS to your Web design bag of tricks, you don't simply abandon HTML. Instead, CSS allows you to modify HTML's tags. In some cases, however, you might find that you want to use some of CSS's features rather than the traditional HTML. For instance, many people think it's better to use CSS positioning tools rather than relying so heavily on tables like classic HTML. Similarly, you might decide to abandon the venerable HTML `<font>` tag in favor of the more powerful and refined text descriptors available in CSS.

Above all, don't be intimidated. CSS is not conceptually difficult, nor is it hard to use in practice.

Getting Practical

Perhaps the single biggest leap of faith that Web page designers must make is to *think beyond HTML* when using style sheets. Many computer programs support HTML — even Office 2003 applications such as Word have Web Page Preview and Save As Web Page options on their File menus. But with CSS, you need to augment your current Web page design habits and tools into a bit of abstract thinking. Academics would say that CSS is primarily a system that allows you to define abstract classes that can be applied with practical results in Web page design. I say that CSS makes design easier.

Look for CSS features in your current software

Doubtless you've used at least one application to build HTML that ends up as a Web page. If you're comfortable with a particular Web page design tool, go ahead and continue using it. But check to see if there are any features in your current software that support CSS. Search the product's Help Index for CSS — possibly you've never noticed a CSS tool sitting right there all the time.

Resources on the Web

As an alternative, you can use popular programming editors like Visual Studio, or dedicated CSS editors, to analyze existing Web pages and abstract CSS style sheets from them — or build a CSS file from scratch. If you don't yet have access to any CSS tools, take a look at the following tip:

You can find many CSS designer tools — some for free — on the Internet. Check out the list of CSS authoring tools at this W3C Web site: www.w3.org/ Style/CSS/. On the topic of CSS Resources, you can often find useful answers to your questions about CSS at this newsgroup: comp.infosystems.www. authoring.stylesheets.

Of course, there's always Microsoft's Web site. At the time of this writing, Microsoft's main CSS index at this address: `http://msdn.microsoft.com/ library/default.asp?url=/library/en-us/vsintro7/html/vxtsk WorkingWithHTMLStyles.asp`. However, Microsoft rarely retains a name or address for its technologies and documentation for long. So you'll likely need to look for CSS using the Search feature on the main Microsoft Web page at `www.microsoft.com`.

Also, considerable information (although somewhat stiffly, academically presented) is available at the Web Style Sheets home page sponsored by W3C at `http://www.w3.org/Style`.

Finally, take a look at Chapter 19, where several additional online CSS resources are described.

Avoiding Browser Compatibility Problems

Early Web page designers faced a peculiar problem: Different Web browsers interpreted HTML in different ways. In those early days, Netscape was still widely used. Fortunately — at least for Web designers — today, more than 95 percent of the people visiting Web sites use Internet Explorer (IE). What's more, most of them can be expected to use a recent version of IE. This makes a designer's life easier. You can expect that most people will see your Web pages as you intend them to be seen — as long as you stick to the specifications and capabilities of the current version of IE.

Many books on CSS spend quite a bit of time listing and describing the incompatibilities between Netscape and Internet Explorer — demonstrating the differing ways that these browsers implement CSS features. Another potential source of incompatibility derives from the differences between operating systems, namely PC and Mac.

But consider the worst case: What happens if a CSS feature is used in your Web page code, but it isn't supported by a user's browser or OS? Nothing happens. Unlike programming languages — with their often baffling error messages that can scare users — browsers are designed to hide problems from their users. The user never sees an error message saying: "This CSS style is unsupported by Netscape." Instead, whatever special effect you were trying to achieve by redefining an HTML element with CSS is simply ignored. If you had redefined `<h1>` as a blue headline, that redefinition is ignored and the default black is just used instead. If CSS is controlling positioning, however, the results can be less benign. But, again, the damage is limited to those few people not using IE.

Browser compatibility isn't nearly as much of an issue now as it was a few years ago when Netscape was more popular. And Mac computers, too, represent a small portion of today's computer market. Fair or not, the browser wars and the OS wars have settled into at least a temporary truce — and Web designers can benefit from the single primary platform they can build for.

Nonetheless, some Web site designers *must* wrestle with the compatibility problem. If the issue concerns you, take a look at Chapter 17, where I discuss various strategies you can employ to at least minimize — if not prevent — the damage done to your great designs by minor or simply out-of-date browsers.

Getting Dramatic with Filters

To give you a taste of how effective and powerful special browser effects can be, take a look at a few filters you can add to your Web pages. *Filters* are a set of special animated effects that Microsoft built into Internet Explorer.

Type this into Notepad or your choice of CSS editor:

```
<html>
<head>

<style>

div.box {width: 300px; height: 200px; padding: 30px;
         font: 46pt times new roman;}
</style>

</head>
<body>

<div class="box" style=" filter:
         progid:DXImageTransform.Microsoft.Alpha

(Opacity=100,
FinishOpacity=0, Style=1, StartX=0, FinishX=0, StartY=0,
FinishY=100)">

Hey...you can modify opacity.</div>


</body>
</html>
```

Now save it to a file named opac.htm, and then double-click on that filename in Windows Explorer. Your Internet Explorer window should open, displaying the text with its opacity adjusted from 0 (can't see through it at all) to 100 (can see through it completely), as shown in Figure 1-4.

Figure 1-4:
You can
adjust
opacity
to suit
yourself by
applying a
CSS style.

Notice in Figure 1-4 that a gradient is created, gradually fading the text. In effect, what's happening here is that the background (by default white) is simply showing through more and more because the text is increasingly transparent.

So what, you might say? I can get the same effect by writing some text in a graphics program like Photoshop, and then applying an opacity gradient. I can then save this text as a graphic file and just import it into my Web page as an image. Sure, you can do that. But creating a CSS style to accomplish the same thing has several advantages. You can apply that style easily to any additional text blocks in your Web site by merely using additional <div> tags. What's more, with a little extra programming, you can cause these kinds of effects to become animated — to be dynamic. For instance, you could use the opacity filter to fade some text, or a graphic, slowly in or out of the page. You could allow items to gently fade in or out in response to something the user does with the mouse. Or how about having entire sections or pages fade relatively rapidly as a transition effect to the next section or page? Lots of cool effects can be achieved when you add a little scripting and some timers to various filters.

Sure, filters are only built into Internet Explorer (version 4 and later). And, technically, they're not exclusively a CSS effect — although CSS does make using them easier. But so what? Filters are increasingly being used by Web page designers as a way of competing with television. Just as adding color was a real improvement over black and white Web pages, so, too, is animation a significant improvement over static pages.

Try a new trick. To create a different gradient — a circular one this time — just make two little changes to your HTML code (shown in boldface). You want to change the opacity `style` attribute from 1 to 2 (this changes the gradient to a circular effect), and provide a color background so you can more easily see the circular radiation of the gradient:

```
<html>
<head>

<style>

div.box {width: 300px; height: 200px; padding: 30px;
        font: 46pt times new roman;}
</style>

</head>
<body>

<div class="box" style="background: green; filter:
        progid:DXImageTransform.Microsoft.Alpha

(Opacity=100,
FinishOpacity=0, Style=2, StartX=0, FinishX=0, StartY=0,
FinishY=100)">

Hey...you can modify opacity.</div>


</body>
</html>
```

Save this HTML to an .htm file, and then double-click it in Windows Explorer to load it into IE. You see that the gradient has become circular, as shown in Figure 1-5.

You'll find lots of special effects you can employ built into IE, several of which you explore in Chapter 13. There are shadows, inversions, reversions, conversions, and a few mild perversions thrown in for the Goth crowd.

As an example of the great variety of effects available via filters, consider transition wipes. Transition wipes — just one of many kinds of effects you can use — provide smooth connections between two elements. These wipes are used in films and video as a way of moving from scene to scene, indicating moving through space or the passage of time, or some other transitional behavior — such as between reality and a dream. You can use them in Web pages for similar purposes. To give you an idea of just some of the effects you can employ, Table 1-1 shows a list of transition wipes.

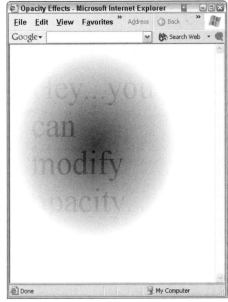

Figure 1-5:
Change the
opacity
Style to 2 to
create
circular
gradients.

Table 1-1	Transition Wipes
Transition Wipe	*Value*
Box in	0
Box out	1
Circle in	2
Circle out	3
Wipe up	4
Wipe down	5
Wipe right	6
Wipe left	7
Vertical blinds	8
Horizontal blinds	9
Checkerboard across	10

(continued)

Table 1-1 *(continued)*

Transition Wipe	Value
Checkerboard down	11
Random dissolve	12
Split vertical in	13
Split vertical out	14
Split horizontal in	15
Split horizontal out	16
Strips left down	17
Strips left up	18
Strips right down	19
Strips right up	20
Random bars horizontal	21
Random bars vertical	22
Random	23

You can combine or blend various effects to generate new effects. I won't say "The possibilities are endless — you're only limited by your imagination," because that's the single most tedious cliché of the computer age. But you can sure do some great visual stuff with CSS and Internet Explorer. If you can't wait to get to the discussion of dynamic animation tricks, flip over to Chapters 13 or 16 and dive in.

Chapter 2

Getting Results with CSS

. . . .

. . . .

*T*his chapter introduces several somewhat theoretical concepts central to understanding CSS. But rather than tire you with boring, abstract explanations of boring, abstract concepts such as *inheritance* and *specificity,* I'm going to entertain you with brief examples and a clever, painless presentation. You'll never know what hit you. Nonetheless, after you try the examples in this chapter, you'll have an almost subconscious understanding of the main theoretical concepts behind CSS.

So, roll up your sleeves and get ready to see how *fun* CSS can be. Never mind that you're also find out about some CSS theory at the same time. The theory comes in through the back door while you're otherwise amused by the interesting examples.

Starting from Scratch

You can write CSS using any plain text editor. Like XML and other contemporary computer languages derived from HTML, CSS makes no attempt to create some strange, specialized *code language* that cannot be easily written or read as simple, English text.

Of course, specialized CSS editors can assist you in various ways, particularly if you want to build heavy-duty, complicated Web sites. But, for now, I start off with very simple examples of CSS in action. And to create these examples, you use nothing more sophisticated than Windows's down-to-earth little Notepad.

A style sheet is often written and saved as a .css file on the hard drive. Thereafter, any HTML (.htm) Web page document that wants to use the styles defined in the .css file merely *references* it as a "link." You see how to link HTML to a CSS file in a minute.

Run Notepad (if you use XP, choose Start ⇨ All Programs ⇨ Accessories ⇨ Notepad). Then type this in to define an ultra-simple style that tells a Web site how you want paragraphs of text displayed:

```
p
{
color: blue;
text-align: right;
font-family: courier;
}
```

Save this style sheet by choosing File ⇨ Save As in Notepad, and then naming the file ParaStyle.css. You can use any name you want, but you need to reference that name in your Web page's HTML code. To do so, delete everything in Notepad, and type in this HTML page that references your ParaStyle.css style sheet file:

```
<html>

<head>
<link type="text/css" rel="stylesheet" href="ParaStyle.css">
</head>

<body>

<H1>Headline Text</H1>

<p>This is body text</p>

</body>

</html>
```

Use Notepad's File⇨Save As feature to save this code to a file named PStyle.htm in the same directory where you saved the ParaStyle.css file.

This highly simplified Web page code illustrates how an external style sheet file works. In the .css file, you specified that the <p> (paragraph) element should be blue, right-aligned, and in the Courier typeface. In your HTML code, you *linked* to a style sheet named ParaStyle.css. This style sheet is located in the same directory as the .htm file.

You have not defined a style for the H1 headline style, so it defaults to the browser's standard size, color, position, font (and perhaps other qualities) for the H1 style. With the Internet Explorer defaults, the headline is left-aligned, black, and a serif font.

But you *did* specify a style for the paragraph tag. So, to see this style in action, double-click on the Web page's filename, PStyle.htm, in Windows Explorer. The page automatically loads into Internet Explorer and displays the default headline style, and your modified paragraph style, as shown in Figure 2-1.

Figure 2-1:
The paragraph of body text is right-aligned, blue, and displayed in Courier font — just as your style sheet specifies.

Selectors and Such: CSS Syntax

The committee that developed CSS didn't take the simple approach and use existing HTML terminology. Instead, they invented special, new CSS words for familiar HTML concepts such as *tag* and *attribute*. Who knows? Perhaps they had a reason for this, but it does require you to get used to some new jargon.

Each CSS style *rule* is divided into three parts: the *selector,* the *property,* and the *value,* punctuated with braces around the property/value pair, like this:

```
{property: value pair}
```

Also, the property is separated from the value by a colon. A complete CSS rule looks like this:

```
selector {property: value};
```

Here's a real-world example of a CSS style. It defines the HTML paragraph `<p>` element as having a value of `blue` for its `color` property:

```
p {color: blue};
```

The CSS *selector* is what in HTML is called the *tag* or *element* — the items in HTML code that are surrounded by angle brackets (such as <h2>, <p>, or <tr>).

A single CSS *rule* is made up of a minimum of three parts:

✔ The *selector*, such as p, which tells the browser which HTML tag (elements) the rule should be applied to later in the HTML code.

✔ The *property*, such as color. This is what HTML calls an attribute. Usually it's the name of a quality of an element, such as its height, font-style, color, and so on.

✔ The *value* of the property, such as blue. This is the actual data specifying the change you are making to the appearance (usually) of the element, such as 45 pixels, Times Roman, or yellow.

The preceding list describes the simplest CSS rule. You can however, group multiple selectors for a single style (h1, h2, p can all be specified in a single rule as green, for example). Likewise, you can group multiple properties in a single rule, as I did in a previous example:

```
p {
color: blue;
text-align: right;
font-family: courier;
}
```

Like HTML, CSS code can be freely rearranged whatever way suits you — lines can be formatted in any fashion. The following rule is interpreted identically to the previous example:

```
p   {color: blue;
text-align: right; font-family: courier;}
```

These two rules mean exactly the same thing to the browser, but CSS programmers have their personal preferences about formatting.

Properties refer to attributes

The CSS *property* is what HTML calls the *attribute* — the name of the quality that you are specifying (such as color or font size). Many computer languages also use the term *property* in this same way.

Finally, the CSS *value* is the actual data about the property: In other words, *black* or *green* can be values of the color property. The value in CSS is the same concept as the value held in a variable or constant in computer programming. Computer programming languages use the term *value* in the same way that CSS does.

Some values are described with more than one word, such as *minty green* rather than *green*. When you have a multi-word value, enclose the value name in quotes:

```
p {color: "minty green";}
```

This notation is similar to how some database software handles multi-word terms.

Also, if you define more than one property for a selector, separate those properties with semicolons, as in the sample CSS style you used earlier in this chapter:

```
p
{
color: blue;
text-align: right;
font-family: courier;
}
```

 You can format a CSS style any way you wish. The braces serve as delimiters (or separators), so the browser knows that a selector's properties end when it comes upon a close brace symbol (}). Some people like to put each property on its own line to make it easier to read.

Grouping

If you wish, you can define a whole bunch of tags (selectors) all at once. This can save time if you want *all* your headline elements, for example, in an Arial typeface. HTML has four headline elements: H1, H2, H3, and H4. Instead of defining each different headline element as a separate style in your CSS file, just pile the selectors all together, separated by commas. In this example, headline sizes from heading 1 all the way down to heading 4 are defined as Arial:

```
h1,h2,h3,h4
{
font-family: Arial;
}
```

Showing Some Class

What if you want to subdivide a given tag (selector) style into several alternatives? It's similar to dividing your Recipes collection into sub-categories like Chinese, Mexican, Thai, and so on.

Say that you want *most* paragraphs in your document to be black, but you want to emphasize a few paragraphs by displaying them in red text. It's easy to do that by adding a *class* definition to a selector, like this example. Here I define a bodytext class and an alert class for the p selector:

```
p.bodytext {color: black;}
p.alert {color: red;}
```

Object-oriented computer languages use a similar punctuation when specifying classes and their properties — dividing the code using periods to separate class from property.

Use whatever word you want as a class name. Instead of p.alert, you can use p.emphasis or p.bridgette or whatever. The only requirement is that once you've defined the style using a particular term, you must later use that same term again when you invoke that class in the HTML. If you've defined a red text paragraph as p.alert in your style sheet, any time you want to invoke it in your Web page code, you must refer to it as p class "alert"). Also, reading your code is obviously easier if you choose terms that have some meaning relating to the end result. For this reason, I suggest that you avoid naming your classes Bridgette.

When choosing a name for a class, try to name it after what it does rather than how it looks. Instead of using p.red above, I used p.alert because alerting the reader with red text is the behavior or purpose of this class, not merely its appearance. I could later decide to make all alerts boldface instead of red. Having named this class red would be a problem if I later did change this style to boldface. I couldn't sensibly allow class=red to turn text boldface and leave it black. To keep the code understandable, I would have to go through the entire HTML code for my Web site and change each and every use of the class name red throughout the HTML files. That would be defeating the purpose of one of the primary values of CSS: That you don't have to search and replace through an entire Web site to make changes to the appearance of your various styles.

After you've specified your members of the p selector class, you can refer to them in your HTML document like this:

```
<p class="bodytext">
This one is black.
</p>

<p class="alert">
This is red.
</p>
```

Specifying All-Purpose Properties

You don't always have to attach a class to a tag. You can specify a generic class that can be applied to *any* kinds of tags in the HTML code. This way, you can avoid having to assign, say, a specific blue color value to each tag that you want to display in blue. You can just assign the blue class whenever you want some element to be blue. (This saves time because styles can be complicated and lengthy, and you only have to specify a CSS rule once. Thereafter in the HTML code, merely use the rule's class name instead of having to repeat all the properties and values in the rule.)

For example, if you want to be able to turn any kind of text blue to highlight it, leave out the selector name, omit the p in p.blue {color: blue} when you define the "highlight" class in the CSS file. The following is a generic class definition of blue:

```
/* This class can be used with any HTML tag */

.highlight {color: blue;}
```

Now, *any* HTML element that uses class = highlight turns blue:

```
<html>
<head>


<link type="text/css" rel="stylesheet" href="ParaStyle.css">
</head>

<body>

<p class="highlight">
I'm blue body text.
</p>

<h2 class="highlight">
I'm a BLUE HEADLINE
</h2>

</body>
</html>
```

If you want to make only part of a paragraph blue, use the <span> tag, like this:

```
<p>I say again, <span class="highlight">and I use blue for
        emphasis here</span> that you need to remember the
        lesson plans</p>
```

Just remember that when you use class selectors, you don't have to define each particular tag as blue in your CSS file. You instead define a `"highlight"` class having a `blue` value for its `color` property, and then just use `class=` `"highlight"` throughout your HTML code whenever you want *any* element to be blue.

If you want to add comments within a CSS file, enclose the comment between `/*` and `*/` symbols. The purpose of commenting your code is to make it easier for you to later read and modify it, or for others to modify your code after you have, say, left the company. You can instantly read the purpose of, or technique used with, the commented code:

```
/* This class can be used with any HTML tag */
```

These symbols are awkward because they're so similar to each other, but yet not identical. A variety of other, more easily typed, and more convenient punctuations could have been chosen. A good choice would have been the single quotation mark ('). But committees designed CSS, so you get inefficiencies from time to time. All in all, CSS is certainly worthwhile, but you might end up wishing that it didn't have so many qualities derived from C programming languages. This is the way C programmers add comments to their code, and C is notorious for being the most difficult, often the most inefficient, of all computer languages.

Using an ID Selector

ID selectors are similar to generic classes — they, too, are independent of specific document elements. But IDs differ from a class in that an ID is supposed to work only *once* on a give Web page — only a single element (the one with the ID) is supposed to be affected. Any references further down in HTML code to an already used ID are supposed to be ignored. Why am I using the phrase "supposed to" so much here? Because ID selectors don't work as advertised. In *practice,* browsers just ignore this "use it only once" rule. For example, I tried this code in Internet Explorer, and the browser didn't enforce the "only once" regulation; all three elements with duplicate IDs get highlighted here:

```
html>
<head>

<style>
#highlight {color: yellow; font-style: italic;}
</style>

</head>
<body>
```

```
<p>ordinary default text </p>
<p id="highlight">highlighted text </p>
<p id="highlight">second attempt to use this id fails
</p>

<h1 id="highlight">highlighted text </h1>


</body>
</html>
```

All three uses of HIGHLIGHT in this example turned the lines of text yellow and italic when I loaded this file into Internet Explorer. What gives? Just the usual. Somebody makes a rule, and somebody else ignores it. In any case, perhaps ID styles will be useful in CSS at some future date, so at least take a brief look at them. (ID *attributes* in HTML code are very useful if you're using ASP.NET or other programming such as scripting. In those cases, the ID allows your programming to affect elements by specifying their unique ID attribute. IDs also play a role in building templates. More on scripting in Chapter 16.)

You use the hash symbol (#) to create a CSS ID rule. This next example puts the CSS definition right in the header of an HTML page. This is called an *internal style sheet.* You can use this option instead of creating a separate CSS file. External, separate CSS style files are considered the best practice for most Web sites, however, because they can enforce rules across multiple pages, and also make it easy to modify the rules in one place only.

For convenience in illustrating CSS in this book, I almost always put style definitions in the header of an HTML page. This way, everything — the definition and its use — is together in the same file. And I also omit some useful, but unnecessary, elements in the HTML such as the <title>. These simplifications make it easier for you to see the idea being illustrated in the code, without unnecessary distractions like two separate files and extraneous HTML code.

In this example, an ID style named HIGHLIGHT is created in the header and then used in the body of this Web page where the ID is referenced.

```
<HTML>
<head>

<style>
#highlight {color: yellow; font-style: italic;}
</style>

</head>
<body>
```

```
<p>ordinary default text </p>

<p id="highlight">highlighted text </p>

</body>
</html>
```

Specifying more than one class

You can use multiple class names in a single HTML element. For example, you can create separate class rules (one for *framed* and one for *pink*) and then combine them by naming them in an element's class attribute in the HTML like this:

```
<p class="framed pink">
```

For an explanation of how this works, and a code example illustrating it, see the section in Chapter 18 titled "Combining Classes."

Capitalizing on case-sensitivity

HTML and CSS code is (usually) not case-sensitive. Tag names, attribute names, and so on can be capitalized any way you wish — and the browser still understands that you're referring to a *single* entity. For example, BODY, Body, body, or BoDy all are allowable body tags and can be used interchangeably.

As always, though, someone decided to get a little funny with this sensible case-insensitivity rule. In HTML or XHTML (eXtensible HTML, which is XML blended into HTML), ID and class values *are* case-sensitive. The CSS style definition's capitalization must match the capitalization in your document. The following CSS style

```
p.yellow {color: yellow;}
```

doesn't match the use of Yellow in this line in the document (the Y is uppercase). This line is not yellow, because the style is not applied:

```
<p class="Yellow">This is black!</p>
```

Another exception to the usual case-insensitivity of CSS and HTML is the value of a TYPE attribute in an OL (ordered, numbered list) element. It is case-sensitive.

Just stay in lowercase

In practice, most people, usually, try to write their programming, HTML, CSS and other code *entirely in lowercase*. For one thing, it's just easier to type. For another thing, if case-sensitivity is in force, you won't run into any problems (or hard-to-track-down bugs) simply because you goofed up and used using uppercase here and there. XHTML, in fact, *requires* all lowercase.

Additional case-sensitive exceptions are escape sequences beginning with an ampersand (&) and Internet addresses (URLs). Not all URLs are case-sensitive, but *some* are. This kind of confusion and inefficiency is really all too tedious and unnecessary. One day, we programmers will get our collective act together and insist that case-insensitivity be required in *all* computer programming situations.

When Styles Cascade

What does the term *cascade* mean for style sheets? It means that a CSS rule tumbles down through the code, and sometimes bumps into a conflicting rule.

The cascade is about what programmers call *precedence*: Who wins when there's a conflict? More than one style can apply to a given tag. For example, there's always the default browser-defined style, such as black as the default text color. If you specify some other color in a CSS rule, the cascade allows your rule to dominate, to have precedence over the built-in style.

But how does the browser decide which style wins out if two CSS rules conflict with each other? Should the conflicting styles be combined? What if the styles are completely incompatible — such as one style specifying italic and the other non-italic?

Visualizing specificity

Several factors determine which style wins out when styles collide: inheritance, the structural tree in a document, and the *specificity* (or *closeness*) of a style (I explain these concepts later in this section). Probably the most easily understood collision rule involves *where* the style was defined. Your CSS styles can be defined in four major locations:

✔ The browser's default styles.

✔ An external style sheet (a .css file containing style definitions that is referenced from within the HTML document with a Link element).

✔ An embedded style sheet (styles defined within the HTML document, inside its <head> tag. This kind of style is also sometimes called *internal*).

✔ An inline style (a style defined as an attribute within an HTML element itself, and whose effect is limited *to that element only*). For example, this is a typical inline style:

```
<p style="border-bottom: blue">
```

This list also illustrates the order in which conflicting styles "win" in any conflict. Think of the order as the style *closest* to the element wins. For example, the inline style — nestled right inside the element itself — is the closest. So if more than one style is specified for that element, an inline style is the style used. This closeness of the style to the element that matches it is more formally known as *specificity*.

The style location with the second highest priority is the internal style sheet located in the HTML document's header. The third highest priority goes to the external style sheet — the separate file. And the weakest priority, the one that all the others trump, is the default style. After all, the default is the look that a style sheet is supposed to alter.

Here's an example illustrating how IE decides between blue and red colors:

```
<html>
<head>
<style type="text/css">

p {color:red;}

</style>
</head>


<body>

<p style="color: blue;">i guess i'm blue. </p>

</body>
</html>
```

To test this document, type the HTML code into Notepad, and then save it using the filename EmTest.htm. Load this Web page by double-clicking its filename in Windows Explorer. You'll see the sentence *I guess I'm blue* appear in blue. The <p> element here was defined in two conflicting ways. In the embedded style, it's defined as red, but that definition is overridden by the inline definition of the color blue.

Try removing the inline style to see what happens. Change the line to

```
<p>I guess I'm blue. </p>
```

Retest it by resaving the Notepad file you just modified.

No need to double-click again on this filename in Windows Explorer to load the new version into IE. After you've loaded a document, it's the default address in IE — in this case, an address of an .htm file on your hard drive. If you modify that file as you just did in this example, all you have to do to see the modification is to press F5. That "refreshes" IE.

Some people prefer to use the browser's built-in source view as a quick way of modifying and retesting CSS code. Choose View⇨Source. You can make changes to the code, and then save it. Both Netscape and Firefox highlight the syntax, which some programmers find useful.

After you load the new version of this document into IE, the line *I guess I'm blue* is now displayed in red. The conflict between the embedded and inline style definitions has been resolved because you deleted the inline style.

You can override the normal rules of priority by using the `!Important` command to specify that this style must be used, no matter what. An `!Important` declaration overrides all other style definitions. You add the command like this:

```
p {color: blue !important;}
```

In CSS1, styles declared important by the author of the Web page override even any styles that the reader has declared important (yes, a Web page reader can specify styles too, as you see later in this book). However, in CSS2, important reader styles win out over important author styles, and indeed over *any* author styles, whether marked important or not.

Understanding CSS specificity

The term *specificity* is also used to describe a second way that a browser calculates which style wins when styles conflict. First, the browser looks for closeness — but what if the closeness is identical? That's when this second technique is applied.

Imagine, for example, that two different style sheets are referenced by the same HTML document (yes, you can attach more than on CSS file to a given Web page's HTML code). But, in one of these sheets, H1 is styled bold, and in another sheet it's styled italic. What's the poor browser to do in this case? Which specification wins?

Unlike the examples of style collision earlier in this chapter, where *closeness* could be used to declare a winner, here you've got both styles located at the *same degree* of closeness (the same specificity). Both of these style definitions are located in external style sheets.

In this case, the browser does a little bizarre math to make the decision about which style to use. As before, the more "specific" style wins. But what counts as specificity in this contest? It's not the same as the "closeness" factor. The browser has to do a bit of strange calculation, but you really can't call this math. It's just an odd kind of accumulation of values where some styles have orders of magnitude more weight than others. Don't bother your pretty head about this stuff if you don't find peculiar calculations interesting.

What does the browser do to calculate the specificity of two competing styles if their "closeness" factor is identical? Three things:

✔ Looks at a style and counts the number of ID attributes it has, if any

✔ Counts the number of class attributes, if any

✔ Counts the number of selectors (you can group selectors in a style like this: h1, h2, h3)

The browser doesn't then *add* these numbers together; it merely concatenates the *digits*. Perhaps this is some kind of arithmetic used by aliens in *their* galaxy, but I've sure never heard of it. Imagine if you got the number 130 by the following concatenation process:

```
1 apple, 3 oranges, 0 bananas = 130
```

This process gives apples ten times the "weight" of oranges, and 100 times the weight of bananas. Here are a couple of examples showing how it works when used to determine specificity in a CSS. Just pretend you're back in third-grade math class.

Attention, class! What is the specificity number for this selector?

```
ul h1 li.red {color: yellow;}
```

Anyone get the answer 13?

The correct answer is 13. You have

```
0 IDs, 1 class attribute (red), and 3 selectors (ul h1 li)
```

That "adds up," so to speak, to 013. Now, kiddies, who can explain how you get a specificity of 1 for the following selector definition?

```
H1 {color: blue;}
```

After the specificity has been determined, the higher number wins. Assume that two styles are in conflict because they both define the color of H1, but define it differently. But because one definition has a specificity value of 13 and the other has only 1, the H1 headline is yellow, not blue.

What if two rules turn out to have the same specificity? I *knew* someone would ask that. In that case (assuming that both are in a style sheet, or otherwise are the same "closeness" to the HTML tag), the rule that was specified last wins.

Grasping Inheritance

Chapter 14 goes into inheritance in depth, but here I want to introduce the idea to you so you won't be completely flummoxed by some of the behaviors that CSS exhibits in the examples in upcoming chapters. Flummoxation is an uncomfortable feeling, as I well know.

You've got to get the idea of inheritance into your head if you want to fully understand CSS. In the computer world, *inheritance* means that a "child" object inherits properties or abilities from its "parent" object.

When you specify a style using CSS, styles are applied both to the element and its "descendants." For example, if you specify that a <p> element should be displayed with a green background, most child elements of that <p> element will also have green backgrounds. Here's how it works:

```
<html>
<head>
<style type="text/css">

p {background: green;}

</style>
</head>


<body>

<p>diagrams <strong>belong in the box!</strong></p>

</body>
</html>
```

In this example, a child "inline element" (<strong>) nestles within a parent element (<p>). The <strong> tag means strong emphasis and results in bold-face. In this example, the strong text is boldface but also *inherits* the green background of its parent element <p>.

Inheritance is useful because you don't have to specify that <strong>, the child of <p>, should also be colored green, or have other characteristics of the parent element. Inheritance is obviously a time-saver with elements such as lists that have many children. All the children turn green at once because they inherit that color from their parent.

A few properties are not inherited, however, because it doesn't make sense in some cases. For example, you don't want child elements to inherit the margins used by their parents. A main purpose of margins is to distinguish parent text blocks from child blocks, so they should have different margins. Likewise, borders, padding, and backgrounds are not inherited.

Chapter 3

Up and Running with Selectors

*N*ow that you've been exposed to the wonders of CSS, you're unlikely to continue to write this kind of HTML:

```
<h3><font color="red">Warning:</font></h3>
```

That's the kind of line you'd have to write perhaps dozens of times in a Web site. Say, for example, that you have a series of warnings throughout your Web site, each preceded by an H3 headline in red. For *each* headline, you had to specify that it was red using the <font> element.

Along comes CSS. Now you can create a single H3 *selector* in a single location, yet it affects all the H3 headlines throughout the entire Web site. That one style makes all H3 headlines red automatically. If you later decide to change H3 headlines from a red color to simply boldface, no problem. You need to make that change only once in the style sheet rule instead of dozens of places to H3 elements scattered throughout the HTML code.

A selector specifies to which element in the HTML code a CSS style rule is applied. For example, use the selector p if you want a rule applied to HTML paragraph <p> elements. Or use the selector h1 to define a CSS rule that is applied to the H1 headline elements in the HTML code. In other words, a CSS selector is just an HTML element with its < > symbols stripped off. Here's an h1 selector (shown in boldface), within a CSS rule:

```
<style>

h1 {color: red;}

</style>
```

This rule means that throughout the HTML code, every H1 element gets *selected* to have the color red applied to it. Selectors tell CSS what HTML elements to target for the application of the CSS rule.

But there's more to selectors than you might have suspected. Consider some of the additional ways you can use selectors. They're more versatile than you might suppose.

Working with Universal Selectors

You might wonder if you can affect *everything* in a Web site — not just certain tags, but all tags? You bet. You can use a * to create a universal selector that has a global effect. Perhaps one day your boss comes in — your boss who has absolutely no taste or sense of design — and says: "Look. I think we should make our Web site stand out from the crowd, so let's make the whole thing boldface! How about that?"

"You mean all the headlines?"

"No, I mean everything from the little captions to the text to the biggest headlines. Everything! What a great idea."

"Why stop there?" you ask, failing to remember that sarcasm is usually lost on your boss. "Why not also make the entire background a bright plaid?"

"Hey, I think you've got something there!" he says, and goes back to his office to think up some other subtle ideas. Well, he is the boss.

To make the whole enchilada boldface without the use of a universal selector, you'd have to create a group of selectors like this:

```
body, p, table, h1, h2, h3, h4, h5, h6, {font-weight: bold;}
```

Actually, you'd have to create an even larger group, grouping most of the tags in your HTML, such as th, td, pre, strong, em, and any others you've used or might use in the future.

Not to worry. Rather than building an enormous group selector, you can just use a *universal selector* and change the text of your entire Web site to bold to make the boss happy, like this:

```
* {font-weight: bold;}
```

An asterisk, by itself, is a universal selector. It means, "Do this to *all* elements in the document." Here you're assigning the font-weight property a bold value for every element. This is obviously a powerful, yet indiscriminate, force — not unlike the boss himself.

Many people avoid universal selectors because they can have unintended side effects involving inheritance. (You probably don't want hyperlinks to inherit universal font styles, for example — hyperlinks need to stand out from surrounding text.) However, if you've got the nerve, go ahead and enforce some mass-rule on your site and try to manage any side effects as they pop up.

Using Multiple Declarations

Remember grouping? Where you specify more than one selector, followed by a style that you want all those elements to share, like this:

```
h1, h2, h3, h4, {font-weight: bold;}
```

Well, you can also use multiple declarations (the property/value pairs inside the braces):

```
h1 {font-weight: bold; font: 18px Courier; color: green;}
```

The thing to remember when using multiple declarations is to separate them with semicolons. Spaces are simply ignored by CSS here, so you can't count on a space as a way of separating declarations from each other.

Many computer book authors don't bother with the final semicolon, leaving it off just before the closing brace (}) like this:

```
h1 {font-weight: bold}
```

However, omitting the final semicolon not a great idea. You should simply always be in the habit of concluding each declaration with a semicolon. Leaving semicolons out of declaration lists is *a very common cause* of browser confusion and errors. Here's an example where you intend to display H1 heads as bold, green, 28 point Arial:

```
<html>
<head>
<style>
```

```
h1 {font-weight: bold font: 28pt arial; color: green;}

</style>
</head>

<body>
<h1>a headline</h1>
</body>
</html>
```

But notice that the semicolon is missing after *bold*. The result is that Internet Explorer becomes confused and fails to recognize `font: 28pt Arial` as a value that can be used with the `font-weight` property (which indeed it cannot be). So the browser simply ignores the `font` property and the associated `28pt Arial` value. It instead uses the default H1 font instead of the Arial you wanted. Likewise, the requested size of 28 points is ignored and the default font size is used instead (which is likely to be smaller than you wanted in this case).

As you no doubt guessed, you can simultaneously group selectors *and* declarations, like this:

```
h1, h2, h3, h4 {color: green; background: white; font-family:
        Arial;}
```

Using Attributes as Selectors

CSS2 defines some new selectors, including *attribute selectors*. Alas, this kind of selector is not supported by Internet Explorer (IE), but I'll cover it. Being familiar with some CSS technologies that IE doesn't support is still a good idea in case IE ever does support them.

And, of course, attribute selectors *do* work with Netscape 6 or 7, Mozilla, or Opera 5 or 6. What's more, CSS can be applied to files other than HTML, such as XML-based files. XML files often endeavor to use "self-describing" attributes, so these attributes often end up being useful as selectors.

Attribute selectors can expand the utility and flexibility of class and ID attributes, in addition to allowing you the freedom to try some useful tricks.

For example, recall that when you use class selectors, CSS compares the selector to each HTML tag — and finds a match only when a class name in the HTML is identical to a class name in the CSS rule (class names you make up, such as `bodytext`, `alert`, `highlight`, `warning` and so on). Here is a typical class selector. It defines a style (display red) that matches any `<p>` tag with class = `"alert"` later in the HTML:

```
p.alert {color: red}
```

In the HTML, this paragraph tag matches the `alert` class:

```
<p class="alert">
This is red.
</p>
```

Pause a moment to be sure that you have the terminology straight (it is a bit confusing). In the following CSS rule, `p` is the selector, `alert` is the class name, `color` is a property, and `red` is a value of that property:

```
p.alert {color: red}
```

And, in an associated HTML document, here's an element that matches this selector:

```
<p class="alert">
```

In this element, `p` is the element (or tag), `class` is an attribute of that p element, and `alert` is the value of the class attribute.

Why is this confusing? Because these items have different names in different locations. In a CSS file, `p` is called a *selector,* but in an HTML file, it's called a *tag* (or *element*). Also, `alert` is a class name (in the CSS file), but becomes a *value* (in an HTML file). You just have to try to memorize these various categories and terms, or you can quickly get confused trying to make sense of CSS. Take a look at Figure 3-1. It compares the terminology in two linked lines of code: first the CSS rule, and then the HTML where that rule is applied:

A Style Definition in a CSS File

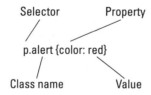

A Matching Element in an HTML Document

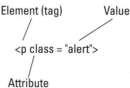

Figure 3-1:
This figure
illustrates a
CSS rule
and a
matching
HTML
element.

The Simplest Attribute Selector

Attribute selectors come in several varieties. The simplest version merely looks for an attribute match and ignores the *specifics* of the attribute. In other words, in the following code, if a <p> tag has a class — *any class at all* — a match occurs. If you want any paragraph with the attribute class = in its tag to be rendered italic, for example, you create this selector:

```
p[class] {font-style: italic;}
```

Notice that here you aren't defining a class *name* (such as the alert in p.alert). Instead, you're merely specifying [class], which means *any class at all*. So, this <p> element in the HTML is italicized because it has a class attribute:

```
<p class="red">
This is red.
</p>
```

And this, too, is italicized. It has a class:

```
<p class="signal">
This is an important point!
</p>
```

Any <p> tag in the entire document with class= as an attribute in its tag — regardless of the actual value specified following the equal sign — is italicized. That's the simplest kind of *attribute selector*.

Another type of attribute selector matches the "value" (the class XML is frequently easy to use with this kind of matching). For example, say that you run a car dealership's Web site and the dealer wants every reference to a car that's on sale in boldface. Here's how you can do that:

```
car[onSale] {font-weight: bold;}
```

This would cause the text of the first and second (but not the third) elements in the following HTML to be boldfaced:

```
<car onSale="5000">Chevy</car>
<car onSale="2999">Ford</car>
<car>Maxim</car>
```

Only the Chevy and Ford text are boldface in this example. Why? Because they have an onSale attribute — that's how the selector is specified.

To make *every* element that uses an `onSale` attribute bold, use the * symbol. Here's how to create that kind of attribute selector:

```
*[onSale] {font-weight: bold;}
```

You can also select for multiple attributes merely by separating them with a space.

```
table[border][width] {property/value}
```

The following table would match this selector because it does have *both* border and width attributes:

```
<table border=0 cellpadding=0 cellspacing=0 width=100%>
```

Matching attribute selection types

This attribute selection technique isn't used frequently, but it can be valuable when you need to match language values, such as `fr` to match French. For example, here's a selector that specifies a blue color for any `lang` attribute beginning with (or equal to) `fr`. This colors French text blue:

```
*[lang|="fr"] {color: blue;}
```

Then, in the HTML, only *one* of the following elements turns blue:

```
<p lang="fr">Pouvez vous prospàrer</p>
<p lang="en-us">May you prosper</p>
```

You guessed it: The first one is `fr`, so it's a match and becomes blue.

Matching partial attribute values

Class names (or *values* if you prefer) can have more than one word, such as

```
<p class="running headline">
```

What if you want to match all elements with a class attribute that includes the word *running*? You can use a kind of wildcard matching against only part of a class name. Write this kind of selector:

```
p[class~="running"] {color: blue;}
```

The wiggly tilde (~) means, "Match if this word appears," regardless of what other words might, or might not, be there.

Matching exact attribute values

The final variation on the attribute selector technique requires an exact match to the attribute value. This selector boldfaces only cars with 2999 as their `onSale` attribute's value:

```
car[onSale="2999"] {font-weight: bold;}
```

This causes the text of the second (but not the first or third) elements in the following HTML to be boldfaced:

```
<car onSale="5000">Chevy</car>
<car onSale="2999">Ford</car>
<car>Maxim</car>
```

Building Your First Style Sheet

You've experimented with small examples — defining a single selector and then trying it out on an element or two in HTML code. Now it's time to try a somewhat larger example to get a more accurate idea of the power of CSS. In this example, you create an HTML page, and then modify it via a CSS file. Finally, you apply two CSS files to the HTML, to see cascading, and specificity, in action.

An easy way to generate an HTML page to practice with is to write a few paragraphs (or just copy and paste them) into Word — and then have Word translate them into an HTML document. To see how this works, follow these steps:

1. **Run Word 2003.**

2. **Type three or four paragraphs.**

3. **Make one paragraph italic.**

4. **Type a few words on a line by themselves, and then press Enter.**

5. **Drag your mouse across this text to select it.**

6. **Choose Format⇨Styles and Formatting.**

7. **Double-click Heading 1 in the list of styles.**

   The headline style Heading 1 is applied to the selected text.

8. **Create a couple of second-level headlines by repeating steps 4 through 7, but instead of choosing the Heading 1 style in step 7, choose Heading 2.**

Your results should look something like Figure 3-2.

Transforming a Word document into a Web page

Now you should have a simple Word document with a few paragraphs — one of which is italicized. You also have a couple of first-level heads and a couple of second-level heads. You now want to save this file as MyFirst.htm. Follow these steps to create an HTML file out of this document:

1. **Choose File⇨Save as Web Page.**

   A Save dialog box appears, asking if you want to save this as an .mht (single file) Web page. This format is a specialized Microsoft format that includes lots of extra information about the document — so it can be edited using all the power of Word. You don't need all that. You just want a simple HTML document generated here.

2. **In the Save As Type list box at the bottom of the dialog box, click the down arrow to see the list of file type options and choose Web Page (*.htm, *.html). Name this file MyFirst.htm.**

   You've now created an HTML document named MyFirst.htm that can be displayed in a browser.

   You may also notice that the text looks smaller when the dialog box closes and you're returned to Word's document view.

3. **Choose View and notice that Web Layout is now the active view instead of the previous Normal view.**

   Now take a look at your new Web page in Internet Explorer by double-clicking MyFirst.htm file in Windows Explorer.

   Your page appears, but it's no longer a .doc file. It's now an HTML file that a browser can read, understand, and display, as shown in Figure 3-3.

Now you're ready to take a look at the HTML code behind this page. Choose View⇨HTML Source in Word. A special Microsoft Script Editor opens, displaying your HTML in all its glory. Even though this is the "pure" HTML version of this page ("pure" compared to the .mht version you rejected in step 1 in the previous step list) — it's still pretty hefty!

Examine the HTML that Word generated, as illustrated in Figure 3-4:

As you peruse the HTML code, you may notice comments (which Microsoft uses to force the browser to ignore proprietary stuff, even some script code in some cases). You also see lots of references to *mso,* which stands for Microsoft Office, and many items in XML format defining properties of the document and other data. Ignore all this. Or if you wish, *peruse* it for a while, but don't get hypnotized because what we're looking for is further down the page.

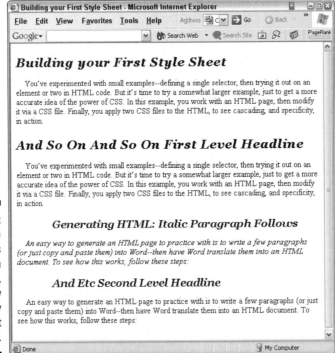

Figure 3-3: This is the same text as displayed in Figure 3-2, but now rendered by Internet Explorer.

Scroll down until you come to the style section, appropriately colored pink. Check out the pink section:

```
strong {color:#400000;}
em {color:#400000;}
p {mso-margin-top-alt:auto; margin-right:0in; mso-margin-
        bottom-alt:auto; margin-left:0in; text-
        indent:12.25pt; mso-pagination:widow-orphan; font-
        size:12.0pt; font-family:"Times New Roman"; mso-
        fareast-font-family:Times;}
```

Notice that both the `strong` and `em` selectors here are defined as having a color with a value of #400000. Because these styles are embedded in this HTML document, they override any external style sheet we link to the document. Embedded styles are closer than external styles to the HTML tags they are intended to modify. "Closer" styles are also described as *more specific*. Therefore, the embedded styles win out if style definitions conflict.

Visualizing levels of specificity

Here are some rules about CSS *specificity*:

▸ Child elements (such as a `<p>` paragraph element within a parent `<body>`) inherit their parent's styles. If `<body>` has a style associated with it that specifies underlining, any `<p>` elements within that parent `<body>` element inherit the underlining. However, if *more specific* styles exist on the Web page (such as an inline style), they override the inherited style.

✔ CSS styles contained within an HTML document (embedded or inline styles) take precedence over external styles (located in a separate .css file and referenced in the HTML code with the `<link>` tag).

✔ A style with an `!Important` command takes precedence, regardless of other factors.

Now, just for fun, try an experiment. Modify this embedded style `strong` in the Word-generated HTML code by following these steps:

1. **In the Microsoft Script Editor, locate this selector:**

   ```
   strong {color:#400000;}
   ```

2. **Modify it in the Script Editor to make the color of <strong> green, by changing it to this:**

   ```
   strong {color: green;}
   ```

3. **Now locate some text in the first paragraph — the text of your document is at the very bottom of the HTML in the Editor. Surround a word or two with the `<strong>` `</strong>` tags, like this:**

   ```
   <p class=MsoNormal>You've <strong>experimented</strong>
           with
   ```

   Notice that once you type the `<` symbol, the text turns red in the Editor. This is to cue you that there is an error in the HTML code. As soon as the code is restored to the correct format (when you type the end `>` symbol), the text turns black again, signaling you that all is now well. Or if not entirely well, at least your HTML code doesn't have a glaring error in it.

   Before saving this file, notice something cool happening in the Word document. Switch to Word now. See the Refresh toolbar as shown in Figure 3-5? Word knows that you've edited the HTML, so the current Web layout view is no longer accurate.

4. **Click the Refresh button on the toolbar.**

   You now see the words that you tagged `<strong>` have turned green, just as your modified style specified.

5. **Choose File⇨Save.**

   The HTML file is now updated to reflect your changes.

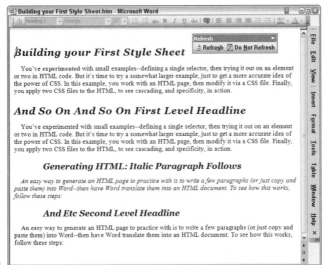

Building your First Style Sheet.htm - Microsoft Word

Figure 3-5:
Word allows
you to see
the results
of any
editing you
do in the
Script Editor
to the HTML
code by
clicking this
Refresh
toolbar.

6. **Switch to IE and press F5.**

   The page is refreshed when you press F5.

   The browser window refreshes by reloading your .htm file, and you see here too the green words that you requested.

Using Word to create Web pages isn't difficult. If you have some Word documents that you want to add to a Web site, using Word's Save As Web Page feature comes in handy. Editing the HTML code in the Script Editor built into Word 2003 is efficient, too: It even has a debugger in the editor.

Creating an External Cascading Style Sheet

Now you build an external CSS file, reference it from within the Word .htm file you just built, and use the !Important command to override the embedded styles with your external styles in the CSS file.

Don't be too disturbed if CSS terminology shifts around. For example, this !Important command is called four different things by four different computer-book authors I've read: Sometimes it's a property, rule, value, or declaration. The official W3 site (www.W3.org) is supposed to have the final word on matters like this, but even they are inconsistent. They refer to !Important as a rule, but also describe ! and Important as keywords. Whatever. For years now, whenever Microsoft cannot figure out a classification for a language element, they've called it a *keyword*. Some language elements are clearly functions or operators and so on. Others are hard to categorize. In effect, *keyword* has no real meaning — it's just the grab bag where unclassifiable concepts are tossed. For these kinds of terms, I prefer the word *command*. So I'm calling !Important a command. And why not? Everyone has a different favorite terminology.

To build a CSS, open Notepad and type the following style definitions:

```
p
{
color: blue;
text-align: center;
font-family: arial
!important;
}
```

Save this CSS as MyFirst.css.

Open the MyFirst.htm file in Notepad. You see something like the following code at the very top of the .htm file. Insert a link to the .css file as shown here in boldface:

```
<html xmlns:o="urn:schemas-microsoft-com:office:office"
xmlns:w="urn:schemas-microsoft-com:office:word"
xmlns="http://www.w3.org/TR/REC-html40">
<head>
<meta http-equiv=Content-Type content="text/html;
        charset=windows-1252">
<meta name=ProgId content=Word.Document>
<meta name=Generator content="Microsoft Word 11">
<meta name=Originator content="Microsoft Word 11">
<link rel=File-List
href="Building%20your%20First%20Style%20Sheet_files/filelist.
        xml">
<link type="text/css" rel="stylesheet" href="MyFirst.css">
<title>Building your First Style Sheet</title>
```

Where in an .htm file you place your various elements is often not critical — although of course you want some things in the header and some in the body. Also, the order in which items are displayed or script code is executed can be affected by their order in the code. However, putting similar elements together if possible is usually best. For that reason, put your new link to the .css file just below Microsoft's link to its own .xml file.

The importance of !Important

Now save the MyFirst.htm file. Test the style sheet by double-clicking MyFirst.htm to load it into Internet Explorer. You should see the results of your !Important styles. In the paragraphs, the black text turns blue, is centered, and changes from the default serif font to Arial's sans serif style, as you see in Figure 3-6.

Try removing the !Important command from the .css file in Notepad. Press Alt+F+S to save the change to this file. Then use Alt+Tab to switch to IE, and then press F5 to refresh the browser (reloading the HTML to update what you see to the latest version). As you see, blue and centering took effect, but the serif Times New Roman font didn't change to Arial as your external style specified. Why did *some* of your CSS files' styles get applied, but not others? The answer is in the .htm code for this page. In the embedded styles, locate the properties selector. You see this:

```
p
            {mso-margin-top-alt:auto;
            margin-right:0in;
            mso-margin-bottom-alt:auto;
            margin-left:0in;
            text-indent:12.25pt;
            mso-pagination:widow-orphan;
            font-size:12.0pt;
            font-family:"Times New Roman";
            mso-fareast-font-family:Times;}
```

Figure 3-6: Your text should change to blue, centered, and Arial for each paragraph in the Web page.

Microsoft's embedded style does not define the color or alignment of `<p>` selector, the selector that determines how paragraph elements look. However, the *font family* is specified in the embedded style:

```
font-family:"Times New Roman";
```

Notice the efficient way you can test CSS effects and modifications. Using Notepad to hold the CSS file, you can make a change to the CSS code and then save the file, simply refreshing the browser to see the results immediately. I mention this edit-test cycle more than once in this book because it's worth repeating.

The importance of being closest

Recall the "closeness" rule in cascading styles: An embedded style takes precedence over an external style. The only way to override the embedded Times New Roman font is to employ the `!Important` command.

Two other important points to remember about `!Important`. You must not precede it with a semicolon and you must use it for *every* property (a "property" in a CSS style has an effect on an "attribute" in the HTML code).

Omit semicolons

For example, this CSS style won't work:

```
font-family: arial;!Important
```

That's because you must *not* use the semicolon between the property's value (`arial`, here) and the `!Important` command. In order to work, your `!Important` command should butt right up against the value, like this:

```
font-family: arial!Important
```

Everything must be important

Also, the following example turns the text blue, centers it (blue and centered don't conflict with other styles), and increases the size to 18 points because of the `!Important` command — but fails to turn the font into Arial:

```
p
{
color: blue;
text-align: center;
```

```
font-family: arial;
font-size:18.0pt!Important
}
```

You have failed to add `!Important` to the `font-family` property. Each property that you want to make `!Important` must have that command appended to it, like this:

```
p
{
color: blue;
text-align: center;
font-family: arial!Important;
font-size:18.0pt!Important
}
```

Adding New Selectors

Now open your .css file and redefine the headline fonts from italic to normal, from the default left-aligned to centered, and to a rather aggressive font family named *Ravie*. First take a look at the embedded style that Word put into the .htm file for the H1 selector:

```
h1
            {mso-style-parent:"";
            mso-style-next:Normal;
            margin-top:14.0pt;
            margin-right:0in;
            margin-bottom:10.5pt;
            margin-left:0in;
            text-indent:0in;
            line-height:24.0pt;
            mso-line-height-rule:exactly;
            mso-pagination:none;
            page-break-after:avoid;
            mso-outline-level:1;
            font-size:17.0pt;
            mso-bidi-font-size:10.0pt;
            font-family:Georgia;
            mso-fareast-font-family:"Times New Roman";
            letter-spacing:.5pt;
            mso-font-kerning:0pt;
            font-weight:bold;
            mso-bidi-font-weight:normal;
            font-style:italic;
            mso-bidi-font-style:normal;}
```

Notice that the font is a typeface called Georgia and it's italic. You have used first- and second-level headlines in your .htm document, so rather than create a separate selector for each, just group the headline styles into a single style specification. Open your .css file in Notepad and add the selector group shown in bold here:

```
p
{
color: blue;
text-align: center;
font-family: arial!Important;
font-size:18.0pt!Important
}
h1, h2
{
font-family: ravie!Important;
font-style: normal!Important
text-align: center;
}
```

Notice that you don't need to add the !Important command to center the headlines because the embedded Microsoft CSS selectors for headlines make no mention of alignment. Therefore, your external style sheet has free reign to make any changes to this attribute that you want.

When Cascades Collide

To see how the browser handles two external files when their styles compete, use Notepad to create a second .css file with this paragraph selector definition:

```
p
{
color: maroon;
text-align: center;
font-family: arial!Important;
font-size:18.0pt!Important
}
```

Save this file as MySecond.css.

Now, link this second .css file to your MyFirst.htm file by adding the link in boldface to the HTML code you've been working with in the previous examples:

```
<link type="text/css" rel="stylesheet" href="MyFirst.css">
<link type="text/css" rel="stylesheet" href="MySecond.css">
<title>Building your First Style Sheet</title>
```

Save this file. Now imagine what will happen. In MyFirst.css, paragraph text is supposed to be blue:

```
p
{
color: blue;
text-align: center;
font-family: arial!Important;
font-size:18.0pt!Important
}
```

But MySecond.css specifies that paragraph text be maroon:

```
p
{
color: maroon;
text-align: center;
font-family: arial!Important;
font-size:18.0pt!Important
}
```

What's going to happen? Both of these selectors have the same "closeness" (or specificity) to the HTML <p> tags in the .htm file because both are in external files. Or do they have the same closeness after all? Does another kind of closeness apply here as well? What do you suppose the color will be?

Load MyFirst.htm into IE to see which of these two external selectors dominates. The text turns maroon. Why? Because the <link> for the second .css file is *closer* to the affected <p> elements in the HTML code. The second .css file link appears lower in the header, therefore closer to the body of the document where the <p> elements reside. If you switch the order of the <link> elements in the header, the text turns blue. Try switching the order like this and then saving the .htm file and refreshing the browser:

```
<link type="text/css" rel="stylesheet" href="MySecond.css">
<link type="text/css" rel="stylesheet" href="MyFirst.css">
```

What is the result? Blue.

Part II
Looking Good with CSS

The 5th Wave   By Rich Tennant

"As a Web site designer I never thought I'd say this, but I don't think your site has enough bells and whistles."

In this part . . .

CSS offers you many efficiencies, including the ability to lay out Web pages *your* way, adjust the space between characters, words, and lines of text, and add color or texture to bring your backgrounds alive. These and other elements of fundamental CSS design are covered in this Part.

Chapter 4

Taking a Position

· ·

In This Chapter

▶ Making it all relative

▶ Getting comfy with absolute placement

▶ Offsetting positions

▶ Stacking elements and adjusting opacity

· ·

*P*erhaps the single most fundamental element of design is positioning. Say someone hands you five objects and tells you to arrange them inside a frame. The texture, color, or shape of those five objects doesn't much matter. If you're talented, you can make them look good inside the frame by *arranging* them in the best way.

Positioning elements on a Web page is likewise crucial to the success of that page. You don't want people to think that the elements just fell there — accidentally located wherever they happened to land.

Several chapters in this book deal with positioning, but here you can get an introduction to the basics of controlling Web page design.

A simple Web page by default arranges its elements from top to bottom, piling them one on top of another, against the left side of the page. Here are two paragraphs, with a picture in between them:

```
<html>
<head>
</head>
<body>
<h1>This Is The Headline</h1>

<P>
<IMG height="292" width="448" src="lake.jpg" >
</P>

<P>This is paragraph two.</P>
</body>
</html>
```

Try saving this file as Simple.htm. Also, in the same folder, add a picture named lake.jpg. Then double-click Simple.htm to view it in Internet Explorer. You should see something like Figure 4-1.

Figure 4-1:
The simplest Web page design merely stacks text, pictures, and other elements on top of each other, along the left side of the page.

Improving the design shown in Figure 4-1 is easy enough: Just add an attribute that centers the headline:

```
<h1 align="center">This Is The Headline</h1>
```

This results in the more pleasing design shown in Figure 4-2.

But there's a problem with centering text this way. It's centered relative to the browser, not to the graphic. So, if the user's browser is any wider than the graphic itself, the centered text moves *off center* relative to the image, as shown in Figure 4-3.

HTML wasn't designed to deal effectively with laying out a page. CSS was developed, in part, to solve this problem. CSS contains a variety of positioning tools, including sophisticated *relative* positioning. You can make the location of one object related (tied to, or *relative* to) another object. This solves the problem of the user resizing the browser window: Relatively positioned objects retain their relationship to each other no matter what happens to the browser itself.

Figure 4-2:
Centering
the headline
adds variety
to this page
and visually
connects
the headline
to the
graphic.

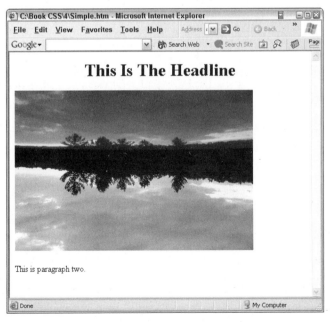

Figure 4-3:
Whoops.
Simple
centering
doesn't tie
the text to
the graphic
— so
different
browser
widths
result in
different
positioning.

Relativity Explained

Relative positioning means that an element is located *in terms of* another element.

Relative location might mean an element is centered in the middle of the other element, or 35 pixels to its left, or 25 percent down from its top. The main point is that the first element's position depends on the other element's location. As you saw in Figure 4-3, a headline can be centered relative to the browser window.

Absolute positioning specifies a particular *number* (pixels, points, inches, whatever measurement system you choose) by which the element should be positioned. Absolute *size* is described by width and height numbers, as in the picture size described in the HTML code earlier in this chapter:

```
<IMG height="292" width="448" src="lake.jpg" >
```

Absolute position is described by two numbers: the top and left. Technically called *coordinates*, these two numbers tell the browser exactly where to put the element within the browser's window. Top 3 inches means put the top of the element three inches down from the browser window frame. Left 2 inches means two inches over from the left side of the frame. Using these two coordinates, you can put anything, anywhere.

Some designers try to make their Web pages extremely flexible so that they can be viewed in many different sizes — from tiny PDA screens to gigantic stadium screens. This is another reason to use relative size and position techniques. Notice that when you choose View⇨Text Size in Internet Explorer, you are shown *relativistic* options: largest, larger, medium, smaller, smallest. You don't see choices like 1 inch, 1/2 inch, 1/4 inch, and so on, which are absolute specs. The people who designed Internet Explorer assumed that people are using different-size screens with different resolutions settings (800x600 and others). So the meaning of "large" should be relative to the resolution, not some fixed (absolute) unit of measurement. What's largest on a PDA is quite a different size from what's largest on a Jumbotron, right?

Of course, as Albert Einstein pointed out, *everything* is relative except the speed of light. So, when we speak of "absolute" positioning, it merely means that we're being somewhat "less relative." What do I mean by this?

You actually cannot sit still, no matter how hard you try. When you think you're sitting still, you're still moving at about a half million miles per hour as the solar system spins around the galaxy. In fact, you're moving through space in a rapid and complex corkscrew path. Even while you're quietly asleep, you're still flying aboard the rotating earth, orbiting the sun, spinning around the galaxy. And the galaxy itself is hurtling through the universe. So you're moving really fast in a dozen different circles all the time. Luckily, so is your bed and everything else in your room. They're all at rest, *relative to you*, but not relative to light.

The same concept applies to absolute positioning. After all, an inch on a PDA screen is quite a different thing from on a giant projection TV set. So, even though an inch is an absolute measurement, its *effect* is relative to the device that displays your Web page. So don't be disturbed by the somewhat slippery concept of *absolute* in CSS styles.

Flow Versus Positioning, Floating Versus Coordinates

If you simply add elements to a Web page — without specifying specific coordinates — they *flow* (stack themselves against the left side, as illustrated in Figure 4-1).

CSS provides two important positioning tools: floating and positioning. Getting your mind around the various interactive features of these tools takes some time, but you'll be glad that you invested that time. For one thing, you can often achieve a great goal that CSS makes possible: ridding your Web pages of tables used for layout.

Chapters 9, 10, and 11 go into CSS positioning features in depth, but getting a sense of what all the excitement's about is a good idea — it gives you a little taste of what you can do.

With CSS *positioning,* you can specify precisely where elements show up on the browser. But note that this specification is *relative* to their default position or relative to other elements, the browser background. (Of course, when you position something in terms of the browser background, you can consider it "absolute" positioning. The browser frame is a Web page's "universe," so you can ignore the fact that a user might move or resize the browser window. An element positioned one inch from the left side of a browser window *stays at that coordinate* through anything the user might do.)

Now look at the various ways you can use to modify the position property in a CSS selector: `static`, `relative`, `absolute`, `fixed`, and `inherit`.

Static is similar to the default — what happens when you don't specify any position value. Static elements flow in the default way (they stack on the left side), but they cannot be repositioned; they remain where they are and you cannot give them coordinates (`top` and `left` properties). Nor can you adjust a static element's position using script, such as VBScript or JavaScript. They remain where they are: *static.*

Relative positioning is like static, but you *can* use `top` and `left` properties to modify the default flow location, *relative* to other objects.

Absolute positioning detaches the element from other objects — its position is *not* relative to them. It's independent. It is located in the browser window some specified distance over from the left side and down from the top. You provide the top and left properties, starting with top: 0px; left: 0px, which would butt the element up against the top left corner of the browser window. (Technically, the top and left properties describe an element's location within its *containing block* — but I leave that concept for a later discussion.)

To see how absolute positioning affects an image, try this example:

```
<html>
<head>
<style>
.absol {position: absolute; top: 0px; left: 0px;}
</style>
</head>
<body>
<h1>This Is The Headline</h1>
<p>
This is a paragraph of text.
</p>
<p>This is paragraph two.</p>
<img class="absol" src="lake.jpg">

</body>
</html>
```

This example illustrates how positioning the graphic at 0,0 (absolute) causes it to partially cover a headline and completely cover a paragraph of body text. The headline and text are flowing (stacking in order of their appearance on the HTML document). The image, however, is *third* in the stacking order, yet positioned first: It's *absolutely* displayed up against the top left, as shown in Figure 4-4:

Figure 4-4:
Mixing flowed with absolute elements can cause one to cover another, like this graphic that covers a headline.

What if you change the position property from absolute to relative? Take a look at this:

```
<style>
.absol {position: relative; top: 0px; left: 0px;}
</style>
```

Changing the position value from absolute to relative causes default behavior. The graphic is positioned where it would normally flow — in the stacking order of the elements based on their order in the HTML code, as shown in Figure 4-5:

Figure 4-5: Change absolute to relative and the default flow order of the elements — with the graphic at the bottom — is restored.

Elements with a *fixed* value for the position property remain in their location in the browser, even if the user scrolls the browser. The *other* elements that are not fixed scroll, but the fixed element does not. This trick can be used to make a running headline, to frame, or to preserve a header or a set of labels at the top of a table. However, using `fixed` has two drawbacks. It can look annoying when the user scrolls — the item can jitter and bounce as it resists scrolling — and, more importantly, this technique doesn't work in IE. If something doesn't work in 96 percent of the browsers in use today, what's the point? Just avoid it.

Controlling Layout with Offsetting

In the previous examples in this chapter, you've used `top` and `left` properties to describe absolute locations. Now, take a further look at offsetting one element relative to another.

`Top` and `left` are specific locations *in relation to* an enclosing object. For example, if your element is not enclosed within another element, the top and left are specified in relation to the browser window (or "viewport").

The World Wide Web Consortium (W3C) is quite vague and sometimes contradictory about some of its terminology. A central problem — aside from traditional academic fondness for airy theory — is that the W3C wants to avoid using the specific, concrete, understandable term *browser*. Instead, they prefer the abstraction of the term *viewport* — a device-independent notion. Given that HTML and its offspring are supposed to be usable on cell phones and large monitors, the idea is that the term *viewport* more accurately expresses the potential variety of output devices. Given that 99 percent of your CSS efforts will end up in a browser, I suggest that you politely ignore the platform-independence abstractions. It's just confusing. So, like most authors of books on CSS, I'll just ignore the viewport problem and use the terms *browser window* and *viewport* interchangeably.

Sometimes elements are positioned *within* other elements (such as a paragraph `<p>` inside a block `<div>`). In that case, specifying top and left are *in relation to* the container element — the `<div>` that surrounds the `<p>`, for example.

Visualize documents as made up of blocks nested inside other blocks. A simple document with just a series of paragraph (`<p>`) elements can be viewed as a `<body>` element containing the `<p>` elements. Here's the official terminology: The body is the *containing block* of these paragraphs.

Notice that the blocks-within-blocks visual description parallels the idea of a "tree-structure" within an XML or even an HTML document. *Parent/child* is another way to describe this hierarchical concept.

Enough theory. Take a look at an example of positioning:

```
<html>
<head>
<style>
div.sidebar {position: absolute; background-color:
          cornflowerblue; top: 0; left: 0; width: 100px;
```

```
height: 75%; padding-left: 6px; padding-right: 4px; padding-
          top: 6px; font-size: 16pt;}
div.maintext {position: absolute;  background-color:
          darkkhaki; top: 0; left: 110px; height: 75%;
width: 75%;}
img.relative {position: relative; left = 35%; top = 20%}
</style>
</head>
<body>
<div class="sidebar"> HERE is a sidebar. You can fill it with
          links, text, whatever... </div>
<div class="maintext">
<IMG class="relative" height="100" width="175"
          src="town.jpg">
</div>
</body>
</html>
```

This code results in the window shown in Figure 4-6.

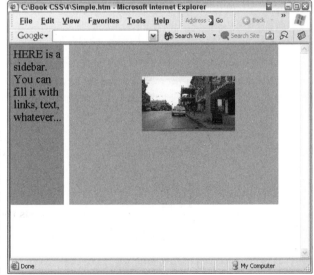

Figure 4-6:
A variety
of CSS
positioning
techniques
are
illustrated in
this figure.

In the header, you define three rules: sidebar, maintext, and relative. The
first style provides information about how a sidebar class of the <div> element should look:

```
div.sidebar {position: absolute; background-color:
          cornflowerblue; top: 0; left: 0; width: 100px;
```

```
height: 75%; padding-left: 6px; padding-right: 4px; padding-
          top: 6px; font-size: 16pt;}
```

This rule specifies that a `<div>` should be absolutely positioned within the browser window at the upper-left corner (`0 top offset` and `0 left`). As we say in North Carolina, that thing is *slap in the corner* — it couldn't get any further up or over to the left. It is specified as 100 pixels wide, but notice that the height is *not* an absolute value. It is expressed as a percentage of the containing block (in this case, the containing block is the browser). As you can see in Figure 4-6, the sidebar `div` on the left side is 75 percent the height of the browser window.

This is an important point: Remember that you can express both size and position as *relative* percentages, even though they are within a style where the position property has been defined as *absolute*.

Try running this example and then resizing the browser window to make it longer. Notice that the browser maintains the 75 percent height ratio between the `div` and the browser window.

The `sidebar` class also specifies some padding on the left, right, and top. This is a useful way to keep text or other elements from looking awkward by butting right up against the edges of a `div` or other block. Without that padding, notice how crude the text looks against the background, in Figure 4-7.

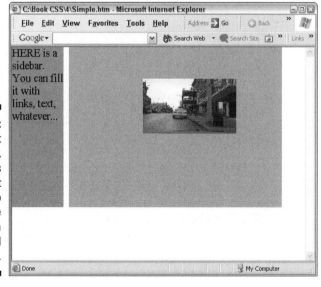

Figure 4-7:
Without padding, text looks crude as it butts up against the sides of a background block.

Moving Deeper into Positioning

In this section, I explore some further refinements of CSS positioning. CSS has lots of ways to assist you in achieving the precise layout you're aiming for in your Web pages.

In the preceding sample of code, the background color is described as *cornflowerblue*. Obviously this is a more readable, understandable, and memorable way of expressing this color than the bizarre RGB equivalent (#6495ED). Browsers other than IE 6 can have problems using descriptive words for colors. So if you're worried about your page looking bad on other browsers, use #6495ED instead of *cornflowerblue*. All browsers can translate #6495ED, even if we humans can't.

But my advice is to just assume that pretty much everyone who'll see your Web page uses IE. Why? Because most everyone *does* use IE.

 I've included the IE color list in this book's Cheat Sheet, which is located inside the front cover. Or you can see the complete color table, with both descriptive and RGB values, at `http://msdn.microsoft.com/library/ default.asp?url=/workshop/author/dhtml/reference/properties/ background_0.asp`. Or, if Microsoft has moved the table to a different URL (not that Microsoft would ever shift one of their site's addresses around!), try searching the MSDN site for *color table*.

Remember the three styles defined in the header of the preceding sample of code? The second style you defined is for the main section in the Web page, called `maintext`:

```
div.maintext {position: absolute;  background-color:
        darkkhaki; top: 0; left: 110px; height: 75%;width:
        75%;}
```

This is similar to the sidebar class, but uses a different color, and offsets the `div` 110 pixels from the left side of the browser window. This is an absolute offset and does not change if the user stretches the browser window to make it wider. Notice the relationship between 110 pixels (defined as the left side of the main section here) and the previous sidebar style, which specified that the sidebar `div` is 100 pixels wide. This way, these two `div`s fit together nicely, with a little 10-pixel-wide stripe. How would you get rid of the stripe? Make the `maintext` class left property 100 pixels, or expand the size of the sidebar to 110 pixels.

CSS units of measurement

You can specify top, left, height or width with the following units:

- **px:** pixels, the smallest unit on a display — the dots of colored light that you can sometimes see if you get close enough to a TV

- **pt:** points, 1/72 inch. Normally this is a typeface measurement

- **pc:** picas, 1 pica = 12 points

- **mm:** millimeters

- **cm:** centimeters

- **in:** inches

- **em:** A measurement of the approximate font size of the current element

- **ex:** the x-height (the height of a lowercase x) of the font of the current element — usually about 1/2 the size of em

For relative size or position, use % for percent. Units of measurement are covered in detail in Chapter 6.

What would happen if you left the `maintext` class at 110 pixels left, but expanded the size of the sidebar class to, say, 130 pixels? Every group always has a joker who wants to see what happens if he violates spaces. Go ahead and try it. The division called `maintext` (which comes after the sidebar in the HTML) covers up part of the sidebar and part of the sidebar's text. You *can* create cool effects by manipulating overlapping blocks and adjusting their opacity (so you could still see the text in the sidebar), but I get to those tricks later.

Notice that with the `maintext` class, you defined both its height and width as *relative*. Both the width and height are 75 percent, but the width is compromised if the user adjusts the width of the browser window because the browser has to make allowances for displaying the sidebar with its absolute width.

The third style defined in the header of the preceding code specifies an image with an entirely relative location *within its containing block*. Unlike the `div` elements, which are contained by the browser itself, the image is contained within a `div`. So the position of 35 percent left means that the left side of the photo is positioned at about one-third of the width of the `maintext` `div`, and at 20 percent, or about one-fifth, down from the top of the `div`. You can see these offsets in Figure 4-6.

```
img.relative {position: relative; left = 35%; top = 20%}
```

If you try stretching the browser wider or longer, the photo moves to maintain its one-third from the left, one-fifth from the top position within its container `div`.

Finally, in the body of the document, you display your elements:

```
<div class="sidebar"> HERE is a sidebar. You can fill it with
        links, text, whatever... </div>
<div class="maintext">
<IMG class="relative" height="100" width="175"
        src="town.jpg">
```

Notice that the image specifies the size that you want the photo to be in absolute terms (pixels are the default unit of measurement, used if you don't specify any other unit). If you don't specify height and width, the image appears at *its* true size.

Stacking Elements on Top of Each Other with the Z-Axis

Clearly, there's more to positioning than mere horizontal (left) or vertical (top) coordinates. Indeed, there's a third axis, known as the *z-axis*. It's what happens when something in a browser overlaps another object, or is "on top of it" in the sense that laying a book on a table puts that book on top of the table.

In CSS, you specify which object is on top of another by using the z-index property. A higher z-index value causes an object to appear on top. For example, recall the experiment earlier in this chapter when you had the `maintext` class at 110 pixels left, but expanded the size of the `sidebar` class to 130 pixels? The `maintext` covered up part of the `sidebar`. You can change this by adjusting the `sidebar`'s z-index to 99 or some number that you know is higher than the `maintext`. This will move the `sidebar` div on top of the `maintext` div.

```
div.sidebar {position: absolute; z-index: 99; background-
        color: cornflowerblue; top: 0; left: 0;width:
        130px; height: 65%; padding-left: 6px; padding-
        right: 4px; padding-top: 6px; font-size: 16pt;}
```

(Note that I also reduced the height of the sidebar from 75 percent to 65 percent so that the overlapping would show up better in Figure 4-8.)

When you add a high z-index value, the sidebar moves on top of the `main text` div, as shown in Figure 4-8:

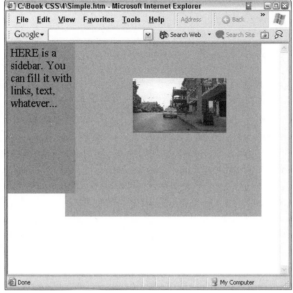

Figure 4-8:
This sidebar
is positioned
"on top" of
the
`maintext`
`div`, thanks
to a high z-
index value.

Combining Stacking with Translucence

Now try a cool trick that combines stacking with opacity adjustments. It's useful for all kinds of design effects and is particularly dramatic when used with scripting that animates the opacity or positioning of the elements dynamically. This kind of animation can be quite compelling when used correctly. This example adjusts the sample code you've been using throughout this chapter, but causes the `sidebar` element to show through the `maintext` element.

CSS3 is working to incorporate an opacity property in some future spec, but why wait? IE 5.5 and later supports an opacity feature you can use right now. How about some stacking, combined with *blending* of elements? Take a look at Figure 4-9.

In Figure 4-9, the `sidebar` is defined as having a lower z-index than the `maintext` `div`. The `sidebar` has a z-index of 1 and the `maintext` has a z-index of 2; therefore, the `maintext` is superimposed on top of the `sidebar`. However, the `sidebar` shows through because the `maintext` is made somewhat transparent by giving it an opacity value of 60. (An opacity value of 0 makes an element fully transparent; a value of 100 makes it fully opaque.)

```
filter:progid:DXImageTransform.Microsoft.Alpha(opacity=60)
```

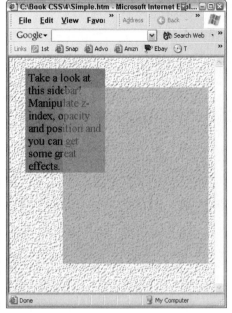

Figure 4-9:
Combine
positioning,
z-index, and
opacity to
create many
cool effects.

Here's the complete code that produces Figure 4-9. Note: This code assumes
that you have a graphic file with a sandstone texture (called sandstone.jpg)
in the same folder on your hard drive as the .htm file. If you don't, substitute
another texture in a graphics file for the background, but name it
sandstone.jpg so that the following code will work.

```
<html>
<head>
<style>

div.sidebar {position: absolute; z-index: 1; background-
        color: cornflowerblue; top: 20; left: 30; width:
        150px; height: 35%; padding-left: 6px; padding-
        right: 4px; padding-top: 6px; font-size: 16pt;}
div.maintext {position: absolute; z-index: 2;
        filter:progid:DXImageTransform.Microsoft.Alpha(opa
        city=60); background-color: darkkhaki; top:
        55;left: 100px; height: 75%; width: 75%;}

</style>

</head>
<body background="sandstone.jpg">
```

```
<div class="sidebar"> Take a look at this sidebar! Manipulate
          z-index, opacity and position and you can get some
          great effects.</div>
<div class="maintext">

</div>
</body>
</html>
```

Imagine the nice fade-in effect that you can generate if you add some scripting to slowly adjust the opacity value while the user is watching. You've probably seen cool effects like fades on some of the better-designed Web sites. By the time you finish this book, you'll know how to create animation with CSS and scripting. But if you're the impatient type who wants to get to it right away, flip over to Chapter 16 now.

If you are concerned about browser-independent code, other browsers than IE also support opacity through proprietary properties. This code enables this trick to work in IE, Mozilla, Safari, and Opera:

```
div.maintext {position: absolute; z-index: 2; background-
          color: darkkhaki; top: 55;left: 100px; height:
          75%; width: 75%;
   opacity: 0.6;    /*supported by current Mozilla, Safari, and
          Opera*/-moz-opacity: 0.6;  /*older Mozilla*/
   -khtml-opacity: 0.6;    /*older Safari*/
   filter: alpha(opacity=60);  /*older IE*/
   filter:progid:DXImageTransform.Microsoft.Alpha(opacity=60)}
```

Chapter 5

All About Text

C SS offers you many ways to style text. If you make wise choices, your overall page design is appealing to your site's visitors. On the other hand, an otherwise elegant, powerful Web page can be ruined if you don't give thought to how text integrates with the graphic effects. This chapter is devoted to CSS text styling.

Thinking About User Interfaces

The user views your Web site as both a graphic and a body of text. As a designer, you are responsible for avoiding obvious problems such as background graphics dark enough to make foreground text unreadable, jumpy animation, distracting colors, poor general design, and so on.

But you're also responsible for choosing text characteristics that are both pleasing and that reflect the image you want to project.

Obviously, a bank site wants to project solidity and conservatism, so the classic Times Roman font is a better choice than the Joker font, shown in Figure 5-1.

Even after you've selected a typeface, you must consider other issues as well when designing your CSS text styles: font size, bold or italic, centered, justified, superscript, initial caps, or underlined.

Figure 5-1:
Choose
fonts that
reflect the
image
you're trying
to project.
The Joker
typeface
isn't
reassuring
to bank
customers.

The First National Citizens & Trust

The First National

Citizens & Trust

Substituting Fonts

A font is a particular design of the letters of the alphabet, digits, and associated symbols and punctuation marks. Two different fonts are displayed in Figure 5-1, and it's easy to see how many different ways you can distort the characters of the alphabet and still leave them recognizable.

Many authors of books on CSS fret that people using various operating systems might not have specific fonts. So, for example, a designer might specify the popular Times New Roman font, but a browser running on Linux might substitute a similar font (perhaps Times Roman, or Garamond) rather than the Times New Roman they specified.

But so what? First, font *families* share enough characteristics that it isn't that crucial. What's more, the great majority of Web users use Windows, which ships with a standard set of fonts, including Times New Roman. The viewer is likely to get exactly what the designer specifies 96 percent of the time.

When memory and hard drive space was scarce in computers, people sometimes deleted fonts to conserve space. No longer. You can count on nearly all users having the full Microsoft set that came with the operating system. Nobody bothers to delete these fonts any more.

My computer has 295 fonts, and I've not added nor subtracted any since Windows XP was installed. However, some of these aren't actually separate fonts — instead they're variants such as Times New Roman Bold, Times New Roman Bold Italic, and so on. On your computer, you'll find fonts for every occasion, and some fonts that are not good for *any* occasion except perhaps scaring away users through sheer bad taste.

Font families are, not surprisingly, specified in CSS rules using the `font-family` property. If you want all paragraphs in your document to use the Arial typeface, you create the rule like this:

```
p {font-family: arial;}
```

Some font names have a space in them, such as Times New Roman or Showcard Gothic. In those cases (and also if the name includes any symbols such as % or @), you should enclose the name in single quotes, like this:

```
p {font-family: 'Showcard Gothic', arial;}
```

Types of Type

Fonts fall into two primary categories, based on whether or not they have curlicues and varied line widths. Take a look at Figure 5-2, which illustrates the sans serif style of fonts — the plainer style with fixed line widths and plain line ends.

Figure 5-2:
Sans serif fonts, like Arial, have lines that don't vary in width, and the ends of lines don't flare — they stop abruptly.

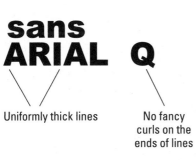

Uniformly thick lines

No fancy curls on the ends of lines

Now consider Figure 5-3, the serif style, that looks a bit more like handwriting because, like characters drawn with a pen, the line widths vary and the ends of the lines taper off to a point or a blob:

The distinction between serif and sans serif is quite stark in the letter *I*. As you can see by comparing Figures 5-2 and 5-3, the sans serif version is like a simple brick. The serif version is more like a roman column, flared at the top and bottom and tapered.

Figure 5-3:
Serif fonts
have
curlicues at
the tips and
their line
weights
vary.

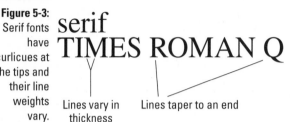

serif

TIMES ROMAN Q

Lines vary in   Lines taper to an end
thickness

Eagle-eyed readers may notice that in Figure 5-2, a few of the lines do vary a little bit in thickness, and some are a tiny bit flared at the end (notice the Q). However, the standard division between sans serif and serif nonetheless overwhelmingly prevails. Over the centuries, various typeface designers have fiddled a little with sans serif fonts to make them ever so slightly less rigid. Likewise, during most of the twentieth century, serif fonts have generally tended to evolve into designs slightly less decorative (or shall we say less *ornate*) in obedience to the modern preference for simplicity, straight lines, and boxy shapes. You've doubtless heard the famous dictum, "Less is more." Today's architects and painters seem to be emerging from the minimalist aesthetic that has ruled for the past five decades, but only time will tell. For now, less is still considered more in most creative fields.

Serif fonts have traditionally been used more for body text, where they are thought to improve readability because the letters have more visual variety. This diversity and the small strokes and flourishes at the ends give letters more individuality than the cleaner but more uniform sans serif styles.

You can think of serif italic fonts as an amplification of the qualities associated with serif, plus they are tilted to the right.

Sans serif fonts and all-caps have traditionally been used more often than serif fonts in headlines because headlines are brief and relatively large, and readability is less of an issue with large text. These traditional design rules, however, are now widely ignored.

One exception to the greater legibility of sans serif faces happens at extremely small sizes. When squeezed into "mousetype," serifs start to obscure readability and the cleaner lines of a sans serif face are actually an advantage. If you don't want people to read the fine print in a contract, be sure to put it in a serif font. Here's an example of small typefaces you can load into your browser to see the difference:

```
<html>
<head>

<style>
```

```
p {font-size: 7pt;}
p.arial {font-family: arial;}

</style>
</head>

<body>

<p>
It's a bit difficult to read text at small font sizes, which
            is an advantage if -- for strictly legal reasons -
            - you don't want someone to see the small print in
            your document.
</p>

<p class = "arial">
It's a bit difficult to read text at small font sizes, which
            is an advantage if -- for strictly legal

reasons -- you don't want someone to see the small print in
            your document.
</p>

</body>
</html>
```

One particularly interesting font design is called *Optima,* which attempts to combine the qualities of serif and sans serif. It is classically proportioned but avoids serifs. It's actually quite a beautiful font.

Figure 5-4:
Optima (or as Microsoft calls it, Optimum) is a hybrid font combining qualities of both sans and serif fonts.

Optima permits itself some slight serifs (see the lowercase *a*) and also a little variation in line widths. So, if you want to combine sans and serif, consider a font like Optima.

Font names vary, but you can usually figure out synonymous fonts because the alias names often closely resemble the official name, as in the classic Palatino and the alias Palomino. If you're unsure how closely two typefaces match, look closely at the uppercase Q and the ampersand (&). These are usually among the most distinctive characters in the typeface alphabet.

Fonts progress from the austere to the ornamental, with sans serif fonts at the austere end of this spectrum, and then progressing to serif, italic serif, and various "cursive" fonts (they imitate handwriting and are best left to wedding invitations and French restaurant menus). At the far end of the spectrum you have the *exotic fonts* (also called ornamental or fantasy fonts). Alas, they are almost never useful. Exotic fonts feature adorned letters (see Figure 5-1 and 5-5). They appeal to very few people over the age of 17, so try to avoid them in most Web page designs. Because most of them are difficult to read, limit their use, if any, to headlines rather than body text.

Figure 5-5: Most of these fonts should be avoided, as a way of preserving your reputation for good judgment.

Perhaps if you're designing a Halloween Web site, or an invitation to a costume ball, you might want to resort to some of the exotic fonts illustrated in Figure 5-5, but for most purposes, they're simply grotesque and to be avoided. For example, the Gigi font might be good for a French-related site, the Magneto for 50s retro designs, Weltron for radiation warnings, and Chiller for horror movie ads. You can visualize using some exotic fonts in specialized contexts; they're attractive in their way. But Baby Kruffy, Jokewood — *where,* on what kind of Web page, could they ever be charming?

Avoiding monospace

I'm also not spending much time on monospace fonts. These fonts — Courier is the most famous — were used frequently until a generation ago. They were used not because they looked good, or were easy to read, but because they solved a technological problem. Monospaced font allot the same width to each character, even when it's senseless to do so. In other words, the *i* is as wide as the *w*. So you have a wad of white space on either side of the i, and other letters have varying amounts of too much or too little room between them.

Why then was monospace so widely used? Most typewriters could not manage proportional (varying) character widths, and some display devices had a similar problem. These issues died along with the typewriter. Computer output devices — printers and monitors — can quite easily handle variations in character width. So just ignore monospaced character fonts. Their day is done, with a single exception: Monospaced fonts like this are sometimes used in books and browsers to indicate computer language code. Try the <code> tag in HTML to see it.

Using system styles

Windows offers a variety of typefaces for its various components. If you want to use elements in your Web pages that look like the Windows fonts (or some other operating system that's hosting the browser), you can use system fonts. The available fonts are caption, icon, menu, message-box, small-caption (for captions on tiny components), and status-bar. Here's an example you can load into Internet Explorer to see these font effects:

```
<html>
<head>

<style>

button {font: caption;}
icon {font: icon;}
menu {font: menu;}

</style>
</head>
<body>

<button>
This is a caption on a button
</button>

<br>
<icon>
ICON FONT
```

```
</icon>

<br>
<menu>
menu font
</menu>

</body>
</html>
```

If you're planning to extensively mimic the OS look and feel in your Web pages, however, you might want to consider using backgrounds created in graphics applications and other special techniques described in Chapter 7.

All Roads Lead to Rome

For most body text, especially for serious, formal Web pages (for example, Web sites that are corporate or religious or wherever sobriety and dignity are expected), a *Roman* font is ideal. All serif typefaces derive from a classic, elegant alphabet designed by an unknown Roman calligraphic genius in the first century AD.

His work quickly spread throughout the civilized world — appearing on everything from public architecture to coins. This seminal typeface consisted originally only of capital letters. It was so thoughtfully designed — close to perfection really — that it continues to dominate Western text, and it probably always will.

Originally carved into marble on temples and statues, the typeface now known as *Roman* proved equally suitable to ink on paper.

Simplicity above all

The other major event in typeface design took place in 1816, and this time we know who to thank. William Caslon IV, scion of a family of famous typeface designers, lopped off the serifs and enforced a single line width for his new typefaces. This represented a return to the long-ignored Greek alphabet of 500 BC, and it anticipated the "Less is more" aesthetic. Now called *sans serif* (*sans* is French for "without"), this typeface dominates headlines, captions, pull-quotes, or any text located apart from, or larger than, body text. Take a look at several popular sans faces in Figure 5-6:

HAETTEN
Sans
Some
Modern
TAHO

Figure 5-6:
Without serifs, letters are sparer but harder to read in body text.

For comparison, here are some famous serif faces, in Figure 5-7:

Palatino
Goudy
Garamond
Times Roman
Calisto

Figure 5-7:
These serif typefaces are all good choices for body text.

As you can see in Figure 5-7, different Roman typefaces have detectable differences in their look and feel. Palatino and Calisto are heavier, so they'll darken a page that has lots of text. Goudy is light, but some consider it and Caslon (also known as Calisto) too "fussy" and old-fashioned.

However, if you've got lots of text and little "white space" (blank areas) on a page, consider Goudy or some other relatively weightless typeface to see if you can lighten things up a bit. Garamond is perhaps the oldest typeface that remains extremely popular. It will likely be around as long as people use Western alphabets. It's an excellent all-purpose choice for body text. Times Roman (of various varieties) is also a safe choice for body text. Times New Roman is the default font displayed in Internet Explorer unless an HTML font element, or a CSS rule, specifies otherwise. The user can also change the default font in IE by choosing Tools⇨Internet Options, and then clicking the Fonts button in the Internet Options dialog box that appears.

When you're not too picky about typeface

If you're not that concerned about *which* particular typeface is used, you can specify generic sans or serif (use `sans-serif` or `sans`), like this CSS style that enables the user's browser to pick a serif font — probably Times New Roman:

```
body {font-family: serif;}
```

Also, because the `<body>` element is parent to paragraphs `<p>` and other children, those children inherit this serif font too (unless a more specific selector insists on another style).

You can combine a specific font request with a generic fallback position. If Garamond isn't available on the user's machine, the user's default serif font is used in response to the following rule:

```
body {font-family: Garamond, serif;}
```

Using Font Variants

When should you use italic, bold, underlining, and other typeface variations? Most typefaces have several variants, with boldface and italic the most common. Boldface is most often used in headlines. It's big and thick. It's rarely used in body text because it's too distracting. Like an all-uppercase font, body text bold can be too much of a good thing.

If you want to emphasize something in body text, use *italics,* not all-caps or bold or any other trick. *Just italics.* (Young people tend to emphasize body text in all kinds of ways. In addition to **c** and ALL CAPS, they reverse the type (white-on-black), underline, draw hearts, add rows of exclamation points!!!!!, and so on. These tactics do add emphasis of a sort, but like someone who thinks that shouting makes their argument stronger, these techniques are not all that convincing and quickly become tiresome. Just use italics in body text when you want to add emphasis.

One special exception: Sprinkle boldface in body text if you want to give the reader a way to quickly scan some text. The bold words act like mini-headlines embedded within the text. The classic example of this technique is the gossip column where the names of the celebrities are bold. You can use this approach in corporate reports, travel advertisements, or anywhere else where you aren't using subheads, yet you want to give the reader an efficient way to skim through the text and locate topics of interest.

Although their use in body text should be limited, boldface, all-caps, and underlining are often useful in headlines and can add necessary variety to your page designs.

Specifying Font Weight

When you want to adjust the *weight* (the darkness, boldness, or lightness), you can resort to these relative CSS values: `normal`, `bold`, `bolder`, `lighter`, `100`, `200`, `300`, `400`, `500`, `600`, `700`, `800`, `900`, `inherit`. The higher the number, the bolder the font weight. Most often, simply use the `bold` value:

```
H2 {font-weight: bold;}
```

The values from `100` to `900` are merely indications of the desired weight, but few user typefaces have this many weights. Although this scheme has no absolutes, you can think of weights `100-300` as roughly equivalent to "light" faces, such as Copperplate Gothic Light, `400-500` as regular (the CSS value `normal`), and `600-900` as bold. However, if a typeface has weight distinctions such as bold, ultrabold, and so on, the numeric weight values add more specificity.

You can use the values `lighter` or `bolder` to specify a boldness relative to the element's parent element, like this:

```
body {font-weight: bold;}
p {font-weight: bolder;}
```

In this case, `<body>` elements are bold, but `<p>` elements are, if possible, displayed in an even heavier face. Times New Roman has no weight beyond bold, so a `bolder` value has no effect. However, in the following case, text outside `<p>` tags is regular, and text inside `<p>` tags is made bold:

```
body {font-weight: regular;}
p {font-weight: bolder;}
```

Using the Font-Variant for Small Caps

The `small-caps` value is a specialized variant on normal letters. It creates capital letters that are about 75 percent the size of the normal capitals. This isn't used often, but it looks good when you need it. You'll see it most often when the terms AD or BC are used to indicate dates, as in the following example.

```
<html>
<head>

<style>

em.smallcaps {font-style: normal;font-variant: small-caps;}

p {font-size: x-large;}

</style>
</head>


<body>


<p>
These vases were created around 4000 <em
          class="smallcaps">b.c.</em>Before glazing was
          invented.
</p>


</body>
</html>
```

The result looks like this:

These vases were created around 4000 BC. Before glazing was invented.

Notice that the BC is displayed in capitals, but compare the *B* to the size of the normal *B* in the word *Before*.

Simple Font-Style

The `font-style` property has only three possible values: `normal`, `italic`, and `oblique`. Because italic is generally used only to emphasize a word or phrase *within* normal text, you generally see the ⟨i⟩ tag used to specify italics within the HTML code. The oblique style is rarely specified in a CSS style — it merely tilts the letters of a normal font to the right so that they lean a little. Oblique is similar to italic, but italic is actually a separate typeface design, with slight changes to the normal font in addition to the tilt to the right. When you specify italic for most serif fonts such as Times Roman, you get the real italic effect. However, many sans serif fonts respond to the request for italics by merely generating a slight offset and tilting the normal letters to the right. In effect, sans serif italics are often actually oblique, although they're specified as italic. In practice, you can just ignore the oblique style.

Choosing the Right Typeface Size

Two things to remember when deciding typeface sizes for a Web page. First, limit yourself to two or three sizes per page; too many different sizes confuse readers and make your pages look cluttered and disorganized. (You can get this same disorganized effect by choosing too many different typefaces.) Second, the size should be appropriate to the space allotted to it on the page. Using a small typeface within a large empty area can be disorienting. Equally unattractive is large type squeezed into a small amount of space.

One more thing to consider about size: Don't worry too much about the impossible goal of browser-independence. Just design your Web page with Internet Explorer set to fullscreen on your 17" or 19" monitor, using 800x600 or 1024x768 resolution, and the result will likely please 96 percent of the people who visit your Web site. They'll be using pretty much the same size monitor and the same browser. So don't sweat it. Trying for the lowest common denominator among open-source software, mini-screen portable devices, and uncommon operating systems has a predictable result: Your Web page looks like the lowest common compromise. Trying to please everybody, you'll please no one. Just go with the overwhelming majority. People surfing the Web with Linux and PDAs are used to seeing strange typeface effects (among lots of other compromises). Your site's awkward appearance on their screen will be no surprise to them; they see stuff like that all the time.

If you're forced to design for different output devices, or even different media types altogether (such as both screen and paper), consider creating separate style sheets, one for each target device or medium. This approach allows you to optimize your design for each target.

Specifying relative sizes

The differences in most people's monitor sizes and resolutions aren't enormous, but using *relative* size (and often position) specifications when possible helps. This way, you get the most predictable proportions on most browsers. Here are the CSS values you can specify for the font-size property: xx-small, x-small, small, medium, large, x-large, xx-large, smaller, larger, length, percentage, inherit.

One way to indicate a size relative to the parent element is to use the values smaller or larger, like this:

```
<html>
<head>

<style>

body {font-size: x-large;}

p {font-size: smaller;}

div {font-size: larger;}


</style>
</head>

<body>

This is the body text

<p>
This is one step smaller than its parent body.
</p>

<div>
This is one step larger than the parent.
</div>

</body>
</html>
```

Load this example into IE and you see results like those shown in Figure 5-8.

The xx-large value is the largest value in the list of possible CSS text size values. However, if you then apply the larger value to a child element within xx-large text, IE follows your request and goes beyond xx-large.

Controlling font size with greater precision

If you want to try for a bit more precision than "smaller" or "larger" but still avoid specifying absolute points or pixels, use percentages. For example, to make a paragraph font 75 percent the size of its parent div, try this:

```
div {font-size: xx-large;}
p {font-size: 75%;}
```

You can also use percentages higher than 100 to increase the child element's size relative to its parent, like this:

```
p {font-size: 145%;}
```

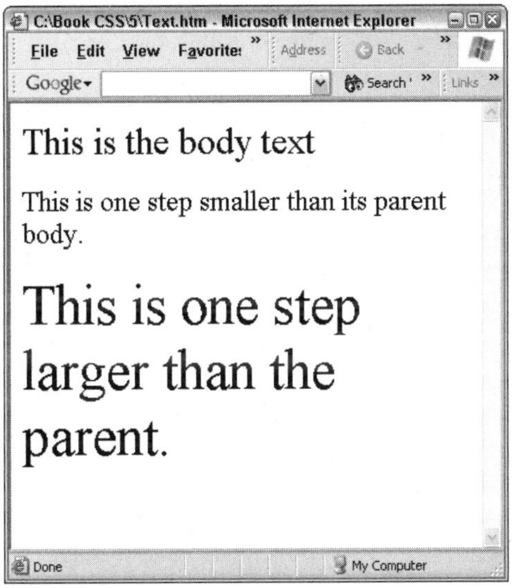

Figure 5-8:
Using the
relative
values
`smaller`
and
`larger`
adjusts an
element's
text size in
relation to
its parent
element.

C:\Book CSS\5\Text.htm - Microsoft Internet Explorer

File   Edit   View   Favorite: Address   Back

Google▼   Search'   Links

This is the body text

This is one step smaller than its parent body.

This is one step larger than the parent.

Done   My Computer

Specifying Absolute Measured Sizes

You can also avoid the relativistic specifications discussed so far and force type size to be a particular unit of measurement, such as .5 inch or 12 points. Recall that the available units of measurement are px (pixels), pt (points), pc (picas), mm (millimeters), cm (centimeters), in (inches), em (the current element's approximate font size), and ex (x-height, the height of the lower-case letter *x* in the current font). This example specifies that paragraph text should be two-tenths of an inch and level-one headlines should be 24 points:

```
body {font-size: .2in;}
h1 {font-size: 24pt;}
```

Most designers use pt or px when specifying font sizes in CSS rules, so you might as well join them. You probably already have a sense of how pt or px work, so stick with what you know.

Font: The All-Purpose Property

Throughout this chapter, you've seen all the many ways you can specify how a typeface should look, using *font-this* and *font-that* properties, like this:

```
p {font-family: Garamond; font-size: 26px;
    font-weight: bold; font-style: italic;}
```

However, you can use a shorthand to create CSS style definitions for type-faces: Just use the all-purpose `font` property. That way, you can leave out specifying each property name (`font-weight`, `font-family`, and so on). Just list the values you want and the browser correctly interprets them. It can tell, for example, that the `bold` value can be used only with the `font-weight` property, and not with `font-size`, `font-variant`, or the `font-family` properties.

This same shorthand feature is available for many other CSS properties, such as the `border` property. Borders can be specified using hyphenated properties such as `border-bottom`, but the shorthand `border` property, followed by a list of values, also works. Whether you use the long or abbreviated format is up to you.

Normally, letting the computer take the burden off the designer or program-mer like this is useful. However, as you might expect, the `font` property isn't as straightforward as it could be. You must memorize and be sure to follow some silly rules, or the browser ignores your style entirely (and, of course, provides no error message to warn you or help you fix the problem).

But if using abbreviations is your thing, go ahead and try out the `font` prop-erty. The p style in the previous example can be condensed in the following way by using the `font` property, like this:

```
p {font: bold italic 26px Garamond;}
```

Both styles will have the same result, but this condensed version saves some time *if* you remember the rules! Here are the rules:

The first two values in the list (`style` and `weight`) can be listed in any order. For example, you can reverse the preceding order with no ill effects:

```
p {font: italic bold 26px Garamond;}
```

You can also throw in a `font-variant` (small-caps) if you wish, and mix and match those first three values any way you want. The browser accepts those values in any order.

However, the last two values *must be* in `size`, `family` order. They *must* be the final two values in the list, *both* must be present in the list, and they *must* be in `size`, `family` order.

Nobody knows why *some* values can be rearranged at will, and others must be in strict order. It's just one of those exceptions to CSS rules that you have to memorize.

This next style rule fails, although different browsers respond in different ways:

```
p {font: bold italic Garamond 26px;}
```

The size-family order is wrong here. This list of values ends with size, and *all* such value lists must end with the `font-family` value. IE goes ahead with bold italics, but it ignores `Garamond` and the `26px` font size.

Sadly, those in charge of the CSS specifications really dropped the ball here. Getting this font value order wrong is an extremely common error, and this strictness is so completely unnecessary. If browsers can distinguish between words like *bold* and *italic*, they can certainly distinguish between digits like *26px* and words like *Garamond*. Oh well.

Adjusting Line Height

You can find a discussion of manipulating text spacing in Chapter 7, but while we're on the topic of the various `font-` properties, I want to take a brief look at how you can manipulate the spacing between lines of text using the `line-height` property.

Line heights are adjusted for two primary reasons. Headlines often look better with *less* white space between the lines; tiny body text sizes are more readable with *more* white space between the lines.

Here's an example showing how you to specify a change to line height. Follow the `font-size` value with a forward slash and the percent adjustment you want to make to the line height. (100 percent is expressed by 1, 120 percent is 1.2, 50 percent is .5, and so on.) A font size of 38 pixels with a line-height adjustment that shrinks the default spacing to 94 percent of normal looks like this: `38px/.94`

Here's an example that specifies two styles. Ordinary H1 headlines are to be bold 32 pixel Arial. But the special class of "narrowed" H1 headlines are to be at 94 percent of the default line spacing.

```
<html>
<head>

<style>

h1.narrowed {font: bold 38px/.94 Arial;}
h1 {font: bold 38px Arial;}
```

```
</style>
</head>
<body>

<h1>
This Is the H1 Style
With the Line Space Default
</h1>

<br>
<br>

<h1 class="narrowed">
This Is Our Superior H1 Style
With the Lines Closer Together
</h1>

</body>
</html>
```

As you can see in Figure 5-9, the adjusted line-height at the bottom of the browser is better looking than the default at the top. Newspapers and magazines, not to mention TV, billboards, and other media, almost always tighten the line spacing in their headlines. It simply looks better than leaving unnecessary white space floating in between the lines.

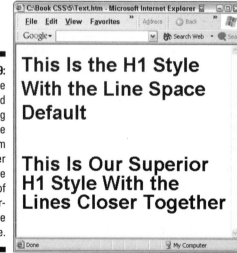

Figure 5-9: The modified line spacing on the bottom looks better and is more typical of contemporary headline style.

Kerning — adjusting the spacing between the individual letters in a headline — is also a common way to add visual appeal to text displayed in large font sizes. You see how to accomplish kerning in Chapter 7. Chapter 7 also covers several additional text management properties that relate to positioning: `word-spacing`, `text-indent`, `indentation`, **and** `vertical-align`.

Decorating Text with Underlining and Strikethrough

For some reason, those-who-know-best (also known as the CSS specification committees) sometimes choose weird terminology. *Decoration* isn't a very good word for underlining and similar text effects. The text-decoration property doesn't actually refer to *decorating* the text, which suggests adding special ornamental designs like monks used to do in medieval times. Rather, this property governs underlining, overlining, strikethrough, and a bizarre effect called *blinking*.

The CSS overlords, in their wisdom, also went a bit whacko when they decided not to call one of the values *strikethrough* like everyone else does. Instead, they thought it might be fun to add a little confusion and call that style *line-through*. Get used to it.

Overlining (a line drawn above the text) can be used for a visual effect, or as a way of separating zones of text. Fortunately, IE in its wisdom, doesn't support the blinking text trick, which to most readers would be a thoroughly annoying distraction.

Underlining, overlining, and strikethrough (see Figure 5-10) are straightforward:

```
<html>
<head>

<style>

h1.over {text-decoration: overline;}
h1.under {text-decoration: underline;}
h1.strike {text-decoration: line-through;}

</style>
</head>
<body>

<h1 class="over">This is an overline.</h1>

<h1 class="under">This is an underline.</h1>

<h1 class="strike">This is a strikethrough.</h1>

</body>
</html>
```

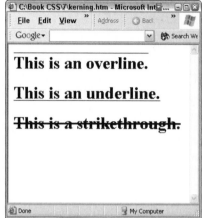

Figure 5-10:
The text-decora-tion properties add various kinds of lines to text.

Transforming Text with Capitalization

If you thought that using the term *decoration* for underlining was strange, consider using "transform" to describe capitalization. With the `text-transform` property, you can specify initial caps, all-uppercase, or all-lowercase.

You might well ask: If you want all uppercase on a Web page, *why don't you just press the Caps Lock key on your keyboard* and forget about this `text-transform` property?

First, you might want to make the text effects dynamic. Say that you want to uppercase a sentence if the user clicks it. You can write a script that adjusts the `text-transform` property to respond to user behaviors. Second, you might want to make the capitalization conditional. Perhaps you want to use initial caps for some headline styles in your site, but in other locations, you want all-caps.

The only strangeness in the value names is that what the CSS leadership confusingly calls the `capitalize` value is, in reality, initial caps.

```
<style>

h1.initcaps {text-transform: capitalize;}
h1.uppercase {text-transform: uppercase;}

</style>
```

This code results in the headlines shown in Figure 5-11:

You might want to avoid using the `transform` property for initial caps. English punctuation usually avoids making prepositions and articles initial-capped. Therefore, the words *into* and *the* should not be capitalized in the headline shown at the top of Figure 5-11.

Shading with Drop-Shadowing

A *drop shadow* is black or gray shading around each letter that makes the letters look as if they were casting shadows. It's often a good way to add dimension and realism to images or text.

Some graphic and typographic effects are best left to graphics applications like Photoshop. Those applications are dedicated to creating visual effects more sophisticated and subtle than any that can easily be achieved via HTML or CSS code. After all, graphics applications have tools that allow you to preview the effects; to use the mouse to assist in designing and modifying the effects; and to compare effects side-by-side. What's more, the built-in effects in a graphics application are carefully designed. For example, their drop-shadow uses a gradient for the shadow rather than a solid, unnatural looking black or gray. Put simply, leave the fancy visuals to applications that specialize in such things.

CSS2 includes a `drop-shadow` property, but mercifully, no browser on earth has implemented this feature. If you want to create a drop-shadow, do it in your graphics application, save it as a .jpg file, and then put the resulting `<img>` element into your Web page. Figure 5-12 illustrates the 3D effect you can get by adding a drop-shadow effect to text:

Figure 5-12:
Drop shadows can be a great visual effect, but create them in a graphics application (like this), not with CSS.

Drop Shadows

Chapter 6

Managing Details in Style Sheets

• •

In This Chapter

▶ Describing units, percentages, and lengths

▶ Adding color to your text

▶ Coloring the background

• •

*A*mong the various features of CSS that Web designers appreciate is the fine control it gives you over such details as color, text spacing, positioning, and size of various elements. Plain HTML comes to seem rather crude and clumsy after you've had some experience playing around with all the freedom that CSS gives you. With CSS, *you* decide just how things should look on your pages.

Specifying Size and Position

In a CSS style definition (or *rule*), you can describe positions and sizes in many ways, using may different units of measurement. You can often choose whatever unit you want, although certain specific kinds of measurements work best in certain situations.

For example, many designers working with paper and ink are used to specifying typefaces in *points*. A point is an absolute length: 1/72 of an inch. Using absolute type size specs for a magazine or book works just fine — after all, the user cannot shrink, stretch, or change the aspect ratio of a page in a book. (*Aspect ratio* is the ratio between height and width.) Browsers, though, can be resized at will. If you drag one side of a browser, you're changing it, making it thinner or fatter. In other words, your changing its shape, its aspect ratio, from, say, a square to a rectangle.

For fonts displayed in a browser, a relative unit of measurement is superior to the traditional points. Unlike absolute measurements such as points or inches, a relative unit scales with font sizes. As a result, you get more predictable results in Web pages with relative units of measurements specifying type size. One of the most useful relative units of measurements for a Web designer is the *em* — more on that later in this chapter. Although the em is useful, in practice, most designers still use points or pixels when specifying type size. Perhaps it's just force of habit, but in any case the results usually look fine in most browsers.

Measuring length

Before I get to an explanation of just what *em* actually means, I first want to take a look at all the units that measure length:

- **px (pixels):** Pixels are the smallest unit on a display — the dots you can sometimes see if you get close enough to a TV. For example, setting your monitor resolution to 800x600 means that it is 800 pixels wide by 600 pixels high.

  Pixels can be a useful way to specify font size, but the drawback is that if you specify pixels, that overrides the custom font size option in Internet Explorer — so users cannot adjust from "large" to "largest" and so on. However, you should always use px to describe *image* sizes. Images are already measurable in pixels (you can see the measurements by loading the image into any graphics application).

- **pt (points):** A point is equal to 1/72 inch. Points (and picas) are classic typeface measurements. Most browsers default to a 12-point serif typeface.

- **pc (picas):** One pica equals 12 points.

- **mm (millimeters):** A millimeter is .0394 inches, so one inch contains roughly 26 millimeters. One centimeter contains 10 millimeters. Much of the world uses this *metric* system.

- **cm (centimeters):** A centimeter is .3937 inches, so an inch contains roughly 2 1/2 centimeters.

- **in (inches):** Inches are a unit in the *English* or *imperial* system — used in the United States. England and a few remnants of the colonial period also stayed with the imperial system for a long time, but caved recently. The British government complied in 2000 with European metrication and it is now a criminal offense to sell by the pound anywhere in Her Majesty's realm. A man in Cornwall, for example, reportedly had to pay court costs after being caught selling mackerel at £1.50 a pound.

  An inch is based on the distance between the first knuckle and the end of a now-forgotten king's thumb. For 50 years, persistent efforts to educate and legislate away the imperial system in favor of the metric have failed in the U.S.

- **em:** Em is a unit of measurement derived from the approximate width of the letter *m* of a font. This is considered generally the best way to specify font size in CSS, although few designers follow this advice.

✔ **ex (the x-height):** Ex is the x-height, or height of the lowercase letter *x*, of the font of the current element. Browsers usually divide em by half to get the ex-height. This unit of measurement isn't currently as useful as the em because it's not as predictable an average for all typefaces.

✔ **% (percent):** Percentages are excellent for specifying relative size (it can be relative to an ancestor, the parent, and so on).

Units of measurement are not case-sensitive. You can capitalize them or not, as you wish. Likewise, in IE, you can include a space between the number and its unit, or not: For example, 2 in is equivalent to 2in. Other browsers don't like the space. For simplicity, using lowercase and avoiding unnecessary spaces is generally a good idea when working with CSS. Just get into the habit of the 2in or 24px format and you'll be fine, unless the CSS committees decide to reverse themselves in the future.

Understanding little em

Because experts recommend that you use em when designing a Web page that you want to look just so, it's worth taking a closer look at what this unit actually means. Traditionally, the em was the width of the letter *m*.

Perhaps you've heard the term *m-dash* or *em-dash*, which is the dash usually employed in publishing. It's a horizontal line — like these — equivalent to the width of the typeface's letter *m* (this isn't strictly a precise equivalent in many typefaces). There's also an *en-dash*. Guess what it's based on.

Em and ex units are *relative* to each typeface. This is useful because it means that the size specified by em changes in a precise way based on the user's monitor resolution, preference settings, and other factors. In other words, using em allows you to specify what happens *relative* to the typeface. The result is proportional to the other qualities of the typeface and surrounding text. Also, relative specifications like em allow people with handicaps to enlarge the typeface in their browser as necessary. Fixed specifications like px or pt don't offer the user this option.

Em and ex are traditional typesetter's unit of measure, but their meanings in CSS are slightly modified. For one thing, computers calculate ex by simply dividing em in half. This is easier to compute, but only an approximation for most fonts. Em in CSS is the font size in pixels. This is useful because you can specify em units and rely on them being relative to the parent (or other) element's font.

Here's an experiment to get the idea of how em is *relative* to another element. In this code, text within the element is defined as 26px, but text within the paragraph element is defined as 1.5em, or, put another way, one and one-half times the size of the parent. Later in the HTML code, the paragraph element is enclosed (parented) by the body element. Therefore, the paragraph text is rendered at 1.5x26 pixels (or 39 pixels).

```
<html>
<head>

<style>

body {font-size: 26px;}

p {font-size: 1.5em;}

p.abs {font-size: 39px;}


</style>
</head>
<body>

some text

<p>
some text (1.5 em of the parent body).
</p>

<p class="abs">
some text (39 pixels).
</p>

</body>
</html>
```

The text in the `abs` class version of `<p>` is rendered the same size as the ordinary `<p>`. The `<body>` element is a parent element of the `<p>`, and `<p>` is defined as `1.5em` of its parent. The parent body uses 26 pixels as its text size, so 26x1.5 results in 39 pixels. You can see the effect of the relativity between em and its parent `<body>` element in Figure 6-1:

Figure 6-1:
The second
line —
a child
element
set to
`1.5em` —
is therefore
1.5 times
the size of
the first line.

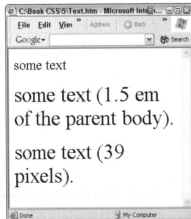

Figuring the Percentages

I switch now from considering ways to specify text size, to the use of percentages as a way of specifying the size or position of larger elements, such as paragraphs. This next example illustrates how you can use percentages to specify the width of a whole paragraph (not the font size of its text). In other words, this percentage value will tell the browser when to break a line of text into two lines (rather than how large to make the characters of text).

If you're familiar with such classic HTML percentage specifications as `<p width="80%">`, you'll have no problems understanding how percentages work in CSS. That HTML code in effect says, "Make this paragraph 80 percent (or four-fifths) as wide as the user's browser." In other words, an element's percentage is *in relation to* its container or parent.

CSS percentages work the same way. Here's an example that combines both CSS and HTML percentage values.

```
<html>
<head>

<style>

p.csspercent {margin-right: 20%}

</style>
</head>
<body>

here's some ordinary body text

<br>
<br>

<table width="80%">
text at eighty percent of the parent.
</table>


<p class="csspercent">
text at eighty percent of the parent.
</table>


</body>
</html>
```

First, this example displays unmodified, ordinary body text that fills the horizontal space in the browser, and then a table defined as 80 percent breaks and starts a new line when it reaches 80 percent across to the right side. Finally, a paragraph behaves the same way as the table, breaking at the 80 percent mark on its line — because you specified that the p.csspercent style had a 20 percent value for its margin-right property. You can see these effects in Figure 6-2:

Figure 6-2:
Setting a table's width property to 80 percent has the same effect as setting a CSS margin-right property to 20 percent — all else being equal.

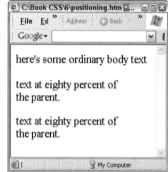

here's some ordinary body text

text at eighty percent of the parent.

text at eighty percent of the parent.

This next example shows how to use the CSS margin-right and margin-left properties with percentages:

```
<html>
<head>

<style>

p.leftside {margin-right: 50%}
p.rightside {margin-left: 50%}

</style>
</head>
<body>

here's some ordinary body text that goes the full distance
            across the browser window, then wraps to

the next line down.

<br>
<br>

<p class="leftside">
here's some ordinary paragraph text that stops half way
            across the browser window, then wraps to the
```

```
next line down.
</p>


<p class="rightside">
here's some ordinary paragraph text that starts half way
            across the browser window, then wraps to

half way across the next line down.
</p>



</body>
</html>
```

Figure 6-3 illustrates the effect of 50 percent margins, both right and left:

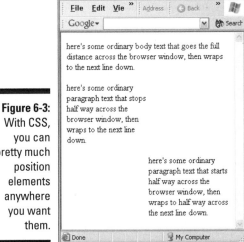

Figure 6-3: With CSS, you can pretty much position elements anywhere you want them.

Adding a Bit of Color

Color is useful for both the design and the organization of a Web page. Choosing effective, appropriate, and harmonic colors contributes quite a bit to the overall success of your page. Perhaps less obvious is the role that color plays in cueing the eye to the structure and logic of your layout.

You can create logical zones with color, just as you do with tables or lines. For example, you can help your users by coloring all your links the same color and grouping them in a separate area on the page — with a common background color underneath. All this helps the visitor to your site understand that these items in this area, with these colors, have something in common. And if you really want to attract attention to them, make them *puce, lavenderblush,* or some other unusual color. You can tie your color choices into the content of the Web page too: For example, use a yellow-orange background for a paragraph that contains a warning about a radioactivity danger.

Even superior to plain color in many situations is a designed background — a gradient, texture, a picture of clouds . . . anything that visually amplifies the message of your site. Many of the best-designed sites load a background image because creating such an image in a graphics program like Photoshop gives you control over every single pixel of your background. You can create pleasing, complex designs of any kind, not simply a single static color:

```
<body background="WaterView.jpg">
```

If you combine graphically designed backgrounds with animation (see Chapter 16), you can aspire to win an award . . . a Web page design award.

Here are some cool sites that can give you some creative inspiration:

```
http://www.philipkoether.com/
```

```
futurefarm.nl
```

```
http://www.tomoco.de/
```

The following page doesn't feature flashy animation, but the page is well-designed and shows off some of what CSS can do (while you're visiting this site, take a look around — it has some great CSS tutorials and resources):

```
http://glish.com/css/noah.asp
```

I have a lot to say about designing backgrounds in Chapter 7 and Chapter 16. For now, consider color alone.

As with setting margins, positioning text, and many other aspects of Web design, CSS is clearly superior to traditional HTML when it comes to managing color. With CSS, you can specify the foreground (text and borders) and background colors of pretty much *every* element. With traditional HTML, your ability to set colors is restricted only to a few elements.

CSS1 and CSS2 group all color into a "Color and Background" set of properties, but in CSS3 promises a new Color family, complete with various new features such as opacity and a new naming system. See Chapter 15 for more details on what CSS3 is expected to offer the designer.

Creating special paragraph styles

Assume that you're writing a Web page that contains special warning paragraphs, and you want these warnings to stand out. In addition to making them italic, you want the text to be a bright pumpkin color. To achieve this effect, just define a paragraph style called *warning* (or whatever you want to name it), and then add the italic and color specifications, like this:

```
<html>
<head>

<style>

p.warning {color: #ffcc33; font-style: italic;}

</style>
</head>
<body>

<p>An ordinary paragraph blah blah</p>

<p class="warning">
Warning: Wow! Here comes a whole bunch of gnats! What to do:
          cover yourself and your loved ones with netting
          and crouch down. Keep your mouth shut, too!
</p>

</body>
</html>
```

Calculating color

How do you figure out that color #ffcc33 is pumpkin and not, say, brown, or even an alarming color like fuchsia? When writing the previous CSS style, I didn't just *guess* the number #ffcc33, did I? After all, the possible color specifications range from 000000 (black) up to ffffff (white). In between are (potentially anyway) nearly 17 million colors. (For you sticklers, the precise number is 16,777,216.) And what kind of number system uses letters of the alphabet anyway? It must be pretty lame. (In fact, it *is* pretty lame, but computer programmers have been using this system for decades, so it's going to take a while yet to get rid of the monster.)

Some people are pretty color-sensitive, but no one is *that* sensitive. What could be less descriptive of a color than a code like #ffcc33? You'll never remember that #ffcc33 produces pumpkin, or that #00ff00 gives you lime green.

You can easily select colors in any of several ways and thereby avoid that bizarre scheme that employs totally useless codes. Here are my suggestions for specifying a CSS color:

✔ Create a background image in a graphics program and use its tools (such as a color wheel or gradient) to select your color.

✔ Use a special Style Editor in programs like Microsoft's Visual Studio to pick a color from a table of colors (as shown in Figure 6-4). It then translates your choice into a color number for the CSS style, such as #ffcc33.

✔ Choose a color from the list of descriptive color names (they work in Internet Explorer). The list is provided below in the section titled "Using the Color List." (You can also find this list in this book's Cheat Sheet inside the front cover.)

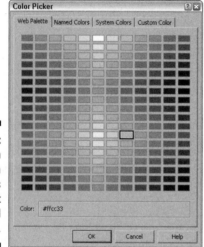

Figure 6-4:
You can click on a color in this palette built into Visual Studio.

You can also see how the colors will look in a browser and at the same time get the values by visiting online browser-safe color charts at sites such as this one:

```
www.primeshop.com/html/216colrs.htm
```

Using the color list

I'm not going to bore you with the details on what the #ffcc33 code means. It's called a *hex number,* but don't put a hex on yourself by trying to figure out what it means and how it works. It's too tedious for words, believe me. I did learn it years ago and, try as I might, I cannot forget it. It's taking up an area of my brain that I wish I could reuse for something important, but it's permanently occupied by useless information, like "The name of the drummer from Cheap Trick is Bun E. Carlos." See what I mean?

I have no idea why people still bother with hex these days (early in computing, several decades ago, hex and binary arithmetic were marginally useful). Manipulating hex numbers themselves is hard enough, but when you try to do arithmetic with them . . . well, it's easier to uncook spaghetti.

When you want to select a color for a Web page element, just pick a color from a *visual* representation (like a color gradient in Photoshop or a tabular palette like the one in Visual Studio shown in Figure 6-4, or an online color chart). Or, if you must, pick one from the list of color names that follows.

Don't try to deal with hexadecimal numbers. Who could possibly memorize which color goes with which "number?" Few people even understand the numbering system itself. And, truly, you don't need to understand it at all.

Here's Microsoft's list of colors that IE can recognize by *name*. No need to bother translating these names into hex values at all:

AliceBlue, AntiqueWhite, Aqua, Aquamarine, Azure, Beige, Bisque, Black, BlanchedAlmond, Blue, BlueViolet, Brown, BurlyWood, CadetBlue, Chartreuse, Chocolate, Coral, CornflowerBlue, Cornsilk, Crimson, Cyan, DarkBlue, DarkCyan, DarkGoldenrod, DarkGray, DarkGreen, DarkKhaki, DarkMagenta, DarkOliveGreen, DarkOrange, DarkOrchid, DarkRed, DarkSalmon, DarkSeaGreen, DarkSlateBlue, DarkSlateGray, DarkTurquoise, DarkViolet, DeepPink, DeepSkyBlue, DimGray, DodgerBlue, FireBrick, FloralWhite, ForestGreen, Fuchsia, Gainsboro, GhostWhite, Gold, Goldenrod, Gray, Green, GreenYellow, Honeydew, HotPink, IndianRed, Indigo, Ivory, Khaki, Lavender, LavenderBlush, LawnGreen, LemonChiffon, LightBlue, LightCoral, LightCyan, LightGoldenrodYellow, LightGreen, LightGrey, LightPink, LightSalmon, LightSeaGreen, LightSkyBlue, LightSlateGray, LightSteelBlue, LightYellow, Lime, LimeGreen, Linen, Magenta, Maroon, MediumAquamarine, MediumBlue, MediumOrchid, MediumPurple, MediumSeaGreen, MediumSlateBlue, MediumSpringGreen, MediumTurquoise, MediumVioletRed, MidnightBlue, MintCream, MistyRose, Moccasin, NavajoWhite, Navy, OldLace, Olive, OliveDrab, Orange, OrangeRed, Orchid, PaleGoldenrod, PaleGreen, PaleTurquoise, PaleVioletRed, PapayaWhip, PeachPuff, Peru, Pink, Plum, PowderBlue, Purple, Red, RosyBrown, RoyalBlue, SaddleBrown, Salmon, SandyBrown, SeaGreen, Seashell, Sienna, Silver, SkyBlue, SlateBlue, SlateGray, Snow, SpringGreen, SteelBlue, Tan, Teal, Thistle, Tomato, Turquoise, Violet, Wheat, White, WhiteSmoke, Yellow, YellowGreen.

Just go ahead and stick one of these (often gracefully descriptive) names like PapayaWhip into your color property specification, like this:

```
p.warning {color: lightslategray;}
```

And you've got a color that looks like . . . well . . . light gray slate.

Nobody's perfect. Microsoft spells *gray* with an "a" most of the time, but elsewhere — in this same list — they use an "e," as in "LightGrey."

Coloring borders

Foreground color doesn't apply only to text. You can also use it to specify the color of borders. In this next example, you set the `color` property of an image to `skyblue`. (Alternatively, you could use the `border-color` property if you wish.) In addition, you set the `border-width` to make it larger than the default. You also must specify a `border-style` property:

```
<html>
<head>

<style>

img {border-style: solid;border-width:25px; color: skyblue;}

</style>

</head>
<body>

<img WIDTH=320px; HEIGHT=264px; src="GrandfatherHouse.jpg">

</body>
</html>
```

If you want to try this example, first save a graphics file in the same directory as this .htm file and name that file GrandfatherHouse.jpg.

As you can see when you test this example, a border in light blue is placed around the graphic. See Figure 6-5.

A monochromatic, plain border is pretty dull. It harkens back to earlier days when computers were straining to provide even simple color effects.

I suggest that you avoid the plain CSS frames and consider generating a cool frame in a graphics program. Then you can drop your image into that frame in the graphics program itself and simply save the whole thing as a new .jpg file. The frame then becomes part of the image itself, and you just load that image file into your Web page. You don't have worry about using the simple built-in border style as a frame — and the one you built in a graphics application is almost guaranteed to be more sophisticated and interesting than anything you can do with CSS. See the example in Figure 6-6.

Figure 6-5:
Borders can be colored with an image's `color` property.

Figure 6-6:
This vignette border was created automatically in Micrografx's Picture Publisher.

Using inset border colors

If you want to create subtle, attractive borders entirely within the capabilities of IE, you can use the `inset` command with colors for the various borders around a graphic. This creates a beveled look that's certainly a step up from the flat, plain border shown in Figure 6-5. Take a look at Figures 6-7 and 6-8:

Figure 6-7:
You can use the `inset` command to create a dimensional, shaded border like this.

The border in Figure 6-7 was created with this code:

```
<html>
<head>

<style>

img {

border-right: silver inset; border-left: silver inset;
border-top: silver inset;border-bottom: silver inset;

border-width:12px;}

</style>

</head>
<body>

<img WIDTH=320px; HEIGHT=264px; src="GrandfatherHouse.jpg">

</body>
</html>
```

Matting means cutting an opening into a mat board that is the same size of a photo, painting, print or other artwork, and then attaching the art to the back of the mat and framing it. This provides a border between the frame and the art. It's almost always used when displaying photos because it provides a bit of distance between the photo itself and the glass in the frame. Matting also emphasizes the artwork.

To get the border displayed in Figure 6-8, make this simple change to the preceding code:

```
border-width:5px;
```

Figure 6-8:
Adjust the
border-
width
property to
get different
effects, like
this simple
matting
effect.

Where does light come from?

As long as we tackle relativity theory in this book, why not also explore the origin of light itself or at least the psychophysics of light sources?

Microsoft darkens the color used for the left and top borders of its inset design (for depressed, clicked buttons in Word, for example), and leaves the right and bottom frame sides light. Buttons just sitting there without being clicked are *outset* and the left and top borders are lighter than the right and bottom borders. Why?

In Windows graphic style (menus, buttons, window frames, and so on), the light is always assumed to be coming from the upper-left corner of the screen. Therefore, a visually *protruding* object like a button picks up highlights along its top and left sides. Shadows fall along the right and bottom of the object. However, if the object is supposed to be sinking into the background — such as an *inset* frame or a clicked button — the process is reversed and the top and left sides are darkened.

This effect actually works pretty much the same way in the real world: When you're reading outdoors, if you're like most people, you maneuver your lounge chair or towel until the sun shines from your left side — and, of course, the sun is above.

Take a look at your work area. Most people prefer to put lamps to the left of and above their desk or reading chair. As an experiment, turn this book upside down and see what happens to your perception of the frame in Figure 6-7. Instead of seeming to be inset, doesn't it now appear to be *outset*? Don't kid yourself: If you weren't prejudiced to think of light coming from the top left, you would just as likely see this upside down frame as *inset* — even with the light coming from down low and to the right of the frame.

Try changing the preceding CSS style code from inset to outset, and then reload the page into IE to see the effect:

```
img {

border-right: silver outset; border-left: silver outset;
border-top: silver outset;border-bottom: silver outset;

border-width:12px; }
```

The outset effect, which looks as if the frame protrudes toward the viewer, is shown in Figure 6-9. Notice that the shadows and highlights are different here compared to the inset style in Figure 6-8.

Figure 6-9:
The outset effect looks as if the frame protrudes toward the viewer.

Other CSS border styles you can experiment with in addition to inset and outset include groove and ridge.

CSS offers many significant improvements on traditional Web design facilities and is far better than classic HTML. With CSS, you can do many things that are visually impressive, as you see in various examples in this book. But don't burden CSS with *all* your graphics effects. For example, if you want to build a background that creates a particular texture, you can sometimes accomplish it by superimposing image files, repeating patterns, and resorting to other CSS tricks. But for heaven's sake, before trying to get some special effect via CSS, first ask yourself: Can this effect be achieved in a graphics program more easily, or with a better result? Often the answer is yes. Don't try to force CSS to do things it's not very good at; graphics programs contain many special tools for creating visual effects. Always ask, "Can Photoshop do this better?" Take a look at the frame in Figure 6-10. A graphics program can do lots of things like this. CSS can't.

Figure 6-10:
Use
graphics
programs
such as
Photoshop
to create
specialized
borders and
other visual
effects.

For those on a budget, or for those who haven't mastered graphics application software and therefore can't use programs like Photoshop, you can find online advice about pushing CSS to its limits. (And remember, you must sometimes limit yourself to CSS when page load time is a major consideration.) Here's one good site that really gets a great deal of bang for the CSS buck:

```
http://www.sitepoint.com/
```

Coloring the Background

The background of an element includes its border and any padding. Padding is explored in more detail in Chapter 9, but essentially, padding adds space around an element. Here's an example that illustrates both the padding and the background-color properties:

```
<html>
<head>

<style>
h1 {background-color: silver; padding: 6%;}
</style>

</head>
```

```
<body>

<H1>Padding around a Headline</H1>

</body>
</html>
```

The result of the style in this code is shown in Figure 6-11:

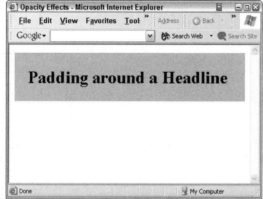

Figure 6-11:
Padding
expands this
background
color
around this
element.

The `background-color` property accepts the same color values as the foreground `color` property. By default, backgrounds are transparent, so any textures, images, or other elements that are on the bottom show through. Also, you can give a background color to almost any element — from inline `em` elements all the way up to the entire `body` element.

Try to avoid lurid color combinations. Some Web page designers are tempted to create "special effects" by using loud, some would even say vulgar, color patches on their pages. Unless you have a very good reason to do this, you should avoid the haphazard, childish appearance of a page splattered with various zones of color. Here's an example of what I mean. This page has a blue background, with lavender, orange, hot pink and other bizarre color combinations. Not only are such pages difficult to read; they're usually just simply ugly as well, as you can see in Figure 6-12.

```
<html>
<head>

<style>

body {background-color: DodgerBlue;}
i {background-color: OliveDrab; color: orange;}
p {background-color: lavender; color: HotPink;}

</style>
```

```
</head>
<body>


<p>Paragraphs are rendered in startling colors!</p>
<p>And <i>italic text within those paragraphs</i> is even
        more annoying</p>


</body>
</html>
```

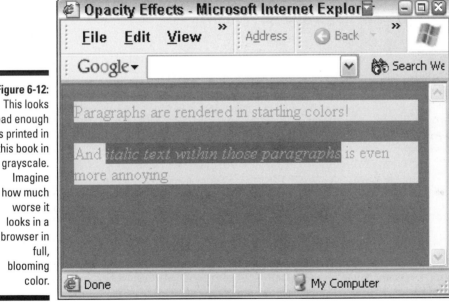

Figure 6-12:
This looks bad enough as printed in this book in grayscale. Imagine how much worse it looks in a browser in full, blooming color.

Chapter 7

Styling It Your Way

· ·

· ·

*I*f CSS did nothing other than give you powerful control over how your Web pages look, it would still be a tremendous improvement over HTML. In this chapter, you explore various ways to enhance the appearance of your Web pages using special tools and techniques. You start by *kerning* — adjusting the space between text characters. Later on in the chapter, you discover how to align text for effect, add textures, and create custom backgrounds.

Kerning for Better Headlines

Kerning — adjusting the space between letters — is sometimes wrongly used for emphasis. Some Web page designers try to add e m p h a s i s by kerning to get extra space between letters. But then, poor text design includes many other ugly forms of "emphasis" in addition to kerning, such as boldface, bright colors, all caps, and so on. These visual tricks should be avoided as a way of emphasizing a word or phrase. For emphasis, use *italics*. And italics *only*.

Widely spaced letters are sometimes used in headlines though, particularly with single-word heads, such as a letters-to-the-editor column like this:

L E T T E R S

Kerning to tighten letter spacing comes into its own in headlines. You *decrease* the space between the letters to squeeze the words together and improve the headline's appearance. Most typefaces (except monospaced typefaces such as Courier) have variations in the distance between the letters to improve the font's readability. Kerning allows you to make custom adjustments to letter spacing — specifically, to bring certain letter pairs closer together. (Sometimes kerning is used to move letters apart, too, such as when an italic character "leans" into a close parentheses mark.)

A simple, less effective kind of kerning can be accomplished in CSS using the letter-spacing property, like this:

```
<h1 style="letter-spacing: -0.06cm">This Headline is Slightly
        Squeezed</h1>
```

Here's a complete example showing the same headline kerned as well as not kerned, as shown in Figure 7-1.

```
<html>
<head>

<style>

h1 {font-size:44px; letter-spacing: -0.12em}
h1.unkerned {font-size:44px; letter-spacing: 0.00em;}



</style>
</head>
<body>

<h1>This Headline is Slightly Squeezed through Kerning</h1>

<h1 class="unkerned">This Headline is Slightly Squeezed
        through Kerning (Not!)</h1>

</body>
</html>
```

As you can see in Figure 7-1, when you use a negative value for letter-spacing (`-.12em` in this example; em being the width of the letter *m*), the headline's letters move together. Traditionally, slightly tightening the space between headline letters is considered aesthetically superior to the unkerned version of the same headline. See if you don't agree that the bottom headline in Figure 7-1 looks a little too loose at the default letter spacing (0em means: no change to the letter spacing).

Why kern headlines? Because your Web pages look more professional and, in fact, are more readable. Studies have shown that people don't read text one letter at a time. Instead, most readers glance at each word and almost instantly recognize the shape of the entire word. If you tighten the interior space, you graphically emphasize that word's individual shape.

Figure 7-1:
Negative
word
spacing
brings
characters
closer
together;
and
headlines
usually look
better when
tightened
up.

You don't need to kern every pair of characters, however. That's why using the CSS letter-spacing property is actually not *kerning,* properly speaking. Kerning involves only adjusting some letter pairs. It's actually a more subtle effect than you see in Figure 7-1.

True kerning

Real kerning is done on a letter-by-letter basis, not wholesale across the entire headline. However, you can use letter spacing to achieve this hand-kerning. Here's an example that defines a tighter than normal letter spacing (-.06em) combined with an even tighter squeezing of the spacing in a class called *kern* (-.16em):

```
<style>

h1 {font-size:44px; letter-spacing: -.06em}
h1.normal {letter-spacing: normal}
.kern {letter-spacing: -0.16em;}



</style>
</head>
```

```
<body>

<h1>This Headline is Slightly Squeezed through <span
        class="kern">Kern</span>ing and Heavier
        Kerning</h1>

<h1 class="normal">This Headline is Slightly Squeezed through
        Kerning (Not!)</h1>
```

The results of this code are shown in Figure 7-2:

Figure 7-2:
Notice in particular the top headline's use of the tighter characters in the first use of the word *Kerning*.

This Headline is Slightly Squeezed through Kerning and Heavier Kerning

This Headline is Slightly Squeezed through Kerning (Not!)

Here in Figure 7-3 is a closer look at the kerned and unkerned word:

Figure 7-3:
The letters *Kerning* are tighter in the top version than the bottom.

Kerning
Kerning

This attention to letter spacing may seem like a bit of trouble — and it is — but if you want your headlines to look better, effective kerning is the key. Of course, you should specify the font size, and perhaps even the font face, to ensure that the results the user sees are the same that you see when kerning the headline. You need not kern every headline, but larger typesizes in particular benefit from a bit of tightening.

If some of the characters in a headline look too loose to you, you might want to take the time for a little manual adjustment. Kerning is often particularly effective when a capital letter overhangs a lowercase letter, the way the *K* overhangs the *e* in Kerning. Without kerning, there's an unseemly gap between the letters, as shown in Figure 7-4:

Figure 7-4:
When uppercase letters overhang lowercase, kerning is especially helpful to improve the appearance of the text.

Switch now to a sans serif font like Arial to see the effect on a typical headline typeface:

```
<style>

h1 {font-family: "Arial Black"; font-size:48px; letter-
          spacing: -.06em}
h1.normal {letter-spacing: normal}
.kern {letter-spacing: -0.20em;}
.ultrakern {letter-spacing: -0.26em;}


</style>
```

Ultra kerning

Notice that I had to adjust the value for the .kern class to .20em when moving to this different font (compare the code in the previous example, which was set to .16 for the Times Roman font). You have to fiddle a bit until you get the desired effect when kerning. I also added a new class named ultrakern for even tighter spacing, and then I applied both classes where needed in this code:

```
<body>

<h1>This Headline is Slightly Squeezed through Kerning and
        Heavier <span class="ultrakern">Ker</span><span
        class="kern">ning</span></h1>

<h1 class="normal">This Headline is Slightly Squeezed through
        Kerning (Not!)</h1>

</body>
```

The result is shown in Figure 7-5. The *e* is shoved under the K using very tight spacing.

Figure 7-5:
You can see the effect of two levels of kerning in the second use of the word *Kerning.*

You can see the effect of kerning even more clearly in Figure 7-6.

Kerning is also frequently used to close the gap between a character and a punctuation mark that follows it. Kerning can also be used to reduce the size of the space character, thereby reducing space between words and bringing words closer together. You explore the CSS word-spacing property shortly.

Figure 7-6:
Kerning
helps the
eye
recognize
unique word
shapes
quickly.

Kerning
Kerning

 Kerning is browser-sensitive, so if you're concerned about making your kerned headlines look good in Netscape or some other browser, load the page into that other browser and see if further adjustments are necessary to achieve the lowest common denominator compromise between Internet Explorer and the other browser.

Vertical Tightening

Multi-line headlines should also be tightened up a bit vertically by adjusting the line spacing: reducing the white space between lines of text, as illustrated in Figure 7-7. Line spacing is known in typography as *leading* because typesetters once shoved in or removed spacers made of lead to separate the lines of type.

Adjusting percentages

Recall from Chapter 5 that you can adjust the line spacing by adding a percent figure to the font size. You follow the font-size value with a forward slash and the percent adjustment you want to make to the line height. In this case, I specified that it be 99 percent, but you can fiddle around with the spacing until it looks good to your eye:

```
<html>
<head>

<style>

h1.spaced{font: bold 48px/.99 "Arial Black"; letter-spacing:
          -.06em;}
```

```
h1 {font-family: "Arial Black"; font-size:48px; letter-
          spacing: -.06em;}
h1.normal {letter-spacing: normal; font-size 48px;}
.kern {letter-spacing: -0.20em;}
.ultrakern {letter-spacing: -0.26em;}


</style>
</head>
<body>

<h1 class="spaced">This Headline is Slightly Squeezed through
          <span

class="ultrakern">Ker</span><span
          class="kern">ning</span></h1>

<br>
<h1 class="normal">This Headline is Slightly Squeezed through
          Kerning (Not!)</h1>

</body>
</html>
```

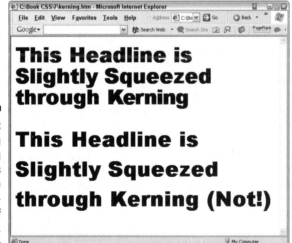

Figure 7-7:
Adjusting
line spacing
also helps
improve
the appear-
ance of
headlines.

If you prefer, you can use the line height property instead of the `fontsize /backslash` technique illustrated in the code example just above. The `line-height` property can take all the usual CSS units of measurement such as `px`, `em`, percentages, and so on. Here's an example:

```
h1 {font: bold 48px "Arial Black"; letter-spacing: -.06em;
          word-spacing: -.46em; line-height:48px;}
```

Understanding baselines

The line-height property specifies the distance between the *baselines* of the lines of text. The baseline is an imaginary line on which the characters rest. Note that this is the line on which the *majority* of the characters rest. In other words, a few characters have *descenders* — parts of the character that go below the baseline — such as p, q, y, g and so on. These descenders are ignored when establishing the baseline. Flip ahead to Figure 7-10 for a look at descenders.

CSS3 Introduces Kerning Mode

If you find hand-kerning more trouble than it's worth, perhaps you'll want to wait until CSS3 properties are available. A new kerning-mode property is part of the CSS3 draft resolutions. You can use the pair value with this property to remove space between letter pairs known to have "extra" space, such as *Ke* or *Yo*. A kerning pair threshold property specifies at what font size you want pair kerning to begin taking effect. Remember that kerning is generally only useful for large font sizes (headlines primarily). An auto value for this proposed kerning pair threshold property lets the browser decide when kerning should be used; an initial value allows you to specify the font size at which the kerning activates. However, unless this proposed automatic kerning property is finely tuned to each different typeface, and to each font size, I doubt it will be able to approach the quality of hand-kerned headlines. And hand kerning isn't all *that* much trouble, is it?

Word spacing

The word-spacing property, like letter-spacing, can be used to create justified text (aligned on both the left and the right sides). However, Web designers can make good use of it for a kerning effect on headlines to reduce unneeded white space between words.

Here's an example that reduces the spaces between words by .56 em:

```
<html>
<head>

<style>


h1.kernSpaced {font-family: "Arial Black"; font-size:48px;
        word-spacing: -.56em;}
```

```
h1 {font-family: "Arial Black"; font-size:48px;}


</style>
</head>
<body>


<h1 class="kernSpaced">This Headline is Slightly Squeezed
        through Kerning</h1>

<h1>This Headline is Slightly Squeezed through Kerning
        (Not!)</h1>


</body>
</html>
```

As you can see in Figure 7-8, tightening the space between words improves
the look of headlines:

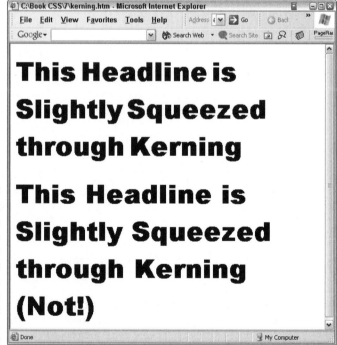

Figure 7-8:
Here the
space
between
words is
reduced a
bit to tighten
the headline
on top.

As with letter and line spacing, you can use any CSS unit for specifying word spacing. However, em is usually the most reliable if, for some reason, another font is substituted by the user's browser. The em measurement is the most accurate *average* character size measurement for most fonts.

You probably want to apply kerning, line space reduction, and word space reduction all at once. This next example does just that, as shown in Figure 7-9.

```
<html>
<head>

<style>

h1.spaced{font: bold 48px/1.1 "Arial Black"; letter-spacing:
        -.06em; word-spacing: -.46em;}

h1.normal {letter-spacing: normal; font: bold 48px "Arial
        Black";}

.kern {letter-spacing: -0.20em;}
.ultrakern {letter-spacing: -0.26em;}


</style>
</head>
<body>

<h1 class="spaced">This Headline is Slightly Squeezed through
        <span
class="ultrakern">Ker</span><span
        class="kern">ning</span></h1>

<br>
<h1 class="normal">This Headline is Slightly Squeezed through
        Kerning (Not!)</h1>

</body>
</html>
```

Notice the line that defines the spacing adjustments:

```
h1.spaced{font: bold 48px/1.1 "Arial Black"; letter-spacing:
        -.06em; word-spacing: -.46em;}
```

You want to fiddle with the line spacing (the /1.1 in this example) and the letter and word spacing values until you get just the look you want. Don't forget that the quickest way to edit and then view the results is achieved by following these steps:

1. **Write your code in Notepad.**

2. **Press Alt+F+S.**

Your HTML code is saved to the disk.

3. Press Alt+Tab to switch to Internet Explorer.

4. Press F5 to refresh the browser.

This cycle of keystrokes allows you to rapidly view your results, and then return to Notepad to try additional adjustments . . . until at last you're completely happy forever after.

Aligning Text

Chapter 4 briefly introduced the idea of aligning elements — usually text aligned to images. In this chapter, you take a closer look at the various possible alignments.

Vertical aligning

The `vertical-align` property specifies how text aligns vertically (surprise!) in relation to another element, such as other text (superscripting, for example) or an image (captioning, for example).

You can give the vertical-align property any of the following eight descriptive values: bottom, baseline, middle, sub, super, text-top, text-bottom, and top. Or you can supply a specific measurement (such as 4px) or a percentage.

Using descriptive values

In CSS, alignment is made relative to any line-height property used with the text. Most of the values that can be used with vertical-align are self-explanatory, but text-bottom means that the baseline is ignored and the imaginary line is drawn at the bottom of the typeface's descenders.

Within block level elements, the vertical-align property has no effect relative to the block. However, the property does work to align elements within the cells of a table.

As you can see in Figure 7-10, the baseline is an imaginary line drawn between characters without descenders.

Figure 7-10:
This image — a rectangle — aligns with the baseline, which is the default if you don't specify a vertical -align property.

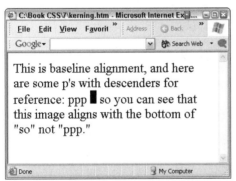

This is the HTML file that produces the result shown in Figure 7-10:

```
<html>
<head>

<style>

img {vertical-align: baseline;}

body {font-size: 24px;}
```

```
</style>
</head>
<body>


This is baseline alignment, and here are some p's with
        descenders for reference: ppp <img
        src="rect.jpg"/> so you can see that this image
        aligns with the bottom of "so" not "ppp."

</body>
</html>
```

Figure 7-11 illustrates superscript alignment.

Figure 7-11:
You can raise an ordinary element or inline text element (a span, for example) using the superscript value.

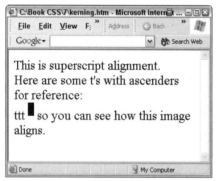

If you use superscript or subscript, note that the text size does not automatically reduce. If you want that effect, you have to specify a smaller size. To get the effect you want (shown in Figure 7-12), you should combine the super value with a percent downsizing of the font-size property, like this:

```
span.super {vertical-align: super; font-size: 70%;}
This is 70<span class="super">o</span> cold!
```

You can also specify absolute distances up or down when using vertical alignment. Just use any of the usual units of measurement, such as px, inches, and so on.

Aligning by percentages

Figure 7-13 illustrates how to use negative or positive percentages as a way of positioning an element relative to its parent:

Figure 7-12:
The
lowercase
"o" works
fine for the
degree
symbol if
you reduce
it to about
70 percent
in the Times
Roman font.

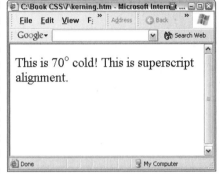

This is 70° cold! This is superscript alignment.

Figure 7-13:
Use
percentages
to specify a
relative
position, as
shown here.

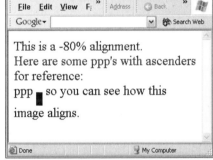

This is a -80% alignment.
Here are some ppp's with ascenders for reference:
ppp ▮ so you can see how this image aligns.

When you specify a percentage for vertical alignment, the baseline of a text element or the bottom edge of an image is displaced relative to the parent element's baseline. As you can see in Figure 7-13, the bottom of the square image is about 80 percent below the baseline of the text (the letters without descenders, such as the "s" and "o").

Horizontal Alignment

Adjusting text horizontally with the `text-align` property is similar to vertical alignment, except the following descriptive values are used: `left`, `center`, `right`, or `justify`, and the results apply to an entire paragraph rather than to individual words.

The values are essentially the same alignment values that you'd find in any word processor. The default is `left` (for Western languages anyway). The `text-align` property can only be used with block-level elements, such as the paragraph `<p>` element, as illustrated in Figure 7-14.

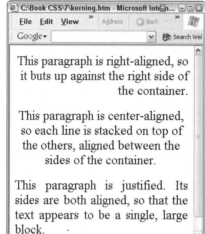

Figure 7-14:
These three paragraphs illustrate right, center, and justified alignments.

The effects in Figure 7-14 are created by these styles:

```
<style>

p.right {font-size: 24px; text-align: right;}
p.center {font-size: 24px; text-align: center;}
p.justified {font-size: 24px; text-align: justify;}

</style>
```

As you see in Figure 7-14, CSS justification isn't too attractive. The spaces between the words are simply too wide. This is somewhat improved when the text lines are wider (the browser window is quite narrow in Figure 7-14). Nonetheless, the true justification that you see in books and magazines is quite a bit more subtle and pleasing. True justification involves adjusting the spacing between letters, not just between words, as IE does it. Also, CSS offers no hyphenation specification — and hyphenation allows word breaks that make the lines of text look better as well.

Indenting Text

Similar to horizontal alignment, *indentation* is frequently used to help readers quickly identify the start of each paragraph, and thus more easily scan text. On a word processor, indentation is typically what happens when you press the Tab key.

HTML didn't have an indentation capability, so people resorted to inserting invisible images and other tricks. (Adding spaces doesn't work because HTML strips extra spaces off.)

CSS came to the rescue with its `text-indent` property. Used with block-level elements like `<p>`, you can specify a unit length like `6em` or `7px`, or a relative percentage.

Here's the way you specify indentation for a paragraph, as shown in Figure 7-15:

```
p {font-size:24px; text-indent: 2em;}
```

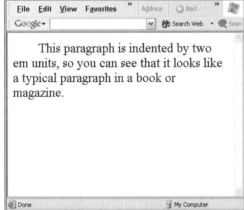

Figure 7-15: In most publications, text is indented. HTML has no provision for indentation, but CSS has the `text-indent` property.

Texturing

Most Web sites look best with some background textures and graphics. Plain background colors are rather crude, but a nice, restrained, pale texture behind your text improves many a Web page. Add some well-placed graphics and you can bring the drabbest page to life. Textures also help to unify a page, tying the various zones together.

As with drop-shadows and many other visual effects that you might want to add to a Web page, your best approach when adding backgrounds is to design them in a graphics application such as Photoshop.

For example, you can create a background out of a small, repeating texture. The example in Figure 7-16 tiles a tiny 1" piece of texture across the entire background of the browser. It works much the same way that tiling textures can be achieved in Windows by right-clicking the desktop, choosing Properties, clicking the desktop tab, and then selecting one of the textures — such as Soap Bubbles — from the list. However, your own textures are pretty much guaranteed to be superior to those supplied with Windows.

Here's an example illustrating how to tile a texture file named *pebble* using the repeat value of the background property:

```
<html>
<head>

<style>


body {background: white url("pebble.jpg") repeat;}

h2 {background: url("coin.jpg") no-repeat left top;
color: blue;
width: 85%;
padding: 30px;
font: bold 48px "Arial Black";
letter-spacing: -.02em;
word-spacing: -.16em;
line-height:48px;
}

</style>
</head>

<body>
<h2>Coins of the Realm</h2>

<h2>European and Asian Available Now!</h2>

</body>
</html>
```

You can set backgrounds for the entire page (in the <body> element), or for individual elements such as Heading 2 (H2) illustrated in the code above. The ability to add graphics or textures behind any visual element via CSS is quite useful to Web designers.

Notice that a photo of a coin is included as part of the definition of the H2 element, so it appears at the top left of each H2. However, additional properties such as width and padding define the spacing of the headline, and spacing properties are used to tighten the headline text.

Even with the spacing adjustments, though, the lettering available via CSS is relatively crude and one-dimensional. Figure 7-17 illustrates how you can use drop shadowing with text in a graphics application to give the page a natural dimensionality: a raised 3D look. Most people would agree that the lettering in Figure 7-17 is more attractive than the simpler, plainer lettering in Figure 7-16.

Figure 7-16:
The background was created in a graphics program, but the text is pure CSS.

Unaltered, the coin photo's background would create a small square behind the coin — covering the background texture. So, in a graphics program, I copied the pebble texture, and then poured it into the small photo's background around the coin. This way, the coin blends into the Web page background. In addition, I added a drop-shadow to the coin photo. One goal when designing eye-catching graphics is to make the page look less *flat.* If your entire design is two-dimensional, with no overlapping elements and no shadowing, you're not exploiting all the possible design tools at your disposal. Besides the traditional x (horizontal) and y (vertical) axes, think about the z axis (the third dimension), where objects stack on top of each other and cast shadows.

When you load a graphic in as your background, as in Figure 7-18, you can have the image only cover part of the background, and the rest of the background filled in via a tiled texture. If *both* textures are identical, as they are in Figure 7-17, the viewer cannot tell where the image ends and the tiled texture background begins.

If you do include a background image, you may want to display hyperlinks, labels, or other elements on top of the image. This can easily be done by specifying some absolute positioning. (If you just add the text or other element in the HTML without specifying positioning, the element appears below the bottom of the image on the page.)

For a good introduction to getting the most out of Photoshop, you might want to take a look at *Photoshop 7 For Dummies* by Barbara Obermeier and Deke McClelland (Wiley Publishing, Inc.).

Here's the code that produces the results shown in Figure 7-17, with a background image created in a graphics application and foreground text superimposed on the image:

```
<html>
<head>

<style>


body {background: white url("pebble.jpg") repeat;}

</style>
</head>

<body>

<IMG src="headlines.jpg">

<DIV style="top: 390px; left: 85px; position: absolute; font:
         32px;" >THIS TEXT IS ON TOP OF THE IMAGE...</DIV>

</body>
</html>
```

This code results in the image you see in Figure 7-18.

Figure 7-18:
Superimposing elements on top of a background graphic is easy.

When you design a Web page in a graphics application, making adjustments to that page later is more difficult. For example, to change the text in Figure 7-17, you cannot merely retype the Heading 2 headline in the HTML code. Instead, you must go to the graphic's application and redo part or all of the graphic.

Background textures and images shouldn't compete visually with the foreground. You want text to remain easily readable, and the overall design of the page — its logic and structure — shouldn't be obscured by a fussy or heavy texture.

Setting Individual Background Properties

In the previous example, you used the background property to specify a whole set of values, like this:

```
h2 {background: url("coin.jpg") no-repeat left top;
```

That is similar to the way that the font property can be followed by multiple values. However, the font properties can be individualized if you wish (font-size for example), and you can also individually specify the background properties if you wish, like this:

```
body {background-image: url(pebble.jpg);}
```

This causes the pebble image to tile throughout the background, covering it. That's because the tiling value (repeat) is the default. If you don't want tiling, use the no-repeat value.

No background inheritance

Background images are not inherited. You wouldn't want a background to be inherited by every element in the document. That would ruin the effect with some kinds of backgrounds (those employing bigger repeating images than the pebble texture used in this chapter). Larger images (a repeating coin image for example) would perhaps look OK as a background for a coin dealer's site — as long as the coin were lightened up enough so that they didn't cause readability problems with the page's text. However, if that image of a coin were inherited, it would tile individually for other elements. Doubtless smaller elements like headlines would cut a line of coins in half, others in three-quarters, and so on. The page would be a mess of varying tile zones. In fact, no background value is inherited.

Special repeats

Unless you specify otherwise, a background image repeats both vertically and horizontally until it fills the window. However, if you want, say, a textured border down the left side, you can specify a vertical-only repeat, using the repeat-y value, like this:

```
<html>
<head>

<style>


body {background-image: url(paper.jpg)
;background-repeat: repeat-y;}

h1 {font-size: 3em;padding-left: 28px}

</style>
</head>

<body>

<h1>Check in to the B & B!</h1>
```

```
<img style="position: absolute; top=100px; left=180px;"
        src=wet.jpg>


</body>
</html>
```

This results in the texture tiling down the side of the browser, as shown in
Figure 7-19:

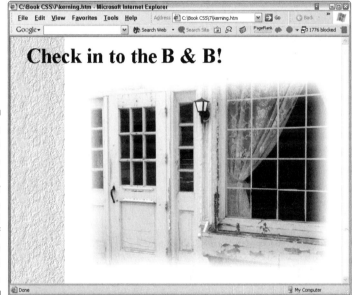

Figure 7-19:
In this
example,
the tiling is
only
vertical,
creating a
column of
texture
down the
left side.

Background Positioning

The background-position property can be specified with the following values:
left, center, right, top, and bottom. You can combine these values like this:

```
background-position: top right;
```

As you probably guessed, you can also use percentages to specify the position of a background image. Percentages work a bit strangely because you
provide two percentages, like this:

```
background-position: 100% 100%;
```

These x/y coordinates are used for *both* the image and the parent element. In other words, `100% 100%` means the position is the lower right. So, the lower-right corner of the image is positioned in the lower right corner of the parent element. Values of `0% 0%` locate the upper left corner of the image in the upper left corner of the element. `50% 50%` centers the image. Any variations of those percentages put the image anywhere you want within the parent. Where do you suppose `40% 60%` would be located?

Here's the code:

```
<html>
<head>

<style>

body {background-image: url(coin.jpg);background-repeat: no-
        repeat; background-position: 40% 60%;}

</style>
</head>

<body>

</body>
</html>
```

This code results in the image you see in Figure 7-20.

Notice that the graphic in Figure 7-20 is not precisely 40 percent from the left and 60 percent down from the top. That's because the top-left of the graphic is not the positioning point. Instead, the point is inside the graphic at *its* 40/60 coordinate.

Absolute positioning units (`inches`, `px`, and so on) can also be used to position a background graphic, using the usual x y coordinate system (the first value is the horizontal position, the second vertical). However, unlike with percentages, the top-left corner of the image is the positioning point.

If you wish, you can supply negative percentages or absolute units, thereby moving the image a bit off the element's box. The following code moves the coin image 20 pixels in both directions off the edge of the paragraph, as shown in Figure 7-21:

```
<style>

p {font-size:32px; background-
        image:url(lightcoin.jpg);background-repeat: no-
        repeat; background-position: -20px -20px;}

</style>
```

Figure 7-20:
This graphic
is located at
the 40%
60%
coordinate.

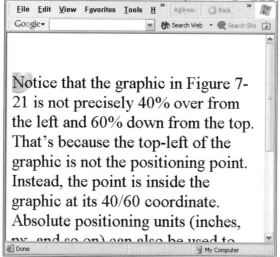

Figure 7-21:
You can
supply
negative
coordinates
to move a
background
image off
the parent
element's
box.

If you specify the background-attachment property's fixed value, you can prevent the background image from scrolling:

```
background-attachment: fixed;
```

The value scroll is the default.

Part III
Adding Artistry: Design and Composition with CSS

The 5th Wave   By Rich Tennant

"Well, it's not quite done. I've animated the gurgling spit sink and the rotating Novocaine syringe, but I still have to add the high-speed whining drill audio track."

In this part . . .

You want efficient pages, but efficiency without beauty isn't much good. Part III explores the secrets of the design masters, including burning questions such as, "How much symmetry is too much?" You also figure out how to apply the famous Rule of Thirds to add a focal point without throwing your page off balance. You see how to manipulate the space between page elements using margins, borders, and padding. Also covered in this Part are lists, tables, and some pretty spectacular visual transition effects.

Chapter 8

Web Design Basics

In This Chapter

▶ Mastering the secrets of the Web design gurus

▶ Handling symmetry

▶ Adding drop caps

▶ Utilizing the rule of thirds (it's easier than you think)

As Shania Twain recently observed, creative people are not necessarily the best judges of their own work. In fact, a disconnect exists between those who create and those who evaluate creative work.

This chapter explores some "rules" about design that you might consider applying to your own Web page efforts. Creative people abhor rules because their job is to make something new, something that, in fact, does not follow the existing rules. So if you're as wonderfully inventive as Andy Warhol or Michelangelo or Jane Austen, by all means ignore the following rules. But if you're one of those rare talents, what are you doing reading this book? You should be at your writing desk or easel.

The rest of us, not so full of genius, are happy to learn how to improve our designs. And rules, even if we sometimes ignore them, can be useful. Try following the rule first. If it doesn't work for you, go ahead and violate it.

The idea of this chapter is to encourage your creativity: Just try new things, move elements around, and otherwise give your ideas a try. When you feel good about a page, take another dispassionate look at it from the perspective of these rules. Perhaps you'll decide to ignore a rule. After all, these are merely guidelines, and some of the best designs *do* ignore one or more of the suggestions in this chapter. But, more likely than not, you might find that taking a second look at your page design with these rules in mind improves the look of your page. After all, they became rules because they generally work pretty well.

Organizing with White Space

Some rules are obvious, and yet you'd be surprised how often they're ignored. Effective use of "white space" is essential to most Web pages. White space need not be actually white: It can be a background color or a texture. It merely refers to the necessity of including areas on the page that contain no text or vivid graphics (a pale background graphic is sometimes OK). In other words, white space is the blank area between images and text.

Your Web sites should avoid alarming people with crowded, text-heavy pages. Users don't want to read all that text. They're not in school: They're surfing the Web. They don't want an *assignment* from you. They want an inviting Web site that promises them entertaining and useful information.

You can make a page attractive and inviting to the reader in many ways. Your primary elements on a Web page are headlines, graphics, text blocks, and white space. Where you position these elements on the page, and their relative sizes, has a major impact on the page's visual appeal. Use these building blocks effectively and you're more than halfway to creating a document that people will want to spend some time looking at.

Take a second look

After you compose a page, put the page aside for a few days and then look at the page with a cold, objective eye (or ask some friends to give you feedback). Check to see if your page has balance, contrast, variety, and the other qualities discussed in this chapter. Also check for some rule violations: crowding, hidden or floating headlines, tombstones (parallel headlines in adjacent columns), or widows or orphans (stranded lines or fragments of text).

Getting on balance

Your primary design goal should be to balance your page. What's balance? It means that the page isn't top- or bottom-heavy, and that the left side balances the right side. In other words, you divide the page into quarters and see if the "weight" is roughly evenly proportioned. What's "weight?" It's not simply the amount of darkness (text is gray, headlines are darker, some graphics are very nearly black, empty space is "white" even if it's a pale color or texture). Instead, think about whether your page holds together visually because you've arranged the elements effectively.

An effective arrangement is *not* completely symmetrical. Few documents look good when perfectly symmetrically balanced. True, a completely symmetrical page is balanced, but it's *too* balanced. Too much of a good thing. Symmetry drains your design of an important quality: variety. The only documents that value extreme symmetry are wedding invitations, and they are often tasteless in other ways too. On some wedding invitations, complete symmetry is combined with script fonts: All that's missing is cheap perfume and they could win the World Championship of Bad Taste.

So now you've got white space, gray blocks of text, black blocks of headlines, and some in-between graphics, photos, charts, and so on. Of all these components, white space (the lighter areas) is usually the most important.

You're doing a *design*, a visual *composition.* You've probably seen paintings by Mondrian. He arranged squares and rectangles into attractive and balanced compositions. He didn't balance his works of art by putting four identical squares in the four quadrants of a page, as shown in Figure 8-1. That's balanced, all right, but it's boringly symmetrical. You face a similar task: avoid symmetry, but achieve a balanced composition.

Another problem with Figure 8-1 is that there's probably too much text (represented by the gray blocks). Adding some white space would relieve the too-gray look.

Figure 8-2 illustrates the opposite extreme: excessive asymmetry. The design in Figure 8-2 manages to avoid the tedium of symmetry, but is not balanced. Also, the two identical headline-text areas are badly positioned. Their positions look haphazard.

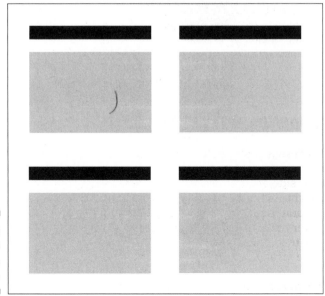

Figure 8-1:
Symmetry is
balanced,
but boring.

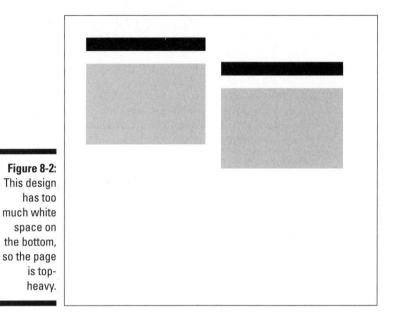

Figure 8-2:
This design has too much white space on the bottom, so the page is top-heavy.

Adding a photo (the darker gray square in the lower left in Figure 8-3) and using text blocks and headlines of varying sizes helps give the page variety.

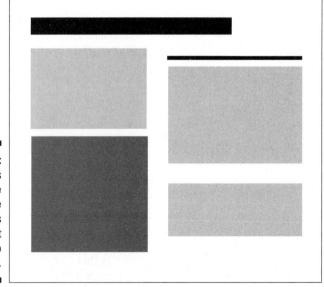

Figure 8-3:
This is closer to the ideal: The page has variety but also balance.

Emphasizing an Object with Silhouetting

A useful technique called *silhouetting* helps break up symmetry by removing most or all of the background of a photo or drawing, and then placing it off-center on the background color or space. When you clean away the existing background, the image's foreground becomes more prominent. It provides an extra dimension, somewhat like adding shadows. The detail on the edge of the foreground is exposed and seems to thrust out of the page toward the viewer.

You can bring an object like the watch in Figure 8-4 to life by first removing the background, erasing it by using tools in a graphics application. Then it looks like Figure 8-5.

Figure 8-4: As shot, this watch sinks too much into the woodgrain background.

Figure 8-5: Often, erasing the background gives the foreground object additional clarity and realism.

By tilting the watch so it's not perfectly vertical and placing it on an offset background, you give it additional prominence, as shown in Figure 8-6.

A primary difference between Figure 8-4 and 8-6 is that in 8-4, the watch is framed by a background. In Figure 8-6, the background doesn't surround the watch, so the watch appears to be placed on top of the screen, not sunk into a background. Figure 8-6 adds motion, dynamism, and dimension to the relatively static, sunken, flat image displayed in Figure 8-4.

Figure 8-6:
This partial
silhouetting
pulls the
watch right
out of the
screen and
pulls the
reader's eye
right into
your page.

Adding Drop Caps

You can apply this same offsetting principle I discussed in the last section to text in various ways. One way is to add an icon — like this watch graphic perhaps — to the side of each of your paragraphs. Flow the paragraphs around the image, or use an enlarged overlapping capital letter at the start of a paragraph. This technique, called a *drop cap,* has been used for centuries as a way of adding variety to pages of text.

Figure 8-7 was created using the following technique. Define a class that specifies a font that's larger than its parent element, that floats to the left of its parent, and, if you wish, give it a different color as well. (In this code, I made the drop cap bold and 400 percent larger than the surrounding paragraph text.) Then use a `<span>` element to add the drop cap to the paragraph:

```
<html>
<head>

<style>

p {font-size:32px;}

.dropcap {font:bold 400%; float:left; color:GreenYellow;}

</style>
</head>

<body>
```

```
<p><span class="dropcap">N</span>otice that the graphic in
          Figure 7-21 is not precisely 40% over from the
          left and 60% down from the top. That's because the
          top-left of the graphic is not the positioning
          point. Instead, the point is inside the graphic at
          its 40/60 coordinate. Absolute positioning units
          (inches, px, and so on) can also be used to
          position a background graphic, using the usual
</p>

</body>
</html>
```

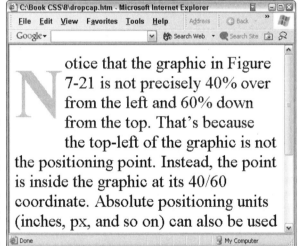

Figure 8-7:
Drop-caps
add variety
by violating
the space of
the parent
paragraph.

An easier way to add a drop cap to every paragraph is to use a pseudo-element. Pseudo-elements are explored further in Chapter 15. Here's a preview, as shown in Figure 8-8:

```
<html>
<head>

<style>
p {font-size:24px;}
p:first-letter {font:bold 300%; float:left;
          color:GreenYellow;}
</style>

</head>
```

```
<body>

<p>
Notice that the graphic in Figure 7-21 is not precisely 40%
            over from the left and 60% down from the top.
            That's because the top-left of the graphic is not
            the positioning point. Instead, the point is
            inside the graphic at its 40/60 coordinate.
            Absolute positioning units (inches, px, and so on)
            can also be used to position a background graphic,
            using the usual
</p>

<p>
You can apply this same offsetting principle to text in
            various ways. One way is to add an icon--like this
            watch graphic perhaps--to the side of each of your
            paragraphs. Flow the paragraphs around the image.
            Or use an overlapping capital letter at the start
            of a paragraph. This technique, called a drop cap,
            has been used for centuries as a way of adding
            variety to pages of text.
</p>

</body>
</html>
```

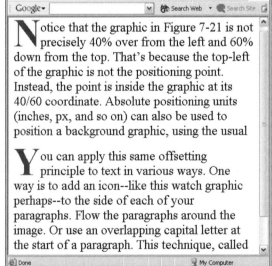

Figure 8-8:
If you want
a drop-cap
at the start
of every
paragraph,
try using the
first-
letter
pseudo-
element.

Trapping White Space

Sometimes white space can look bad. If you've surrounded a white area with text or graphics, you've managed to create what is called *trapped* white space. This kind of trapped space looks bad and can make your page look blotchy and jumbled as shown in Figure 8-9:

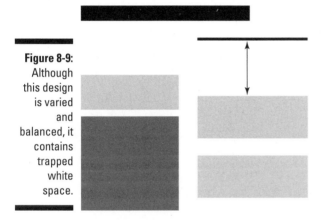

Figure 8-9:
Although this design is varied and balanced, it contains trapped white space.

The problem in Figure 8-9 is the distance between the H3 (the thin horizontal black line) on the right side and the text it describes. Headlines, captions, and other descriptive items should almost always be right next to the photo or paragraph they describe. Figure 8-10 shows how adjusting the items on the page can remove the trapped white space and put the headlines next to the text they describe.

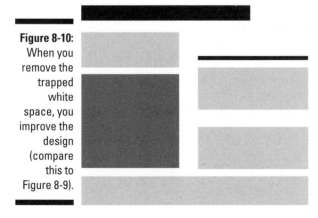

Figure 8-10:
When you remove the trapped white space, you improve the design (compare this to Figure 8-9).

Following the Rule of Thirds

Like any good painting or photograph, your Web pages benefit from having a *focal point* — an object that represents the main topic or most prominent visual element. This can be a photo, a sketch, or whatever is the first thing the viewer notices. It stands out from the rest of the page. Perhaps it's as simple as an unusual shape — something that doesn't match the other shapes on the page, as in Figure 8-11:

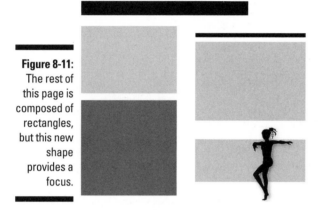

Figure 8-11:
The rest of this page is composed of rectangles, but this new shape provides a focus.

Figure 8-11 is an improvement over Figure 8-3, but invoking the rule of thirds strengthens the composition even more. Draw imaginary lines dividing your Web page into thirds both vertically and horizontally, as shown in Figure 8-12. Where the lines intersect is the best location for your focal point.

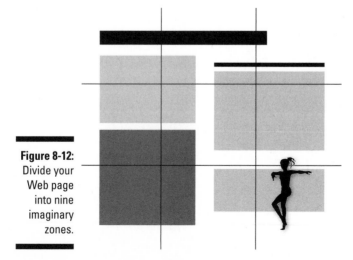

Figure 8-12:
Divide your Web page into nine imaginary zones.

The four hot spots

A Web page contains four "hot spots." These locations are where you should try to center your focal point. See if you don't think that Figure 8-13 is an improvement over Figure 8-11, now that the dancer has been moved to a hot spot:

Figure 8-13:
The focal point is now on a hot spot in the page.

Try moving the focal point to one of the other hot spots; you'll see that it looks good in those locations as well. Remember, you've got four hot spots to experiment with. In Figure 8-14, the dancer is positioned in the upper-left hot spot. Also notice that the dancer has been reversed from her position in Figure 8-13, so she dances *into* the page in Figure 8-14. If you have motion (an arrow, a dancer, anything that points or moves), ensure that the motion moves into, not out of, your page. The focal point is the first thing the viewer sees, and it should lead the eye into the page.

Figure 8-14:
This dancer looks good in this other hot spot as well.

However, the design in Figure 8-15 isn't as successful, even though the dancer is positioned on the lower-left hot spot. Why?

Figure 8-15:
The focal point is positioned in one of the hot spots, but the surrounding dark area swallows the dancer and frames her as well.

Recall the positioning of the watch in Figures 8-4 and 8-6. One of the rules of good composition is that you should violate white space, moving a focal point so that it's not framed or sunk into its background, but instead pokes into the surrounding white space. In Figures 8-13 and 8-14, the dancer leaps out of the background into the white space. That's the better choice.

Of all these page designs, Figure 8-13 is probably the best. It's the most balanced because the dancer counteracts the weight of the large headline at the top of the page. But the final choice is, as always, up to you.

Background image positioning

The same concept of hot spots also applies to background images. Most people would center the background image shown in Figure 8-16, thinking: Why not? It's balanced if it's in the middle, right? True, but always remember that you want balance combined with interest, and unity combined with variety.

When you center your background on a hot spot, you maintain balance (hot spots do precisely that) while adding interest to your composition.

In Figure 8-17, the background radiates from the hot spot.

As I've often commented in this book, there's really no substitute for using a graphics application when designing a Web page. CSS is great for many things, but you simply cannot make it do everything. The words *Deals on Wheels* in Figure 8-18 are not composed of a special metallic font; the 3D metallic effect was added in a graphics program to an ordinary, flat, black typeface. CSS can manipulate text in many ways, for example, but it cannot add that metallic effect. When you need to take text or graphics to the next level, move to a dedicated graphics application like Photoshop that has many such capabilities.

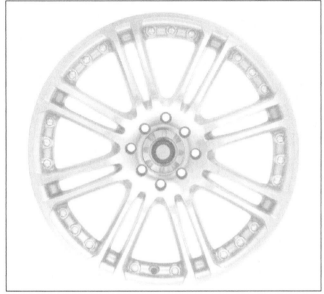

Figure 8-16: Most amateur Web designers drop a background graphic smack in the middle of their page like this.

Figure 8-17: This is better composition: centering the wheel on the upper-left hot spot.

Figure 8-18:
Combine some text with an offset background and you're on your way to a well-designed Web page.

Keeping It Appropriate

I conclude this chapter with a cautionary note for those designers who, now and then, neglect to *think*. I'm not talking about you, of course. I'm talking about some friend of yours that you might lend this book to.

Please do ensure that the symbols, shapes, clip art, and other focus elements you add make sense for your Web site's content. The clip-art silhouette added to Figure 8-11 is great for a dance studio's Web site. It's not so great for a site sponsored by Concerned Mothers Against Filth on TV.

In the latter Web site, you expect sober, down-to-earth graphics. *Anything but a leaping dancer.* The dancing woman just doesn't symbolize the CMAFTV philosophy very well, does it? That dancer would be out of place, too, in the Web sites of most churches and government agencies.

I'd like to recommend some specific sites to illustrate the principles discussed in this chapter. However, Web sites change their content so often that any site I point out will likely have changed by the time you read this book. However, you can do a little surfing on your own and find Web pages that are visually compelling. (Or just look at magazine layouts or ads.) You're likely to find at least some of this chapter's principles illustrated in any good Web page.

Chapter 9

Spacing Out with Boxes

· ·

· ·

*T*o gain a command of precision positioning using CSS, you must understand the concept of the *box*. After you understand that, you can get a
good feel for the ways that elements are positioned within the browser
window. In this chapter, you find out how to use boxes and padding to position elements on your Web pages.

Getting a Grip on Boxes

Each visual element in a CSS has an imaginary box around it that causes it to
perhaps take up more space on the page than its contents (the text or graphics of the element) actually use. In other words, you can add optional padding,
border, and margins to an element that expand the area that the element uses.

The box is a virtual diagram of the content (text or graphics), plus any
padding, border, or margin added to that content. Figure 9-1 illustrates
how padding, borders, and margins radiate out from the central contents.

CSS defines two main types of elements: block-level (such as paragraphs) and
inline elements (such as `<span>`). Block-level elements are positioned in
ways that you can fairly quickly visualize. Inline elements can be less intuitive. (A *containing* block is simply a block-level element that has one or more
child elements that it contains. The concept of *containing block* is used when
discussing CSS inheritance features.)

To understand how padding, border, and margins interact, think of the job of hanging paintings in an art gallery. Each painting consists of the actual canvas area, which is the content in this CSS scenario. Next you can add an optional matte that separates the outer edge of the canvas from the frame. A matte is equivalent to the padding in a CSS box. The frame around the painting is equivalent to the CSS border. Finally, how far apart you hang the paintings on the wall is equivalent to CSS margins.

Figure 9-1:
An element's box is composed of its contents, plus optional padding, border, and margins.

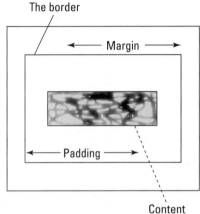

The border

Margin

Padding

Content

The width and height of the content area depends on whether you've specified a value for the `width` or `height` properties, whether the content is a table (or other specialized element), whether the content contains other boxes or text, and so on.

The width of an element's box is determined by adding the content width to any left and right margins, borders, or padding. Likewise, the height of an element's box is the sum of the content height, plus any top and bottom margins, borders, and padding.

The background (visible) styles of the zones of a box are specified using these properties:

- ✔ **Content area:** The element's `background` property
- ✔ **Padding area:** The element's `background` property
- ✔ **Border area:** The element's `border` properties
- ✔ **Margin area:** No background, margins are always transparent

The padding, border, and margins can each be specified with different values for their top, bottom, left, and right sides. Some of these properties are `padding-top`, `border-bottom-width`, and `margin-left`.

You can use these properties to create various special effects within boxes. However, you could specify only a bottom border, for instance, and draw that border in quite a few different ways. In fact, the `border-bottom` property can specify a series of values that apply *only* to the bottom line of the four possible border lines.

Adding a border

If you want a paragraph to be underlined with a one-inch thick blue dotted line, use this code to get the result shown in Figure 9-2:

```
<p style="border-bottom: 12px blue dotted">
You can apply this same offsetting principle to text in
          various ways.
</p>

<p>
This is the next paragraph.
</p>
```

Figure 9-2: A border-bottom property specifies blue, 12-pixel dots for the bottom border line only.

Adding padding

Now add padding to the previous example to see how space is added between the bottom of the text (the bottom of the content area) and the border. The content in Figure 9-3 is *padded*:

```
<p style="border-bottom: 12px blue dotted; padding-
          bottom=.5in;">
You can apply this same offsetting principle to text in
          various ways.
</p>
```

Figure 9-3:
Here space
is padded
between the
paragraph's
content and
border. A
border is
like a frame,
although a
CSS border
isn't
required to
have four
sides.

Adding a margin

Finally, add a *margin* that separates the paragraph element from a nearby element; in this case, the next paragraph below, as shown in Figure 9-4:

```
<p style="border-bottom: 12px blue dotted; padding-
          bottom=.5in;margin-bottom=1in;">
```

Figure 9-4:
Add space
between the
first
paragraph
and the
following
paragraph
by adjusting
the
`margin-
bottom`
property.

In each of the previous three figures, the *box* around the first paragraph has grown in height, although its width did not change. Remember that the box height is the combination of content, border, padding, and margin height.

Vertical Positioning

If you specify no positioning, your Web page elements flow into the page using default flow: The browser simply stacks the elements along the left side of the screen in the order that you locate them in the HTML code, as shown in Figure 9-5:

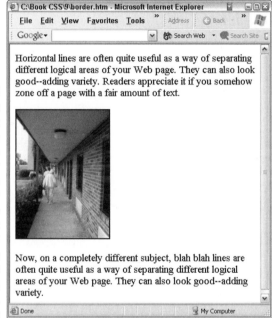

Figure 9-5:
Default positioning enables the browser to decide how your elements should stack up, and the results can be as unappealing as this.

This default positioning takes effect unless you specifically use positioning or floating to violate the normal stacking behavior.

Also by default, the height of an element is, at the most basic level, determined by the element's content. For example, the image in Figure 9-6 is this size in the browser because it is this size in reality. That's the size that the lure.jpg graphics file defines for this image.

```
<img style="border: thin solid"; src="lure.jpg";>
```

Images can be resized in graphics applications, but you can also resize them via CSS using specific width and height properties. The result is shown in Figure 9-7:

```
<img style="border: thin solid; width=380px; height=240px;"
        src="lure.jpg";>
```

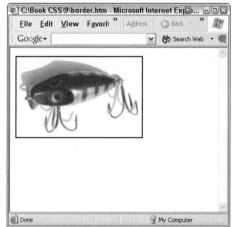

Figure 9-6:
If you don't specify otherwise, the image is as high and wide as its file specification says it should be.

Figure 9-7:
Specify a height value larger than this graphic's default height and you cause elements beneath it to move down on your page.

Obviously, you've affected the height of this element by specifying a `height` property. This, in turn, affects the default vertical positioning of any items below this element. (You can affect the positioning of these lower items by using positioning properties for them.)

Similarly, you can affect the height of a paragraph of text by making the paragraph narrower, requiring that the paragraph grow in height to display all the text. Specifying that a paragraph should be only 35 percent (of the browser width) can cause the paragraph to flow off the bottom of the browser and force the browser to add a scroll bar, as shown in Figure 9-8:

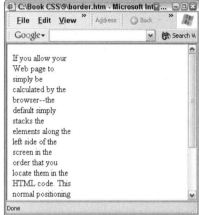

Figure 9-8:
When you
adjust a
paragraph's
height, you
can force
elements
beneath it
down, even
out of the
window at
the bottom.

Here's the code that produces Figure 9-8:

```
<body>

<p style="width: 35%;">
If you allow your Web page to simply be calculated by the
            browser--the default simply stacks the elements
            along the left side of the screen in the order
            that you locate them in the HTML code. This normal
            positioning takes effect unless you specifically
            use positioning or floating to violate the normal
            stacking behavior.
</p>


</body>
```

To understand the box height of an element, you may need to consider a total of seven properties that can be involved:

- ✔ height (the actual content of the element)
- ✔ padding-top
- ✔ padding-bottom
- ✔ border-top
- ✔ border-bottom
- ✔ margin-top
- ✔ margin-bottom

The box's bottom determines where the top of the box surrounding the next element just below can be positioned (in the default normal flow positioning).

An element's height and the top and bottom margin properties can be set to `auto`. If you want to specify the padding property (to add space between the content and any border), or the border width itself, you must specify those with actual units of measurement, or percentages, but not `auto`. However, `auto`, for margin tops and bottoms, defaults to zero.

Horizontal Positioning

Western browsers read from left to right, so when elements are positioned horizontally, they start on the left side. But you must always remember that its *box* can be larger than the element's contents.

Consider this example that displays a background color to illustrate the `width` property of this paragraph element. The result is shown in Figure 9-9:

```
<style>

p {width: 100px;background:tan;}

</style>

</head>

<body>

<p>This paragraph is only 100px wide.</p>

</body>
```

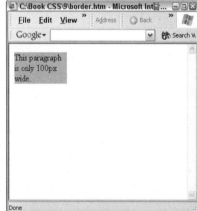

Figure 9-9: The width here is simply specified by the paragraph style's `width` property.

But if you add padding and a margin to the paragraph, you increase the paragraph's box's width:

```
<style>

p {width: 100px; padding: 30px; margin: 40px;
          background:tan;}

</style>

</head>

<body>

<p>This paragraph is only 100px wide.</p>

</body>
```

Notice that compared to Figure 9-9, the paragraph element shown in Figure 9-10 has a wider background color (because padding has been specified) and is also positioned horizontally further away from the left side of the browser (because a margin has been specified).

Figure 9-10:
Here, the paragraph has a larger background color block and is indented from the left of the browser window.

Web page designers often mistakenly believe that when they provide a value to the width property of an element, they're specifying the distance between its left and right border lines. Or worse, some think their width value specifies the entire visible distance between the element and the next element. In fact, padding, border widths, and margins must *all* be taken into account.

This applies as well to the `height` property, where you must take into account padding, borders, and margins too.

Some designers temporarily add a background color to their elements to enable them to more easily visualize the boxes (see Figure 9-9). But always remember that a background does not include any margins, as you can see in Figure 9-10. So simply adding a background doesn't always make the virtual box visible.

Positioning also involves concepts such as the `auto` value and floating. These and related issues are covered in upcoming chapters.

Breaking Up Text with Horizontal Lines

For some reason, horizontal rules aren't used as much in books and other media as they once were. It's a shame, in my view, because they're both attractive and functional.

Horizontal lines are often a quite effective way of separating different logical areas of your Web page. They organize things visually for the reader in a way that's both unobtrusive and efficient. They can also improve the aesthetic appearance by adding variety.

Readers appreciate it if you somehow visually break up a page that contains a large amount of text. Headlines and subheads help to do this, as do borders and background colors or textures. But one of the best ways to indicate that a group of paragraphs belongs together logically is to simply insert horizontal lines as needed.

Probably the easiest way to employ horizontal lines is to use the `<hr>` (horizontal rule) element, like this:

```
<style>

hr {
  margin-top:5px;
  width: 80%;
  height: 1px;
  color: blue;
}

</style>
</head>
<body>
```

```
Horizontal lines are often quite useful as a way of
          separating different logical areas of your Web
          page. They can also look good--adding variety.
          Readers appreciate it if you somehow zone off a
          page with a fair amount of text. Headlines and
          subheads help with this, as do borders and
          background colors or textures. But one of the best
          ways to indicate that a group of paragraphs
          belongs together logically is to simply insert
          horizontal lines as needed.
<hr>

Now, on a completely different subject, blah blah lines are
          often quite useful as a way of separating
          different logical areas of your Web page. They can
          also look good--adding variety.
```

Some CSS experts suggest using the top or bottom border properties of elements to provide horizontal rules, but I've never quite understood why. These experts insist that you should *always* try to separate content, the HTML, from presentation, the CSS, but that seems extreme to me. After all, such elements as <i> for italics are surely easy to embed within body text, rather than setting up a CSS rule for the same effect. The experts further argue: "What if you decided to change italics to some other method of emphasis?" My answer to that is threefold: You should always use only italics for emphasis. But if you are ever faced with going through and changing each <i> tag to a different element, how hard is it to use a search and replace utility to globally make the change throughout your code? It only takes a few seconds, so what's the big deal? And lastly, if you don't like search and replace, you could alternatively redefine the <i> element by creating a new CSS rule with i as the selector, right? Anyway the <hr> element works just fine for adding lines. If you provide a percentage width for it, as in the preceding example, the line is the right size in relation to the parent element. Generally, limiting a dividing line to around 80 percent of the parent is best, as shown in Figure 9-11.

You can use most of the CSS properties you'd expect with <hr>, including, in the example above, a little bit of top-margin to space the line nicely below the first paragraph.

Although a plain, black, or gray line usually suffices, if you wish, you can fiddle around with the shape and size of your dividing line, like this, where the margins, height, width, and color are all changed from the previous example:

```
hr {

  margin-top: 3px;
  margin-bottom: 5px;
  height: 14px;
  width: 60%;
  background-color: mediumspringgreen;
}
```

Figure 9-11:
Use
horizontal
rules to
separate
groups of
paragraphs.

For a list of all the colors available in Internet Explorer, including such favorites as LavenderBlush and WhiteSmoke, see the Cheat Sheet inside this book's front cover.

If you are really adventurous, you can experiment with the line's `back ground-image` property and transform your line into a graphic. However, if you want to divide your paragraph groups with images, I suggest two things:

✔ Just use the `<img>` element to employ graphics rather than twisting the horizontal rule element into something it was never intended to be.

✔ Consider carefully the visual effect of using graphics instead of simple lines to separate your paragraphs.

If you must try it, here's the code. Figure 9-12 illustrates what happens when enthusiasm triumphs over common sense:

```
<style>

p {font: 24pt;}

hr {
 background-image: url(globe.jpg);
 background-repeat: no-repeat;
 border: none;
 width: 400px;
 height: 800px;
 }
</style>
```

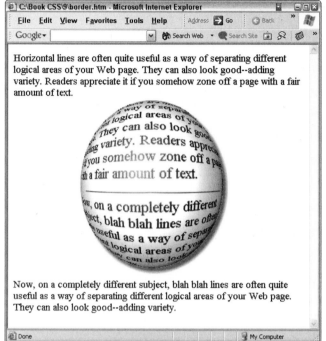

Horizontal lines are often quite useful as a way of separating different logical areas of your Web page. They can also look good--adding variety. Readers appreciate it if you somehow zone off a page with a fair amount of text.

Now, on a completely different subject, blah blah lines are often quite useful as a way of separating different logical areas of your Web page. They can also look good--adding variety.

Figure 9-12:
Using images as a way of separating paragraphs — though possible — is often not very wise.

The trick used in Figure 9-12 is more likely to confuse viewers rather than guiding them. Graphics, generally speaking, just aren't a great a way of organizing text zones. Even subtle graphics, like a small, tasteful border of diamonds or dots, are usually just a distraction to the reader and are best avoided.

Chapter 10

Organizing Your Web Pages Visually

● ●

In This Chapter

▶ Creating effective borders

▶ Floating elements

▶ Using the `clear` property with floats

● ●

*T*his chapter focuses on two ways to visually organize a Web page: adding borders around elements, and floating elements on the page.

Borders can be a good way to help your viewers understand the layout of your page, its various zones, and their purposes. Paragraphs are a way of dividing text into logical units — the reader knows that a paragraph division indicates a new idea, or further expansion of the idea in the previous paragraph.

Similarly, paragraphs themselves can be grouped into larger logical units. For example, a Web page may be subdivided into a section describing your company, another section containing links to various locations in the Web site, and yet another section advertising your latest product.

Each of these sections might contain several paragraphs, but you group them together because they belong together logically.

Paragraphs can be grouped in many ways. Headlines or sub-heads, for example, group the paragraphs that follow them. Horizontal lines (`<hr>`) can be used to effectively divide groups of paragraphs. Or you can resort to less-elegant visual zoning by coloring the background of the paragraph groups using different colors (this last approach isn't recommended except for Web sites designed for kids).

Finally, you see how to exploit the useful `float` property to allow elements to flow around each other, such as a paragraph of text that seems to enclose a photo.

Managing Borders

If you choose to surround elements of a Web page with borders, you're in luck: CSS offers quite a variety of ways to employ borders, and it allows you to add borders to any element you want to.

A *border* is a frame, just a line usually, that surrounds an element. However, you can selectively leave out any of the four lines of a border or define them each differently using the `border-top`, `border-right`, `border-bottom`, and `border-left` properties individually.

A border surrounds the content, and, optionally, any padding that you've specified for an element. Any optional margin specified is not surrounded by the border, but instead separates this element from surrounding elements.

Borders can be given values indicating how you want them to look: color, thickness, and style (dotted, inset and so on). The thickness or width of the border can be specified in the usual CSS variety of ways (using the units of measurement described in detail in Chapter 6, such as `px`, `in`, or `em`), including the default *medium*, which is two or three pixels wide. The default color of a border is the text color of the element, or if an element has no text (an image, for example), the text color of the element's parent is inherited.

If people want to know why you use CSS, you can tell them that one of many reasons is the `border` property. It can be applied to any element, and, like many CSS features, the `border` property is flexible, attractive, sensible, efficient, and useful. Without CSS, you'd have to resort to really nasty solutions like torturing the `table` element into serving as a frame.

Specifying a simple border

You'll find all kinds of borders at your disposal when using CSS. The simplest border specification just uses the `border` property followed by a series of three values (`width`, `style`, and `color`) separated by spaces, like these:

```
<html>
<head>

<style>

body {font-size:24px;}
p {border: thick solid green;}


</style>
</head>

<body>
```

```
<p>Absolute positioning units (inches, px, and so on) can
        also be used to position a background graphic,
        using the usual x y coordinate system.
</p>


<p style="border: 10px groove gray">Absolute positioning
        units (inches, px, and so on) can also be used to
        position a background graphic, using the usual x y
        coordinate system.
</p>

<p style="border: .4in ridge mintcream">Absolute positioning
        units (inches, px, and so on) can also be used to
        position a background graphic, using the usual x y
        coordinate system.
</p>

<p style="border: 6px double blue">Absolute positioning units
        (inches, px, and so on) can also be used to
        position a background graphic, using the usual x y
        coordinate system.
</p>

</body>
</html>
```

Save this code to a file with an .htm extension in Windows Explorer, and then double-click that .htm file. Internet Explorer opens and loads the page you see in Figure 10-1:

Notice in the preceding code that you follow the border property with values for width, style, and color, in this way for an inline CSS style:

```
style="border: 6px double blue"
```

Or like this for a general CSS style:

```
p {border: 6px double blue;}
```

If you don't specify a style, you get no border. The default style is none. So don't assume that if you specify other border-related properties like border-width or color, you'll end up with a border. The border-style property is required.

The difference between external, embedded, and inline CSS styles is described in the section titled "Visualizing Specificity" in Chapter 2.

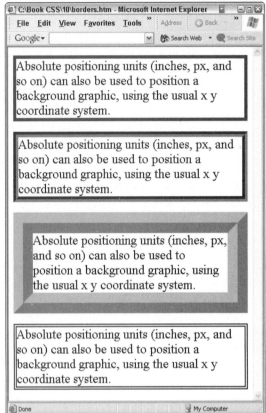

Figure 10:1:
You can
create all
kinds of
borders.
These styles
are, from
top to
bottom,
solid,
groove,
ridge, and
double.

Choosing from lotsa border styles

You can specify eight different border styles: solid, dotted, dashed, double, groove, ridge, inset, or outset. Figure 10-2 illustrates each style, although some of them are a bit wider than you'd normally want to use. I'm specifying that each border here be a generous eight pixels for illustrative purposes so you can easily see them in this book. Generally speaking, the only styles you should usually make thick are the frame-like designs: groove, ridge, inset, and outset. These are designed to display shading (by varying the lightness of the lines), so you want the lines large enough so the viewer can actually see the shading. Here's the code:

```
<p style="border: 8px solid">This is the SOLID border style.
          No color is specified, so it defaults to black.
</p>
<p style="border: 8px dotted">This is the DOTTED border
          style.
</p>
```

```
<p style="border: 8px dashed">This is the DASHED border
            style.
</p>
<p style="border: 8px double">This is the DOUBLE border
            style.
</p>
<p style="border: 8px groove">This is the GROOVE border
            style.
</p>
<p style="border: 8px ridge">This is the RIDGE border style.
</p>
<p style="border: 8px inset">This is the INSET border style.
</p>
<p style="border: 8px outset">This is the OUTSET border
            style.
</p>
```

Figure 10-2 illustrates the eight border styles:

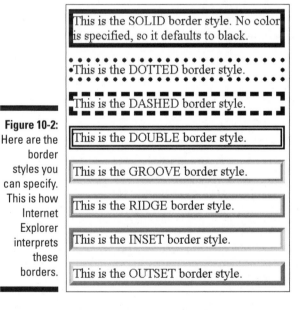

Figure 10-2:
Here are the border styles you can specify. This is how Internet Explorer interprets these borders.

Other browsers interpret the border styles slightly differently. Figure 10-3 shows how Mozilla Firefox displays the styles. For example, Firefox thinks "dotted" means small dashes. Firefox also employs black, rather than the more subtle gray, for the shadows in the bottom four frame-like borders, as shown in Figure 10-3:

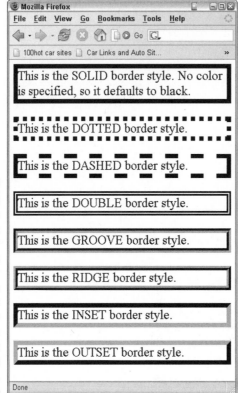

CSS3 is developing a border-radius property that allows you to further refine the appearance of borders by rounding the corners; a border-image property that you could use with fancy graphics to build ornate frames; and some associated properties to rotate and otherwise transform ornate borders. Progress marches on.

Mixing and matching styles

If you like, you can use only a one-sided border (or two- or three-sided). You can even to mix and match styles so that, for example, one side is dotted and the rest are double lines. Why you would ever want to do this is another issue, but here's an example of a graphic bordered on the top and right with the dotted style, the bottom with no border, and the left side the dashed style:

```
<html>
<head>

<style>

IMG {border-style: dotted dotted none dashed;}

</style>
</head>

<body>

<IMG src="woofie.jpg" >

</body>
</html>
```

This code results in the odd, mixed-border look in Figure 10-4:

Figure 10-4:
Mix and match borders, or you can even use *none* to remove a border. This image has no bottom border.

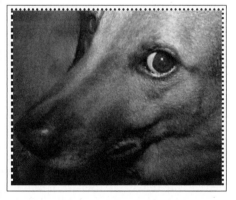

 In CSS styles, when the four sides of a border, margin, or other property are specified with a list of values, the order is always top, right, bottom, left. You can remember this value order because it's simply clockwise, starting from midnight at the top. Thus, dotted dotted none dashed translates as a dotted top and right side, no border on the bottom, and a dashed border line on the left side, as shown in Figure 10-4.

Specifying border width

Border width can be specified using the usual CSS set of units (px, in, em, and so on), or by using the descriptive values thin, medium, or thick. The following code using the thick value produces the result shown in Figure 10-5:

```
<style>

P {background-color: lightsalmon; padding: 12px;
   border-style: double; border-width: thick;}

</style>
```

In addition to altering the border style, you can also vary the *size* of each individual border (as you can with margins), although this too is useful for few Web page designs. If you wish, use these properties to display a multi-thick border: `border-top-width`, `border-right-width`, `border-bottom-width`, and `border-left-width`. Figure 10-5 illustrates the thick size.

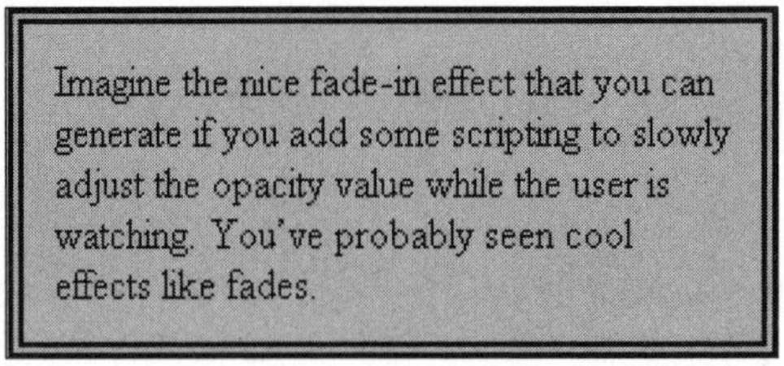

Figure 10-5:
This border is rendered in the `thick` border width.

Imagine the nice fade-in effect that you can generate if you add some scripting to slowly adjust the opacity value while the user is watching. You've probably seen cool effects like fades.

Coloring a border

Border color is specified with the `border-color` property. No surprise there. Just use any of the CSS color values described in detail in Chapter 6. Remember that if you omit this property, the border takes on the color of the surrounding text, or the text of the parent element, if the local element has no color (such as an image element). The default border color is, therefore, usually black.

If you want to play around with some lighting effects to give your borders a dimensional quality, you can specify four different colors, one for each side of the border, like this:

```
<style>


P {padding-left: 6px; padding-right: 4px; padding-top: 6px;
   border-style: double; border-width: thick;

   border-color: lightskyblue lightskyblue darkslateblue
           darkslateblue;}

</style>
```

When you assign dark colors to the right and bottom sides, you produce the "outset" protruding lighting effect, even though you're not using the outset style for your border property. Figure 10-6 illustrates one way to do this:

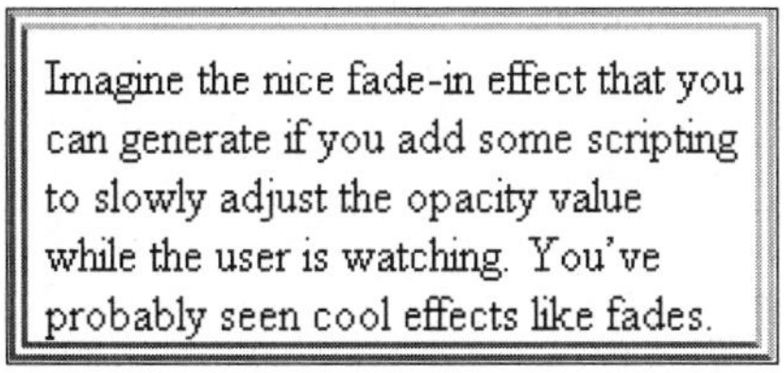

Figure 10-6:
By specifying different values for different sides of this border, you get a 3D lighting effect, similar to the outset border style.

> Imagine the nice fade-in effect that you can generate if you add some scripting to slowly adjust the opacity value while the user is watching. You've probably seen cool effects like fades.

Although you can add borders to inline elements, avoid that trick. It can look pretty messy and overdone. Borders aren't meant for inline elements.

Floating About

CSS permits any element to float, just as it extends many other properties to *all* elements that were in traditional HTML limited to only a few. Designers were able to flow (or *wrap*) text around an image or table by using the align="right" code in HTML, but now you can pretty much float anything you wish. Here again, CSS gives designers far greater freedom to *design* than was previously possible.

Figure 10-7 illustrates how the following code looks, *without* using the float property:

```
<body>

<h2><img src="woofie.jpg" style=" width: 200px; height:
        150px; margin: 0 3% 0;">Illustrating how a
            gradient effect works</h2>
```

```
<p>You can apply gradients to various images, as you wish.
     Imagine the nice fade-in effect that you can
     generate if you add some scripting to slowly
     adjust the opacity value while the user is
     watching.</p>

</body>
```

Figure 10-7:
Without the
`float`
property,
many Web
page
designs are
almost
guaranteed
to include
unneces-
sary white
space, like
this.

But when you add the `float` property, text and other elements wrap around the floated element. In this next example, the image is floated within both the parent headline and the text that follows it, as shown in Figure 10-8:

```
<body>

<h2><img src="woofie.jpg" style="float: left; width: 200px;
height: 150px; margin: 0 3% 0;">Illustrating how a gradient
     effect works</h2>

<p>You can apply gradients to various images, as you wish.
     Imagine the nice fade-in effect that you can
     generate if you add some scripting to slowly
     adjust the opacity value while the user is
     watching.</p>

</body>
```

Notice in the above code that the image is an inline element, nested inside the H2 element. When you nest elements like this, you help ensure that most browsers align the top margin of the headline text and the image.

Figure 10-8:
Use the
`float`
property to
tighten your
designs and
offer the
viewer this
more
professional
look.

Figure 10-9 shows a right float, using the preceding code but with one change:

```
float: right;
```

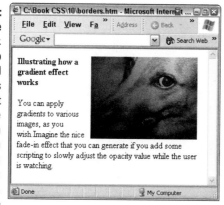

Figure 10-9:
Change the
`float`
value to
right, and
you get this
effect. Right
floats are
more often
used when
inserting
photos than
left floats.

Left floats are often used to add special effects to text, such as drop caps (described and illustrated in Chapter 8) or bullets or icons that you want to insert at the start of each paragraph.

If you want to float both left and right, go ahead. Figure 10-10 illustrates this double-float. Here's the code:

```
<h3><img src="woofie.jpg" style="float: left; width: 100px;
height: 75px;">
<img src="woofie.jpg" style="float: right; width: 100px;
height: 75px;">
Illustrating how a gradient effect works</h3>
```

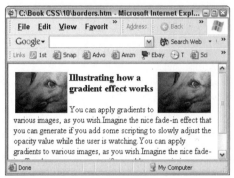

Figure 10-10:
You can combine left and right floated images, like this.

Canceling a Float with Clear

Text listed in the HTML following a floating image usually flows down alongside the image, as the various figures in this chapter demonstrate.

But what if you want to force some text to detach itself from the image it would normally flow around? What if you want to move it down below the image? Sometimes you *don't* want text associated with a particular image.

Also, consider that the actual number of words needed to flow from the top to the bottom of any given image can vary considerably. The user might resize the browser window, for example, which has a big impact on the flow. Likewise, the user's preferred font size, the resolution of the screen, and other factors can impact the amount of text that flows. In these situations, you may want to specify that some of your text must be displayed beneath a floated image — regardless of how much the user resizes the browser or other factors. That text must *always* ignore the floating and appear below the image.

One problem with floating arises when you have several images on the page. The clear property can assist you in ensuring that the each element of text appears next to the image it's associated with.

The CSS version of clearing is similar to the traditional HTML <br> element used with a clear attribute. In CSS, you use the clear property, along with the values left, right, or both. Only employ <br> with this CSS style to force the text following the <br> to move down below any existing margins (in other words, to move down into the next *clear* area on the page).

Here's an example illustrating the effect that the clear property has. The following code inserts a plain <br> tag, but it doesn't move the paragraph of text following the <br> beyond the floated image. All the <br> does is move the text down one line, as shown in Figure 10-11:

```
<body>

<img src="woofie.jpg" style="float: left; width: 200px;
height: 150px;">

<p>You can apply gradients to various images, as you wish.
        Imagine the nice fade-in effect that you can
        generate if you add some scripting to slowly
        adjust the opacity value while the user is
        watching.
<br>
We want this paragraph to be disassociated from the previous
        paragraph and from the floating image. You can
        apply gradients to various images, as you wish.
        Imagine the nice fade-in effect that you can
        generate if you add some scripting to slowly
        adjust the opacity value while the user is
        watching.</p>
</body>
```

As you can see in Figure 10-11, inserting a plain <br> element merely creates a paragraph break (moves the text down to the following line). But what we really want to do with this text is move it all the way down past the image.

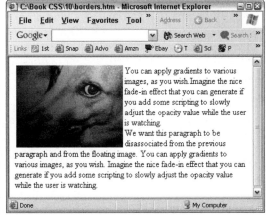

Figure 10-11:
Using an ordinary <br> simply moves the text down one line.

However, by adding the CSS clear property and specifying a left value, you force the text to move down beyond the floated image, as Figure 10-12 illustrates.

```
<br style="clear: left">
```

Figure 10-12:
When you
want to
move some
text down
beyond a
floated
element,
just use the
clear
property.

Use the left value, obviously, when you want to override an element floating left. I'll leave it up to you to figure out when the right and both values are used.

As is usual with CSS (and impossible in traditional HTML), you can apply the clear property to any element, not just text and images. So, if you run into a situation where you want to ensure that an element is positioned below a floating element, use clear.

If you do a lot of clearing in a page or site, you might want to create a generic class that can be applied with a div or span tag, like this:

```
div.spacer
{
    clear: both;
}
```

Chapter 11

Designing with Auto and Inline Elements

A CSS element's box is a virtual, imaginary shape composed of an element's contents, plus its optional padding, border, and margin, if any. The box dimensions are not necessarily the same as the visible contents or the visible border. If padding is used, the box grows to include the padding dimensions. If a border or margin are further added, they, too, increase the size of the box. However, padding is never itself visible — it merely creates space between its element and surrounding elements or the browser frame.

When you understand the concept of the virtual box, you're well on your way to managing effective page layout. And, as you discover in this chapter, CSS offers you further control over the behavior of content and margins by allowing you to use the `auto` value. CSS even allows you to add features such as borders and margins around inline elements, such as the italics (`<i>`) element. In this chapter, you explore both topics — auto and inline manipulations — to see what to employ and what to avoid.

Employing Auto to Control Layout

Of the four possible zones of a Web page — content, padding, border, and margin — only two, the element's content and optional margin, can be set to `auto`. Auto allows the browser to automatically resize content and margins: This enables you to do some pretty interesting things, such as stabilizing a graphic in the center of the Web page, no matter how the user resizes the browser.

This next example allows the browser to automatically adjust the size of the right margin, to ensure that a paragraph remains at a fixed size and at a fixed distance from the left side of the browser window.

You can individually specify the left, right, top, and bottom margins using, for example, code like this:

```
p {width: 150px; margin-right: auto; margin-left: 150px;}
```

This interesting style says that the content should be fixed at a width of 150 pixels, and that the left margin is fixed at 150 pixels. The parent element is, in effect, the browser window itself (technically, the parent is the `<body>` element if no other parent is involved, but the browser window certainly *seems* to be the parent). In other words, the total distance from the left side of the browser window to the right side of the content (the paragraph's text) must be maintained at 300 pixels. The right margin, however, automatically adjusts to maintain those two other fixed widths. The effect of the `auto` property is to freeze the paragraph at a specific horizontal location within the browser window, even if the user stretches or shrinks the browser window by resizing it (or if some other event causes resizing).

To understand this effect, take a look at Figure 11-1. This paragraph uses no CSS style. No `auto` value is in effect, so when the user widens the browser window (the window on the right side), the text widens to fill the width of the window.

Figure 11-1:
When you don't use `auto`, a paragraph stretches as necessary to fill the width of the browser window.

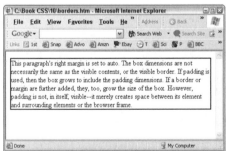

The browser on the left in Figure 11-1 is stretched and ends up looking like the browser on the right. The paragraph of text widens to accommodate the new browser width.

In Figure 11-2, by contrast, you see the effect of adding a CSS style employing auto. Here's the code that causes the paragraph to freeze in one position (a stable distance from the left side of the parent browser window, in this example):

```
<html>
<head>

<style>

p {width: 150px; margin-right: auto; margin-left:
        150px;border: 2px solid;}

</style>
</head>

<body>

<p>This paragraph's right margin is set to auto. The box
        dimensions are not necessarily the same as the
        visible contents, or the visible border. If
        padding is used, then the box grows to include the
        padding dimensions. If a border or margin are
        further added, they, too, grow the size of the
        box.
</p>
</body>
</html>
```

Figure 11-2:
With the right margin set to auto and the left margin and width specified, this text doesn't move or resize when the user resizes the window.

 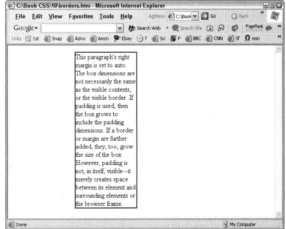

Figure 11-2 demonstrates that stretching the browser window wider (right) does not stretch the paragraph wider. The right margin in this figure automatically adjusts to whatever size necessary to maintain the paragraph's size and position.

If you set all three width properties — `width, margin-left, and margin-right` — to a specific, absolute size (such as 150 pixels), you've created an impossibility. What can the browser do when the user stretches the browser window? One of these three width measurements must become flexible. They can't all remain fixed, can they? In this situation, the browser automatically changes the margin-right property to `auto` and ignores your specified size.

Specifying margins

If you specify left and right margins, but don't specify width, an element stretches its width to accommodate and maintain the requested margins. For example, if you specify that the left and right margins should be 150 pixels, the `width` property of the paragraph then becomes (of necessity) `auto`.

```
p {margin-left: 50px; margin-right: 50px; border: 2px solid;}
```

Figure 11-3 illustrates that specifying both left and right margins but omitting a width specification causes the browser to assume that the width is `auto`.

Figure 11-3:
When you specify this paragraph's margins, but not its width, the paragraph adjusts its width as if you had set the width to `auto`.

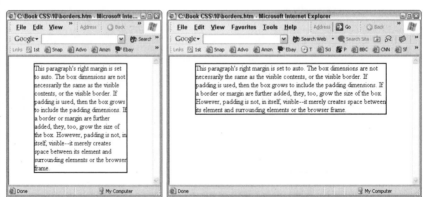

This next style has the same effect as the previous style in the preceding code:

```
p {width: auto; margin-left: 50px; margin-right: 50px;
          border: 2px solid;}
```

Centering

Figure 11-3 illustrates one way to center a paragraph, but what if you want to freeze its size as well as centering it? In other words, you want it to remain in the middle of the browser and resist being resized (as in Figure 11-3) if the user stretches the browser window. The following code is *supposed* to do just that:

```
p {margin-left: auto; margin-right: auto; width: 200px;}
```

However, at the time of this writing, Internet Explorer version 6 chokes on the preceding code and simply sticks the paragraph against the left side (using no left margin). Mozilla Firefox and other browsers get it right, however, as you can see in Figure 11-4:

Figure 11-4:
Mozilla can handle using auto margins to center an element. IE cannot.

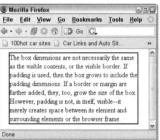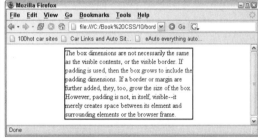

This is one of the few instances where Internet Explorer 6 fails to correctly interpret a CSS style. This technique of setting margin left and right to auto is technically the correct way to center and freeze the size of elements in a CSS style. I'm hoping that IE gets on the bandwagon soon.

Using !DOCTYPE to force IE to comply

You can make IE render the previous example (and some other kinds of CSS rules) by inserting the following line of code at the *top* (above the <html> element) of your page of code. Here's how it looks:

```
<!DOCTYPE HTML PUBLIC "-//W3C//DTD HTML 4.0 Strict//EN" >

<html>
<head>

<style>
p {margin-left: auto; margin-right: auto; width: 200px;}
</style>
```

This !DOCTYPE declaration can have unintended side effects such as changing proprietary IE behaviors that you might be exploiting (relative font sizes, for example, can render differently). But if you want to try using the declaration, it does force IE 6 to switch to its CSS standards-compliant mode.

Vertical Positioning with Auto

Just as you can set three properties to auto when sizing and positioning horizontally (width and the left and right margins), so, too, can you in theory use the auto value with the equivalent vertical properties: height and the top and bottom margins.

Strangely, centering an element when using normal flow (the default) is rather difficult because if you try to use auto as the value for the margin-top or margin-bottom properties, the value is evaluated as zero! Auto is just ignored in this case. Recall from the discussion of horizontal centering earlier in this chapter that auto margins can be used for centering — and indeed using auto margins is the recommended technique for CSS centering.

You can freeze the top position of an element using the following code. Just specify the top-margin value, but ignore the element's height:

```
p {width: auto; margin-top: 100px; margin-bottom: 100px;
        border: 2px solid;}
```

Figure 11-5 shows how an element can be put in place in a specific vertical location, but its height is *not* frozen. Adjusting the browser (or parent element) shape can add or subtract from the element's height (see how the paragraph loses some height on the right side of Figure 11-5, when the browser is widened).

You can fiddle around with absolute or relative positioning and achieve vertical positioning that works in some of the minor browsers, but these workarounds still don't work in Internet Explorer. Also, don't be tempted to fiddle with the vertical-align property. It's designed to manipulate the position of inline text elements (such as superscripting); the vertical-align property has no effect on block-level content.

Here's example code that does work fine in Firefox and Netscape:

```
div {
height: 100%;
width: 100%;
display: table;
```

```
position: fixed;}

p
{
display: table-cell;
vertical-align: middle;
}
```

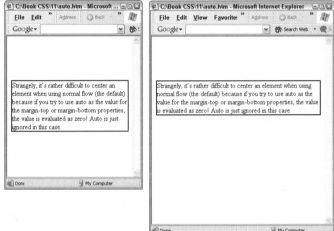

Figure 11-5:
Center
vertically by
freezing the
top margin.

Handling Inline Elements

In CSS, an inline element is a small element right within a line of text (such as the <em> or <i> elements). You can fool around with inline elements in text in many ways: drawing borders around individual words or phrases, padding, including margins, inserting extra large characters or words, dropping graphic images into the middle of a paragraph, and other annoying tricks.

Why annoying? These kinds of adjustments to text are almost always ugly and unsophisticated. Just because CSS allows you to apply virtually any property to any element doesn't mean that you *should*.

Text manipulations, generally speaking, are best left to those who designed the typeface in the first place. Start adding inline frames, borders, margins, large characters or graphics in a line of text and you begin to approach the unattractive, hard-to-read, text effects found in ransom notes and a child's first attempts at printing.

The only exception to this is the `vertical-align` property, which can be valuable if you need to make text superscript or subscript. This topic is covered in Chapter 7.

However, for the sake of completion, I briefly cover some of the nasty, spooky things you can do via repositioning and otherwise molesting perfectly good text. (Never let it be said that you don't get your money's worth from a . . . *For Dummies* book.) This section of the chapter should serve more as a warning than a guide.

Inline elements, unlike block elements, are generally rather small and, as their name suggests, in a line of text. You can insert nonreplaced elements such as `strong` (which makes text darker) or drop in replaced elements like an image. (Replaced elements are those such as an image, where the content is inserted on the fly, rather than existing in the code itself. A nonreplaced element, on the other hand, is a word of text: It's in the actual code of the Web page, so it doesn't need to be replaced by content in some outside file.)

You can take a perfectly good paragraph of text and mess it up by adding an inline element, a `span` in this case, defined with a CSS border, as shown in Figure 11-6:

Figure 11-6:
A border
stuck into
some text.
It's like a
necklace
around a
parrot's
neck — it
catches
your eye,
and then it
looks
ridiculous.

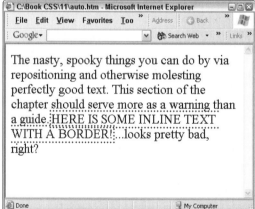

The crime in Figure 11-6 was committed by this code:

```
<html>
<head>

<style>

span {border: 3px dotted;}
```

```
body {font-size: large;}

</style>
</head>

<body>

<p>The nasty, spooky things you can do by via repositioning
            and otherwise molesting perfectly good text. This
            section of the chapter should serve more as a
            warning than a guide.<span>HERE IS SOME INLINE
            TEXT WITH A BORDER!</span>...looks pretty bad,
            right?</p>
</body>
</html>
```

I don't want to annoy or shock you with multiple examples of tortured inline positioning resulting in distasteful text layout. Instead, I content myself with one more example involving applying padding to an inline element. It not only looks bad, but part of the text also becomes unreadable as a result.

Here's the code that produces the special effect shown in Figure 11-7:

```
<style>

span {background: linen; padding-top: 16px;}

</style>
```

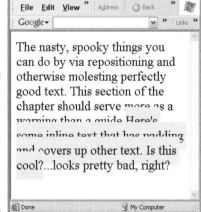

Figure 11-7:
A new low in tormented text, thanks to padding used with an inline element.

Truthfully, I've yet to see — or even imagine — a use for these kinds of inline element manipulations, but I'm equally sure that someone, somewhere has invented a clever technique involving just these properties applied to just these inline elements. If you know of any, please e-mail me at `richardm52@hotmail.com`.

Chapter 12

Handling Tables and Lists
(And Doing Away with Tables)

Ah, now I come to the classics. The venerable backbone of classic HTML — tables. *What* would Web designers ever do without tables? They've been to traditional Web page layout what frames are to houses or what chicken wire is to a parade float: It's what you attach everything else to.

In *theory,* you're supposed to be able to create vibrant, complex Web page designs without using tables at all, thanks to CSS. In practice, most of today's Web pages are still — behind the curtain — held together by tables. Think I'm toying with you? Go to almost any well-known site like www.cnn.com or www.bbc.com, choose View➪Source in Internet Explorer to see the HTML, and I'll bet you don't have too look far to find your first <table> element. You won't have to look much further to find dozens more.

In this chapter, you see what impact CSS has had on HTML lists, and then go on to explore how CSS can either embrace tables, or, perhaps, somehow, even replace them altogether.

This chapter has two focal points. First, it explores what CSS contributes in the way of special properties for lists and tables. (The answer, for you impatient types, is, "Not much.") Second, you see how you can free your Web pages from dependency on tables for their structure and layout. *This* — the CSS positioning features — is a big contribution that CSS has made to Web page design and one that, sooner rather than later, all Web page designers should embrace. The CSS positioning features are just a much more sensible way of doing things than using those old, cumbersome table techniques.

List Styles O' Plenty

Lists, of course, are the simpler cousins of tables. Instead of items spread out in two directions — both horizontal and vertical — as in a table, a list limits itself to a simpler horizontal stack of items. A list is like a single column in a table. And because it's a simpler format, lists normally don't need the help of borders to frame the individual cells. Bullets, dingbats, or numbers generally serve to visually separate one list component from the next.

But lists do have their uses, as Martha Stewart would surely agree. (I've long suspected that Martha has so many lists that she probably needs a master list of all of her other lists.)

CSS allows you to manipulate lists in many ways that are not possible in HTML. You can use one of three graphic symbols as bullets with an unordered (also known as an unnumbered or bulleted) list. Obviously, even a list with bullets is not haphazard, as the term "unordered" suggests. The three symbols are

- **Disc:** the most common symbol, a black, filled dot, and it's also the default CSS list style
- **Circle:** an empty outline of a circle
- **Square:** a filled square

Here's code that produces Figure 12-1. Notice that I didn't specify the first style, but instead simply used the `<ul>` (unordered list) element. That's because the disc (a dot) is the default unordered list style:

```
<html>
<head>

<style>
body {font-size: large;}
</style>
</head>

<body>

<ul>
<li>first
<li>second
<li>third
</ul>

<ul style="list-style-type: circle;">
<li>first
<li>second
<li>third
</ul>
```

```
<ul style="list-style-type: square;">
<li>first
<li>second
<li>third
</ul>

</body>
</html>
```

Figure 12-1:
The three bulleted (unordered) list styles are dots, circles, and squares.

Here are the six styles of numbered (ordered) lists:

- decimal: 1. 2. 3.

- lower-roman: i. ii. iii.

- upper-roman: I. II. III.

- lower-alpha: a. b. c.

- upper-roman: A. B. C.

- none: The items in the list are indented like all other lists, but with no graphic or numeric symbols.

CSS2 adds a few languages to the group of styles (Armenian, lower-Greek and so on). CSS2 also includes a decimal-leading-zero style that inserts a 0 in front of all numbers below 10 (01. 02. 03.).

Getting exotic with the list-style-image property

If you want to use a different graphic as a bullet — something more exciting or exotic than the supplied disc, circle, or square — use the `list-style-image` property, as illustrated in Figure 12-2.

```
<html>
<head>

<style>

li {list-style-image: url("shadow.jpg");}
body {font-size: large;}
</style>
</head>

<body>

<ul>
<li>onezee
<li>doozee
<li>thrice
</ul>

</body>
</html>
```

Figure 12-2: You can easily substitute your own custom buttons, rather than merely relying on the built-in discs, circles, or squares.

If, as you can see in Figure 12-3, the graphics don't align in the middle of the text characters, it's not your fault. The text is forced to align with the bottom of a `list-style-image`.

Figure 12-3:
Unfortun-
ately, these
bullets
are not
centered;
they're a
bit too high.

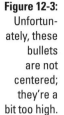

The solution is to go back to the graphics application where you designed the bullet graphic and chop off the bottom of the graphic, thereby lowering it. This is illustrated in Figure 12-4:

Figure 12-4:
Adjust the
white space
around
a bullet
graphic to
reposition
it in the
Web page.

You cannot resize the `list-style-images` using, for example, `height` and `width` properties. Instead, you must resize your image in a graphics application such as Photoshop.

Positioning lists

If you want to adjust the way your bulleted or numbered lists indent (when a list item contains multiple lines of text), you can specify `inside` or `outside` values for the `list-style-position` property. The effect is relatively minor, but if you specify the `inside` value, you get a drop cap-like effect — nesting the bullets or numbers within the text — as shown in Figure 12-5:

Figure 12-5: Use the inside value with the list-style-position property to move the second line of text over to the left.

This code produces the inside effect shown in Figure 12-5:

```
ul {list-style-position: inside}
```

The default is the outside position, shown in Figure 12-6.

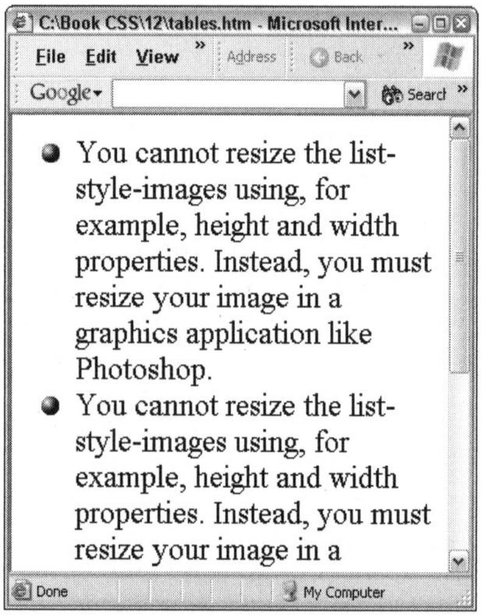

Figure 12-6: This default indent style is the one almost always used in books and magazines.

Why is the style displayed in Figure 12-6 (the default) the most popular? It looks better, and it helps the reader in the same way bullets and numbers are supposed to: helping them quickly recognize the items in the list.

Putting it all together

As you might expect, CSS offers a shorthand format for list formatting. The `list-style` property combines the features of the three previously described properties: `style-type`, `style-image`, and `style-position`. It looks like this:

```
<style>
li {list-style: circle inside}
</style>
```

Or, to include your own bullet, use this code, where shadow.jpg is the name of the graphic file you would like to use as a bullet:

```
<style>
li {list-style: url("shadow.jpg");}
</style>
```

Or, to define a particular `<ul>` element:

```
<ul style="list-style; square inside">
```

Managing Tables

Nowadays, tables are used in Web pages for far more than they were originally intended. The plan was to simply use them to display tabular data — an ordinary table of information. However, tables have served for years as a grid upon which to build the entire Web page.

The fundamental problem is that HTML did not provide a viable way to arrange the various components or visual zones within a page. Designers who work with magazines, in advertising, and other fields expect to be able to position page elements precisely where they want them to go — down to the tiniest unit of measurement. (On a computer monitor, that unit of measurement is the pixel.) But with HTML, even when you used tables as a way to hang your other content, you never got pixel-level control.

Stalking invisible .gifs

Then designers, notably David Siegal, author of *Creating Killer Web Sites* (Hayden, 1997), came up with the idea of using a single-pixel .gif graphic as a way of positioning content using tables. The graphic can be easily resized to whatever space you need to fill to make your page look good. Just adjust the `width` and `height` properties to suit your purposes, as illustrated in Step 5 below. What an invisible table cannot accomplish by positioning your elements on a larger scale, you can fine-tune by inserting invisible graphics images.

To see how prevalent the use of this kind of spacer image is now, follow these steps:

1. **Open Internet Explorer, type msn in the Address field, and press Ctrl+Enter.**

    Internet Explorer fills in the www. and .com and other necessary redundancies (as if you were looking for this in some *other* location than the World Wide Web, and as if it didn't have a *com* extension).

    You go to the msn.com site.

2. **Choose View⇨Source.**

    Notepad opens, displaying the source code for the MSN Web page.

3. **In Notepad, choose Edit⇨Find.**

    The Find dialog box opens.

4. **Search for c.gif.**

5. **Press F3 repeatedly and notice how many times you find this graphic referenced.**

    You're likely to find quite a few references to this image (although the width and height are variable):

```
<img src="http://hp.msn.com/c/home/c.gif" width="25"
      height="20" />
```

By changing this image's width and height, you can create space. You'll find it inside table elements, too. Lotsa times.

Or look at the source code for other sites such as www.cnn.com, where you are likely to find mystery .gif files that have no visible content (but do have width and height attributes). They're often located inside tables, as you'll see. I found an interesting one named px.gif.

Before I get into how CSS enables you to design pages without using tables as a backbone, first consider the table-layout property, a feature that CSS brings to actual tables. By *actual tables,* I mean tables that behave like traditional tables: displaying information to the user in tabular format, as opposed to tables hiding behind the layout of the Web page, merely providing the framework upon which you hang your page's visible content.

Employing the table-layout property

The CSS table-layout property allows you to specify whether your table cells should expand to display their entire contents, or remained fixed. The default value is auto, which means that the browser is burdened with the job of calculating each cell's size before laying out the table. However, you can use the fixed value for the table-layout property and speed things up by specifying a maximum size for the cells. This can, however, cut off part of a photo, as shown in Figure 12-7:

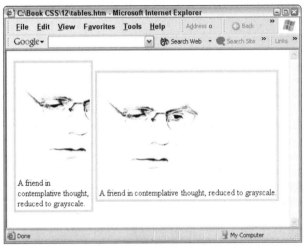

Figure 12-7: When you use the fixed value for table-layout, you can cause the contents to be cut off, as in the table on the left.

As you can see in the following code, the figure on the left (the first figure specified in the code) is in a table with its table-layout property set to fixed. No amount of resizing the user's browser stretches or shrinks this figure. It's fixed at the width specified (150 pixels here). (The height of the table's cell is unaffected by all this.)

```
<html>
<head>
<body>

<table>
<tr>
<td>

<table style="table-layout: fixed; width: 150px; border:
        solid">
<tr>
<td><img src="thought.jpg"><br />
A friend in contemplative thought, reduced to grayscale.</td>
</tr>
</table>
</td>
<td>

<table style="table-layout: auto; border: solid" >
<tr>
```

```
<td><img src="thought.jpg"><br />
A friend in contemplative thought, reduced to grayscale.</td>
</tr>
</table>
</td>
</tr>
</table>


</body>
</html>
```

The second table is set to auto, and thus the browser is allowed to stretch those cells so that they widen to display the entire contents, as you can see in the table on the right in Figure 12-7. (For a detailed discussion of auto, see Chapter 11.)

Avoiding properties not supported by IE

The caption-side property is intended to add a brief bit of descriptive text or a caption or title, to the top, right, bottom, or left of a table. It doesn't work in Internet Explorer 6 or earlier, so avoid it. Plus, it's pretty ugly even when it's working.

IE ignores or improperly handles these three CSS properties as well: border-collapse, border-spacing, and empty-cells. These properties attempt to govern how borders are displayed, including drawing no border if a cell contains no content (empty-cells). However, until IE responds to these properties correctly, employing them is clearly not a good idea.

Doing Without Tables

For years, the dream of many Web page designers has been to find some way to avoid relying on the extensive, bloated code required to lay out a Web page using tables and spacer images. CSS positioning brought us much closer to that elusive goal. If you assume that 95 percent of your Web page's audience is using Internet Explorer, and that very few are using the old renegade Netscape 4, you can move a table-based layout over to CSS style without feeling guilty or worrying that some users see havoc on their screen. CSS positioning is now widely accepted and results in essentially predictable effects in browsers. Here are the two primary advantages of designing a page using CSS rather than tables:

> ✔ You accomplish most of your style definition in one location in your CSS code, rather than having to specify multiple attributes throughout all kinds of table elements.
>
> ✔ Your code (markup) is much "lighter" (less verbose and complex), making it easier to read and maintain.

Truth be told, Netscape browsers have provided more support for CSS properties like positioning and float than IE. It's only now that IE is supporting these properties that designing without tables has at last become practical (given that most people use IE for their browser). CSS has been ready to make this change from tables to table-free positioning; IE has not.

Positioning where you will

Tables are cumbersome and include loads of elements within elements, so avoid resorting to them when possible. When you don't force tables to do jobs for which other techniques are better suited, pages load faster. Pages have less code to send, less code for browsers to figure out, and the code is more easily understood and modified by the designer and programmer.

Multicolumn layouts are perhaps the most common style of organization for Web pages, just as you find columns of text in newspapers and magazines. The columns serve to organize the contents horizontally, just as elements such as paragraphs, rules, and headlines help the reader see how the information is organized vertically. The result, in most pages laid out in this kind of grid, is essentially a table, a set of "cells" containing paragraphs or groups of paragraphs. And for years now, nested tables were the only viable solution to creating many kinds of Web pages.

CSS specializes in describing how things should look, including how they should be positioned. The `top`, `left`, and `position` properties allow you to create styles describing the various zones on your page.

Placing content willy-nilly

Sometimes you want to break out of the more formal columnar, grid-like layout so common in Web pages. You want to position a few paragraphs here and there, willy-nilly — wherever your design sense tells you they look good. In this section, I show you that approach first, before doing a more text-heavy, column-based layout.

The trick when using CSS positioning is to create classes or IDs that specify where you want your zones located. (You can throw in formatting, coloring, and other qualities, as well, if you wish.)

Using the `absolute` value with the positioning element causes the element to be positioned without reference to the normal flow in the page. The element has no influence on, and is not influenced by, other elements except for its containing block. In the examples below, the containing block is the body. Any space that the absolutely positioned element might have used up in the normal flow is ignored during the page layout. The element thus has no effect on other elements at all.

Notice in the following code that I use absolute positioning, which causes each division to be placed independently of all the other divisions. They don't bump into each other like train cars. Also, because percentages are used to describe position (the `top`, `left`, and `width` properties), when the user resizes the browser, the elements move around to maintain their relationship to the body, as the body element takes on different shapes.

In the following code, I've eliminated some of the actual paragraph text to avoid wasting space:

```
<html>
<head>

<style>

.topheadline {
padding: 10px;
font-size: xx-large;
font-family: arial black;
 left: 12%;
 top: 0%;
 width: 75%;
 position: absolute;}


.biggestcolumn {

 top: 25%;
padding: 10px;
 font-size: small;
 left: 50%;
 width: 40%;
 text-align: justify;
 background: lightgrey;
position: absolute;}


 .mediumcolumn {
padding: 10px;
```

```
top:40%;
 left: 5%;
 width: 35%;
 background: lightsalmon;
 position: absolute;}


.smallcolumn {
padding: 10px;
 left: 45%;
 width: 25%;
 top: 65%;
 background: lightsalmon;
 position: absolute;}

</style>
</head>

<body>

<div class="topheadline">
THIS IS THE MAIN HEADLINE
</div>

<div class="biggestcolumn">
The biggest column: Here you are specifying that you want the
         first paragraph displayed in a special green
         version of the highlight class, but ...
</div>

<div class="mediumcolumn">
The medium column: Here you are specifying that you want the
         first paragraph displayed in a special green
         version of the highlight class, but ...
</div>


<div class="smallcolumn">
The small column: Here you are specifying that you want the
         first paragraph displayed in a special green
         version of the highlight class, but ...
</div>

</body>
</html>
```

As you can see, a set of classes is defined in the style at the top of the code. Each class describes a position on the body of the page. In the body section of the code are a set of divisions, each referencing one of the classes. The result is shown in Figure 12-8:

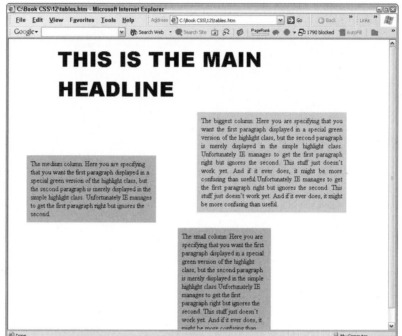

Figure 12-8:
This design
avoids the
traditional
grid layout.
Sometimes
designs
like this
are called
free-form.

Figure 12-8 does have its problems, though. It violates some of the design principles you explored in Chapter 8. For example, it isn't as balanced as it could be, tending to be weightier toward the top left, and it has no focal point. Nothing is in the hot spots to attract the eye. What if we added a background graphic?

```
<style>

body {
  background-image: url(backfish.jpg);
  background-repeat: no-repeat; }
```

This background contains a floating ball focal point, and also helps unify the rest of the page with the light, abstract, circular design. To further tie things together, adjust two of the divisions (text blocks) to remove their background and drop the text into the background. These text blocks are also repositioned:

```
.biggestcolumn {

 top: 25%;
padding: 10px;
 font-size: medium;
 left: 50%;
 width: 40%;
 text-align: justify;
```

```
position: absolute;}

.smallcolumn {
padding: 10px;
 left: 25%;
 width: 25%;
 top: 70%;

 position: absolute;}

</style>
```

Finally, lower the main headline on the page:

```
.topheadline {
padding: 10px;
font-size: xx-large;
font-family: arial black;
 left: 12%;
 top: 10%;
 width: 75%;
 position: absolute;}
```

Figure 12-9 shows the results of these improvements.

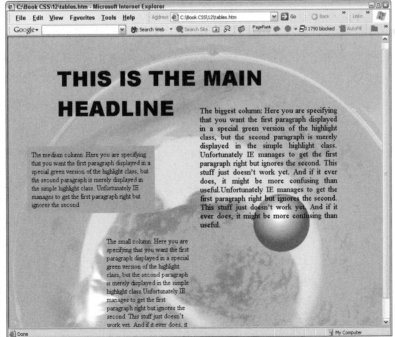

Figure 12-9:
You can
improve
the design
by adding
some
graphic
elements
and fiddling
with the
positions
of the
blocks
of text.

Loving your layout a little too much

If you have a design that you can't stand to see move around a bit, use specific measurement units (along with the absolute position value) to fix the size and position of your text blocks and other elements.

The designs discussed earlier, and illustrated in Figures 12-8 and 12-9, are somewhat plastic, fluid, and unfixed. If the user lengthens the browser, for example, that changes the meaning of top: 10%. A <div> specified at that position must, therefore, move down the stretched browser to maintain its ten percent distance from the top. In other words, ten percent isn't the same distance if the user resizes his browser windows.

However, you can refuse to allow your precious, hard-won positioning to be disturbed. You can pin your <div> elements to their positions (relative to each other), so even if the outer frame (the browser window) is resized, the *internal design* — the visual relationships between the graphic elements on the page — remains fixed. The way to do this is to replace all the percentage values with specific units of measurement such as inches or pixels.

Here's how fixed-unit code looks. This code creates the results shown in Figure 12-10:

```
<html>
<head>

<style>

body {
  background-image: url(background.jpg);
  background-repeat: no-repeat; }

.topheadline {

font: bold 48px/.99 "Arial Black"; letter-spacing: -.06em;
padding: 10px;

left: 100px;
  top: 85px;
  width: 475px;

  position: absolute;}


.biggestcolumn {


  padding: 10px;
  font-size: medium;

left: 200px;
```

```
top: 200px;
width: 370px;

text-align: justify;

position: absolute;}


 .mediumcolumn {
padding: 10px;
 font-size: medium;
 top:420px;
 left: 80px;
 width: 350px;
 position: absolute;}


.smallcolumn {
padding: 10px;
 left: 590px;
 width: 200px;
 top: 430px;
 position: absolute;}

</style>
</head>
```

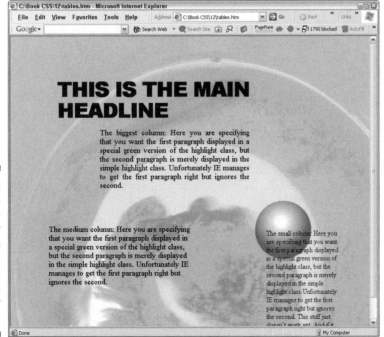

Figure 12-10:
Used fixed units if you want your design to remain unaffected by adjusted browser shapes.

Notice that the headline in Figure 12-10 is tightened up, by removing space between both the letters themselves, as well as between the lines. These useful techniques contribute to an attractive Web page and are discussed in detail in Chapter 7:

```
font: bold 48px/.99 "Arial Black"; letter-spacing: -.06em;
```

Figure 12-11 shows the same page as Figure 12-10, but the browser has been resized. Notice that the internal design — the size and position of the elements — has remained stable and fixed.

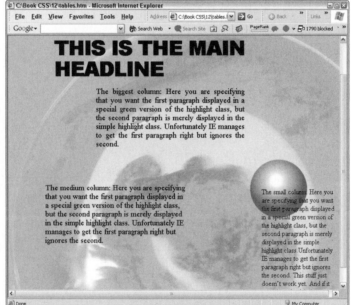

Figure 12-11: No matter what the aspect ratio of the containing browser, these various text blocks remain in position.

Creating Columns that Resize with the Browser

Of course, the free-form designs demonstrated in the previous examples aren't appropriate for every Web site. In fact, most businesses continue to prefer the more staid, often more text-intensive, classic grid layout that tables have been supporting for so long in Web pages.

But you can overturn the tables; just throw them out. Use techniques similar to those described for the free-form layout, but when you define your styles, float the blocks (they're really *columns* now that they're horizontally lined up next to each other). In this next example, you use two columns of text that resize if the browser is widened or narrowed. (For additional details on using `float`, see Chapter 10.)

Figure 12-12 and Figure 12-13 illustrate how to use classic columns that resize in a graceful way when the browser is resized:

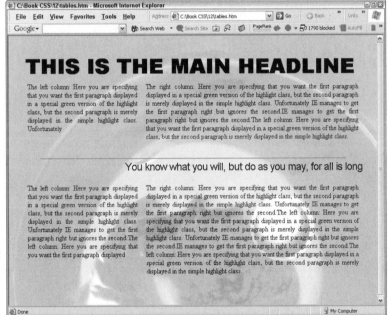

Figure 12-12:
This two-column design is created without resorting to tables. It's pure CSS.

Here's the code that produced Figures 12-12 and 12-13, with some of the body text removed to avoid wasting space:

```
<html>
<head>

<style>

body {
  background-image: url(background.jpg);
  background-repeat: no-repeat;
  padding: 24px;
```

```
    }
.topheadline {
font: bold 48px/.99 "Arial Black"; letter-spacing: -.06em;
padding: 5px; }


.leftcolumn {
float: left;
width: 35%;
padding: 10px;
text-align: justify;}

.rightcolumn {
float: left;
width: 65%;
padding: 10px;
margin-bottom: 23px;
text-align: justify;}

.midhead {
 clear: both;
 font: 24px/.99 "Arial"; letter-spacing: -.06em;
 text-align: right;
 padding-bottom: 15px;

}

hr {
 clear: both;
 height: 2px;
 width: 90%;
 background-color: mediumspringgreen;
}

</style>
</head>

<body>


<div class="topheadline">
THIS IS THE MAIN HEADLINE
</div>

<div class="leftcolumn">
The left column: Here you are specifying that you want the
          first paragraph displayed in a special green
          version of the highlight class, but the second
</div>


<div class="rightcolumn">
```

```
The right column: Here you are specifying that you want the
        first paragraph displayed in a special green
        version of the highlight class, but the second
</div>

<hr>

<div class="midhead">
You know what you will, but do as you may, for all is long
</div>

<div class="leftcolumn">
The left column: Here you are specifying that you want the
        first paragraph displayed in a special green
        version of the highlight class, but the second
</div>


<div class="rightcolumn">
The right column: Here you are specifying that you want the
        first paragraph displayed in a special green
        version of the highlight class, but the second

</div>

</body>
</html>
```

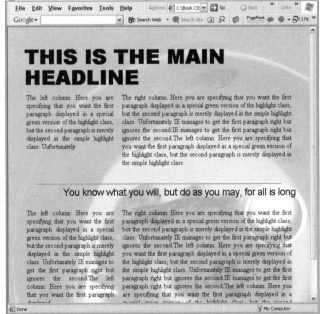

Figure 12-13: Here you see how the columns have gracefully readjusted after the user resized the browser, making the browser narrower.

Because this design uses two columns, you specify a `float: left`, but also ensure that the two columns (plus any padding, borders, or margins) don't add up to more than 100 percent. In this example, the `leftcolumn` class is specified at 35 percent the width of the body, and the `rightcolumn` class at 65 percent. This way, no matter how the user might resize the browser (making it wider or narrower), the widths retain their relative sizes, as Figure 12-13 illustrates. The left column is about half the size of the right column.

If you want three or more columns, just create additional classes for `column-three` and `columnfour` (or whatever you want to call them). And give them percent widths so that all of the columns (their boxes) added together don't exceed a width of 100 percent.

In the above code, the `clear` property is used for the horizontal rule and the middle headline. Recall that using `clear` forces the element to move below a floating element (such as our columns). For more on the `clear` property, see Chapter 10.

In this example, the right column aligns to the left side of the browser in Firefox and Netscape (probably to maintain the width of 35 percent in the left column). If you specify that the right column should float right, the problem is eliminated in those browsers. Also note that the order in which elements appear in the markup affects how they are rendered (especially when using `float`). For example, placing the right column markup above the left column flip-flops their display. Changing the right column to float right makes it float right regardless of whether it appears before or after the left column markup.

Building Fixed Columns

Freezing your column widths (rather than allowing them to resize as illustrated in Figures 12-12 and 12-13) is easy to do. Use a `position: absolute` property-value and specify the position and size of your columns (their `left`, `top`, and `width` properties) with fixed units of measurement such as pixels. Here's how such a column style looks:

```
.topheadline {
position: absolute;
top: 25px;
font: bold 48px/.99 "Arial Black"; letter-spacing: -.06em;
padding: 5px; }

.leftcolumn {
 position: absolute;
 top: 135px;
 left:25px;
 width:200px;
 text-align: justify;}
```

```
.rightcolumn {
position: absolute;
top: 135px;
left:260px;
width:200px;
text-align: justify;}

.thirdcolumn {
position: absolute;
top: 135px;
left:495px;
width:200px;
text-align: justify;}
```

When using absolute positions, you're responsible for ensuring that the `left` properties of your columns work as they should. The width of the leftmost column, for example, helps you determine what the `left` property of the next column should be. In this code, the leftmost column is 200 pixels wide (with 25 pixels added to that for its `left` position). You position the `rightcolumn` class further over by giving it a value of 260 pixels for *its* `left` position. The third column starts at 495 pixels.

Because these are absolute positions, any padding built into the body is ignored.

If you want to add additional columns *below* these blocks of text (see the four blocks of text in Figure 12-13), you have to create additional classes for them. The three existing column classes in this code — `leftcolumn`, `rightcolumn`, and `thirdcolumn` — have a fixed, specific `top` property (130 pixels for all three of the columns). Obviously, columns lower on the page require a greater `top` property value.

When you create fixed columns like these, no matter how the user resizes the browser window, the text columns remain in the same position (relative to the top left of the window) and also do not change their size or shape.

Figures 12-14 and 12-15 show how these fixed columns do not yield their positions, or change their shapes, when the browser is resized.

The body of your page includes the various divisions (the columns in this case); their positions are governed by the classes you created in the style section:

```
<body>

<div class="topheadline">
WHEN SHIPS HEAD TO SEA
</div>

<div class="leftcolumn">
```

```
The right column: Here you are specifying that you want the
         first paragraph displayed in a special green
         version of the highlight class, but the second
</div>


<div class="rightcolumn">
The right column: Here you are specifying that you want the
         first paragraph displayed in a special green
         version of the highlight class, but the second
</div>


<div class="thirdcolumn">
The right column: Here you are specifying that you want the
         first paragraph displayed in a special green
         version of the highlight class, but the second
</div>

</body>
```

Figure 12-14:
Here's a
fixed-
column
layout with
three
columns.

TIP

If you need to build a form (such as a series of text boxes for the user to fill in to register with your site, or order some goods), you might be tempted to revert to tables. But, like tables, forms can easily be built using CSS alone. Create CSS rules for the row, label, label value, left side of the form and right side of the form. Now build a row in the HTML code of your page, insert the left content, right content, and then use a spacer to clear the floats. Next build another row. You can even get fancy and include headers and footers for forms, too. Building forms with CSS can be painful at first, until you learn the techniques, but it has the usual benefits of resulting in less markup code and more control over the final result.

Figure 12-15: When the browser is resized, the columns remain frozen in place.

Nesting boxes within a page box

Consider these suggestions to help you more quickly reposition an entire Web page at once.

The downside about absolute positioning is that it makes moving everything on the page at once difficult. Each placeholder must be moved individually. Instead, you may prefer to create an outermost box that you name "page" and use it to relatively position all your elements within.

Here's why: What if you complete a site using CSS layout and absolute positioning, but the boss later tells you that all corporate Web pages must now be 798 pixels in width, and centered in the browser with a white border around them. What the boss says, goes, right? You've got a pretty big revision to do if all your elements are positioned absolutely.

To solve this problem, create a page box as the outermost box, and then relatively position everything within that outer box. This way, you can move the whole "page" down, over, centered, or wherever you want without having to manipulate the positions of each element inside. Consider, for example, using an absolutely positioned outer box with areas for a header, footer, sidebars, and so on. (Note that those inner elements *are* relatively positioned.)

Another useful technique is to first draw a template on paper for your Web page. This is very helpful: Relative nesting of boxes gets confusing if you try to do it ad hoc on the computer. After you've drawn the overall design, write the CSS code to make that design come to life on the screen. Add content to the page and relatively position it within the template. You can easily rearrange your pages by swapping headers, footers, sidebars, or main content areas just by changing the CSS for those areas.

Chapter 13

Creating Dramatic Visual Effects

• •

In This Chapter

▶ Adding static filters

▶ Increasing excitement with dynamic transitions

▶ Transitioning between pages or sites

• •

A well-designed Web page is a wonder to behold, but it's not a joy forever. Right now, your Web pages primarily compete with magazines and other static media. This won't always be the case, however. Eventually, Web pages must go up against the excitement offered by television and other active, dynamic, animated media. In fact, the Web may well one day blend with digital TV into a single medium. After all, a pixel is a pixel, and all that separates the Internet from television is some hardware restrictions, some old habits that are a little hard to break, and, above all, the fact that television production and Web design are — for the time being anyway — two different jobs.

Given current Internet bandwidth restrictions affecting more than half of the visitors to your site, you can expect that these 56K modem-connected folks won't sit still and wait for your page to download heavily animated moving picture shows. (*Bandwidth* refers to the amount of info that can stream through.) However, at least 40 percent of urban home users in the United States now have high-speed Internet. And that trend shows no sign of slowing down. Experts estimate broadband penetration may reach 70 percent relatively soon.

For one thing, nearly 80 percent of American workers are exposed to broadband Internet, usually at their workplace. And after you've tried broadband, you don't want to go home to a pokey 56K modem.

Now that you're convinced that Internet bandwidth will make animated Web pages increasingly popular, why not get your feet wet by exploring some of the cooler tricks currently available? In this chapter, you explore transitions — ways to segue your users (or should we call them *viewers*?) from one image to the next, or between Web pages. You also get a little taste of adding the power of scripting to CSS — writing some simple programs that react to the user clicking a button on your page.

Impressing with Static Filters

I discussed filters briefly in Chapter 1. Use filters if you can assume that people not using Internet Explorer won't suffer from not seeing them. Filters are a Microsoft-only technology, and though you can use them with CSS styles, CSS itself hasn't yet progressed to embrace animation (unless you consider hyperlinks that change color when clicked a form of animation). However, many filters are merely used to add some nice visual effects and those who browse without IE only miss some beauty (not much information) by not seeing them.

Here's an example of a static filter. (A *static* filter doesn't change over time; we'll get to dynamic filters, or *transition* filters, in the section called "Dazzling with Transition Filters.") Try this code to see a filter that adds drop shadows to text, ⟨div⟩ blocks, and so on:

```
<html>
<head>

<style>

p {height: 350px; width: 450px; font-size: 44pt;

filter: progid:DXImageTransform.Microsoft.Shadow
(color='gray', direction=120, strength=6)

}

</style>
</head>

<body>

<p>
Get a Drop Shadow Effect
</p>

</body>
</html>
```

Adjust the direction value to anything from 0-360 to rotate the light source around the object casting the shadow. Because I believe that most natural shadows fall on the lower right of objects, I like to use 120 as the value. Microsoft agrees with me. (Or is it the other way around?) Take a look at the shadowing on Windows elements such as buttons, icons, and window frames:

The shadowing on these elements indicates a light source coming from the upper left of an object. Adjust the `strength` value to lengthen the shadow. Figure 13-1 was generated from the preceding code:

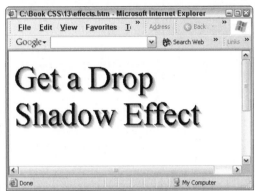

Figure 13-1: Adding shadows is one of 16 static filters you can add to your page elements.

In my view, you're generally better off creating an image in a graphics application like Photoshop if you want to add drop shadows and most other "filter" effects. In other words, just shadow some text in the graphics application, and then save the result to a .jpg file. (I think .jpg offers better quality than the .gif format sometimes used in Web pages.) Then simply import the finished, polished result into your Web page using the `<img>` tag. Photoshop and similar applications specialize in such effects, and the results are generally more subtle and more fine than you can get by trying to trick things up via CSS. Browsers aren't designed to achieve the most sophisticated graphics effects, and browsers generally cannot compete with the delicacy and variety of the tools in Photoshop, Picture Publisher, and other graphics applications. CSS has many uses, but I think you're asking too much of it when you try to use it for special graphic effects.

For people with slow modems (who turn graphics off) or those who have visual or other impairments, always including the `alt` tag with each image is good practice. That way, if someone can't see your graphics, or is *listening* to the text of the page being read out loud, they'll still get the necessary information. Here's an example of how to use `alt`:

```
<img src="seashore.jpg" alt="This is a pleasant, if cliched,
          photo of a typical, deserted Aussie beach.">
```

I don't use `alt` in this book for clarity; I avoid including code that distracts from the main point being made in each example. However, you should include `alt` in your Web pages.

Here's the list of the 16 static filters you can experiment with: alpha, basicimage, blur, chroma, compositor, dropshadow, emboss, engrave, glow, ICMfilter, light, maskfilter, matrix, motionblur, shadow, and wave. These static filters — and more dynamic ones — are Microsoft extensions to the "official" CSS specifications. You can find a complete reference to the filters and their arguments (or *values* as CSS prefers to call them, or *attributes* as HTML prefers) at this address, Microsoft's "Visual Filters and Transitions Reference":

```
http://msdn.microsoft.com/library/default.asp?url=/workshop/
        author/filter/filters.asp
```

In the example shown in Figure 13-1, using gray with the shadow filter produces a respectable drop shadow, but experiment with some of the other filters if you wish. The dropshadow filter is separate from the shadow filter, for example. But whereas the shadow filter provides a convincing gradient (a shift from dark to light), the dropshadow filter offers only a solid shadow. Paradoxically, the dropshadow filter doesn't produce as good a drop shadow as does the shadow filter. So, if you do decide to use static filters despite my advice in the preceding tip — well, a curse upon you! Whoops . . . I momentarily lost it. I meant to say that you'll just have to try the various effects, and their associated values, to see what looks good to you.

Change the filter to the dropshadow type and see the results in Figure 13-2:

```
filter:progid:DXImageTransform.Microsoft.dropshadow(OffX=5,
        OffY=5, Color='gray', Positive='true')"
```

Figure 13-2:
This drop shadow effect doesn't include a gradient, as does Figure 13-1. Experiment until you get the effect you like.

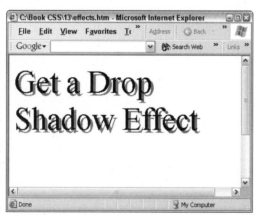

Here's one more example of a static filter. This one's called motionblur, and the effect can be similar to drop shadows, as you can see in Figure 13-3:

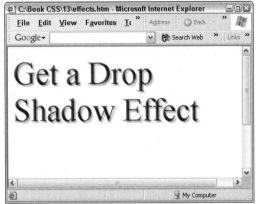

Figure 13-3:
The `motion-blur` filter can provide a gradient shadow effect, if used cautiously.

Here's the code that produced Figure 13-3:

```
<style>

p {height: 350px; width: 450px; font-size: 44pt;

filter:progid:DXImageTransform.Microsoft.MotionBlur(Strength=
        5,Direction=120);}
```

The subtle effect in Figure 13-3 is achieved through restraint. I kept the `strength` at a low value of 5. To see what happens if you use this filter as intended, look at Figure 13-4:

Figure 13-4:
Changing the direction and increasing the strength of the `motion-blur` filter creates this special effect.

The result shown in Figure 13-4 is achieved with this code (note I increased the `strength` to a value of 45):

```
filter:progid:DXImageTransform.Microsoft.MotionBlur(Strength=
       45,Direction=270);}
```

In Chapter 16, you experiment in depth with *dynamic* code, which allows you to change CSS styles while the user is viewing your Web page. For example, if the user moves the mouse pointer over, say, some small text, its `font-size` CSS style can be modified and can then resize from 10 pixels to 25 pixels, right before their startled eyes. Chapter 16 also covers the related concept of script programming in depth.

Dazzling with Transition Filters

I might get a little ahead of myself here, introducing a bit of *scripting* (programming for Web browsers), but what the heck? Chapter 16 goes deeper into this interesting topic. However, just for fun, I want to show you how to trigger some interesting transition filters (also known as dynamic filters) using script.

When you write script, you have to decide between the two great families of programming languages: Basic and C. My preference is Basic, but many people (mostly professional programmers) prefer the C-like scripting language JavaScript. For this first example, I'll provide a script for both languages if you're interested in comparing them. Here's the Basic version:

```
<html>
<head>

<SCRIPT LANGUAGE=vbscript>

dim toggle

function fader

    mydiv.filters(0).Apply

    if toggle = 1 Then

        toggle = 0
        mydiv.style.backgroundColor="indigo"

    else
        toggle = 1
        mydiv.style.backgroundColor="lime"

    end if

    mydiv.filters(0).Play

End Function
```

```
</SCRIPT>


</head>

<body>



<DIV ID="mydiv" STYLE=" background-color: indigo;
        height:400px; width:500px;

        filter:progid:DXImageTransform.Microsoft.Fade
        (duration=3);">

</DIV>

<br>
<button onclick="fader()">Click Me!</button>

</body>
</html>
```

For those who prefer C and Java, here's the JavaScript version of the same function:

```
<SCRIPT>

var toggle = 0;

function fader() {

    mydiv.filters[0].Apply();

    if (toggle) {
        toggle = 0;
        mydiv.style.backgroundColor="indigo";}
    else {
        toggle = 1;
        mydiv.style.backgroundColor="lime";}
    mydiv.filters[0].Play();
}

</SCRIPT>
```

Microsoft has long promoted VBScript, but someone decided to make JavaScript the default scripting language for Internet Explorer. Therefore, you need not specify JavaScript in your code, as in `<SCRIPT Language=Java Script>`. You can just use `<SCRIPT>`.

As you can see, the differences between these two scripts aren't massive. The primary difference, actually, is that the C languages insert lots of unnecessary semicolons and braces all over the place. But in other programming, the C languages use reverse syntax (the opposite of the way it would be expressed in ordinary English) and other complications.

Try executing this code and you'll see a large square fade from purple to green when you click the button. Click it again and the fade reverses back to purple.

This cool effect is brought to you courtesy of the fade filter. When the button is clicked, the browser responds by doing whatever is assigned to the onclick attribute. In this case, it's a function (a behavior described in programming code, script in this case) named fader. (You can name your functions whatever you want.) So, the browser carries out whatever instructions are in the fader function. Here's the code that triggers the fader function:

```
<button onclick="fader()">Click Me!</button>
```

That function begins by setting up a variable named toggle that, like a light switch, is toggled between two states. As with functions, you can name variables whatever you want to: You could call it *MarthaWashington* if you wanted. But programmers like to name variables in a way that reminds them of what the variable is supposed to do, so I called it toggle.

Inside the function, you first *apply* (set up) the filter in the mydiv element:

```
mydiv.filters(0).Apply
```

Mydiv, too, is just another name I made up. It's just the ID for the <div> tag. The script knows which div to manipulate thanks to this ID name.

Don't worry about why you use the (0). It's a quirk of computer languages that makes no sense — they start counting up from zero rather than one. Just use the code and don't bother your pretty head about it. Just *apply* this filter.

Next is a common programming structure, the if . . . then. Actually, it's a pretty common situation in life, too. It means, *if* the toggle variable holds a 1, *then* change the color to purple indigo (and at the same time, put a zero into the toggle variable). That way, the next time the user clicks this button, something *else* happens. Namely, the color changes to lime and a 1 is assigned to the toggle variable:

```
if toggle = 1 Then

    toggle = 0
    mydiv.style.backgroundColor="indigo"
```

```
else
    toggle = 1
    mydiv.style.backgroundColor="lime"

end if
```

Finally, after the background color has been changed, the `play` method is triggered and the transition fades as you requested:

```
mydiv.filters(0).Play
```

`Play` is a function that's built into the IE browser, so you don't have to write this function. You can just name it. Same with the `apply` function.

For tricks on debugging script (fixing things that don't work right because you didn't do the programming correctly), see Chapter 17.

If you want to use this script with a different kind of transition, just make a simple change to the name of the filter and perhaps tweak the attributes. To see the `blinds` transition (it looks like Venetian blinds), all you have to change is the name of the filter in the code, like this:

```
filter:progid:DXImageTransform.Microsoft.Blinds(duration=3)
```

Make this change, and then load the file into Internet Explorer and click the button. You see the result shown in Figure 13-5:

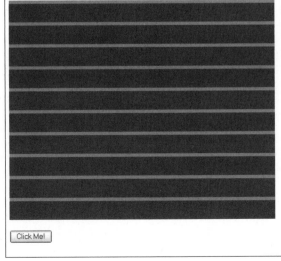

Figure 13-5:
The
`blinds`
transition
effect
looks as if
someone is
opening
Venetian
blinds.

You can play around with additional parameters for transitions as well. Find them described and listed at

```
http://msdn.microsoft.com/library/default.asp?url=/workshop/
            author/filter/filters.asp
```

For example, the blinds transition has arguments (or *attributes*) in addition to the duration argument used in the previous example. You can also specify the direction in which the blinds open and close, as well as the number of bands. If you want vertical blinds, try this:

```
filter:progid:DXImageTransform.Microsoft.Blinds(duration=3,
            direction = 'right')
```

And if you want more bands (*blinds* . . .why can't they call things what they are?), specify the number. The default is ten bands (as you can see in Figure 13-5), but go wild and ask for 20. You get the transition effect shown in Figure 13-6:

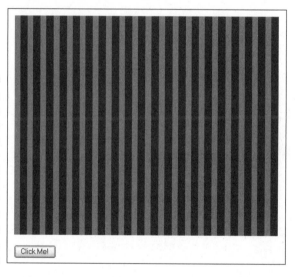

Figure 13-6: You can specify both the direction — vertical here — and the number of blinds for this transition.

```
filter:progid:DXImageTransform.Microsoft.Blinds(duration=3,
            direction = 'right', bands=20)
```

A famous transition called the wipe consists of a single large line moving across the screen, replacing, for example, one image with another as if it were sliding into view. You can do various kinds of wipes by setting the blinds transition's values to (direction='up', bands=1). Vary the direction property to vary the wipe direction.

Fading Between Images

Another really useful, attractive effect is to fade or wipe or otherwise transition between two images. You've doubtless seen this technique. It's used in all browsers because it can be applied via JavaScript. Some of the best-designed Web sites use delicate fades — often triggered when you first view the page as a kind of introduction, with one image gently dissolving into another.

If you want to see some good examples of JavaScript code for "rollovers," fades, and other transitions, visit this site:

```
http://brothercake.com/site/resources/scripts/transitions/
```

To try this next example (IE-only), ensure that you have two .jpg files in the same folder on your hard drive where you save the .htm file. These files must be named first.jpg and second.jpg. You must also include a graphics file named texture.jpg that can fill the background with some kind of light texture.

```
<html>
<head>

<SCRIPT LANGUAGE=VBScript>

function fadethem()

    myimage.filters.item(0).Apply()
    myimage.src="second.jpg"
    myimage.filters.item(0).Play()

end function

</SCRIPT>

<style>
H1 {font-size: 42px;padding-left: 3%;}
BODY {background-image: url(texture.jpg);}
</style>


</HEAD>

<BODY>

<br>
<H1> Join us! We Have all Styles of Houses</h1>

<IMG ID=myimage width=60% height=70%
```

```
src="first.jpg"
           style="filter:progid:DXImageTransform.Microsoft.
           fade(Duration=2);
border= 14px solid peru inset; position=relative; left=20%;">

<br><br>

<INPUT type=button style="position=relative;left=83%;font-
           weight: lighter;

font-size: 20px; width: 120px; font-family: 'times new
           roman'; height: 44px"
value="See More" onClick="fadethem()">

<IMG src="first.jpg" style="width:1;
           height:1;visibility:hidden">
<IMG src="second.jpg" style="width:1; height:1;
           visibility:hidden">

</BODY>

</html>
```

The script in this example is simple because you merely click the button once to exchange the images — no toggling. But it's all as smooth as butter, and looks pretty impressive. Sites that use this effect stand out from the crowd. Notice that the two images are defined as having a hidden value for their visibility property, but the first image is in the code twice. The first occurrence defines the size, border, and position for both images. That occurrence also seeds the first image so that the visitor to your site sees the first image when the page loads.

Figures 13-7 through 13-9 illustrate the transition effect, where one "house" gradually changes places with the other:

If you prefer to use JavaScript in the above code, you just need to dump a bunch of extraneous punctuation into the preceding VBScript code:

```
<SCRIPT LANGUAGE=JavaScript>
function fadethem()
{
    myimage.filters.item(0).Apply();
    myimage.src="second.jpg";
    myimage.filters.item(0).Play();
}
</SCRIPT>
```

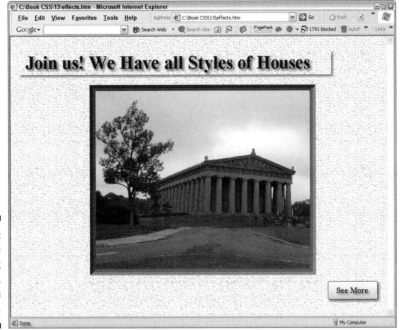

Figure 13-7:
Before
you click
the button,
you see this
building.

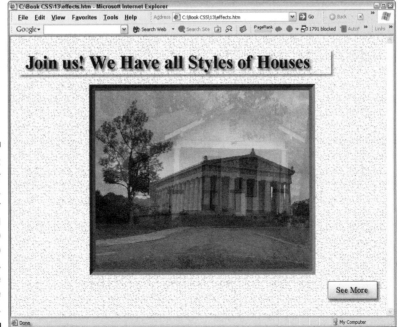

Figure 13-8:
After
you click,
the other
building
starts to
fade into
the picture,
as the
first house
fades out.

Figure 13-9:
After the
transition
is finished,
you see
only the
second
graphic.

When you write script for a browser, it's like embedding a computer program into your HTML. Clearly a Web site run by someone from the dark side — those disturbed, childish virus authors — could easily cause some damage if you visited their site. The script languages have some built-in safeguards. For example, they have no commands to access the hard drive. However, canny evildoers know ways around this, so some people configure their browsers to refuse scripts. (To do this in Internet Explorer, choose Tools⇨ Internet Options⇨Security⇨Custom Level and select the Disable or Prompt (Ask First) buttons under Scripting.) Also, if you've installed the latest Microsoft security packs, you'll see a small message at the top of Internet Explorer (see Figure 13-10) when the preceding .htm file is loaded into the browser. It warns that your page contains "active content." If the user clicks the warning, the scripting on the page is then allowed to execute.

Transitions between Pages

Would you like your entire Web page to fade in (or otherwise transition) when the user first visits your site? You can do whole-page transitions by just adding a little so-called "meta" code to your HTML code.

Will they ever get their act together?

The mayhem never ends: Those in charge of defining punctuation, diction, and other elements of computer programming are never content to have just *one* way of describing something. That would be too easy and efficient. No, each new committee insists on putting its stamp on things — not all that different from children scratching their names in wet concrete: JASON WAZ HERE! These committees of "experts" from Microsoft, other companies, or academia seem to come up with some new, incompatible variant diction at every standards meeting. Nor do they allow these variants to act as synonyms (each working just fine in all contexts). No, that would be too logical. It would prevent bugs and confusion. It would be efficient. Instead, they usually require that each context have its unique usage, so that you have to learn lots of extra rules and regulations. You can imagine how much pleasure this kind of muddle gives the hearts of little bureaucrats everywhere. For example, here are four *different* ways that you can describe a graphics file in a Web page. And they cannot be substituted for one another — each variation is required in its special context.

In the `<style>` element, you specify the graphics file value by using a colon (not an equals sign) and then `url` followed by the filename in parentheses, followed by a semicolon, like this:

```
body {
  background-image: url(back-
    fish.jpg);
}
```

However, when you specify a graphics file as an attribute within an HTML element definition, it's all different. You must now use quotation marks around the filename and remove the parentheses. The attributes are not separated by semicolons, just by spaces, like this:

```
<body background-image="tex-
    ture.jpg" font-size: 24px;>
```

Yet another variation involves the `<img>` tag. You specify *its* file using the attribute `src` with an equals sign and quotation marks like this:

```
<IMG src="texture.jpg">
```

Finally, if you use the shorthand background property, you separate the values with spaces, use a colon after the property, use `url`, quotation marks, and parentheses, like this:

```
h2 {background: url("coin.jpg")
    no-repeat left top;
```

You must memorize these variations. Face the fact that you're bound to get them confused now and then and have to waste your time looking up the correct punctuation and usage. These committees are often made up of tedious people with no idea of the confusion and chaos that they cause. Think of the cumulative effect of this sloppy and never-ending manipulation of computer languages: Huge amounts of collective programming effort is being wasted trying to figure out why code doesn't work, and why programmers can't make their intentions clear to the computer. If you've ever done any programming, you know the effect: The first time you write a line of code, it often simply does not work. Even if you've written CSS or other kinds of computer code for years, you'll still find that your first stab at a line of code often fails. Don't blame yourself. Blame those whose egos are injected into the process of creating these languages. No wonder we call their results *code.*

Figure 13-10:
Some users
see this
warning
when a
Web page
employing
scripts
loads,
telling them
of potential
danger.

Put this code within the `<head>` element, the same place you normally put scripts and, sometimes, CSS styles. Try this simple Web page to see some really cool transitions:

```
<html>
<head>

<meta http-equiv="page-enter"
content="progid:dximagetransform.microsoft.wheel(duration=4)"
       />

<meta http-equiv="page-exit"
content="progid:dximagetransform.microsoft.stretch(duration=3
       ,stretchstyle='spin')"

  />

</head>
<body>

<h1> Visit Us Often! We Have Lots of Great Transitions</h1>

</body>

</html>
```

Now save this file as effects.htm to your hard drive. Double-click on it in Windows Explorer and it loads the page into Internet Explorer. If you see a security warning, click the warning and permit this page to load. Then try pressing F5 to reload the page. Watch the cool "wheel" effect when the `page-enter` condition (event, as it's called) happens. Now to see the `page-exit` transition, the `stretch` effect, click one of your links or the home page icon to go to a different Web site. Then press Backspace to return to this page once again.

Try various other transitions you'll find listed here:

```
http://msdn.microsoft.com/library/default.asp?url=/workshop/a
            uthor/filter/filters.asp
```

If I were you, I'd avoid using the `page-exit` transitions unless you have a multipage Web site and you want to use them between your own pages. (No matter what, make them of short duration.) Transitions do take a bit of time and some people might be annoyed with you for making them watch your page grudgingly yield to the site they're trying to visit next. You can also replace the `page-enter` and `page-exit` events with `site-enter` and `site-exit` events if you wish.

Microsoft's FrontPage Web design application makes it easy to configure the transitions discussed in this chapter (and plenty of other transitions as well). In FrontPage, choose Format⇨Page Transitions.

Part IV
Advanced CSS Techniques

The 5th Wave   By Rich Tennant

"Look into my Web site, Ms. Carruthers. Look deep into its rotating, nicely animated spiral, spinning, spinning, pulling you in, deeper... deeper..."

In this part . . .

This Part is all about advanced CSS techniques — stuff even the CSS gurus sometimes don't know. You wrestle the concept of CSS inheritance until you have pinned it to the ground and can provide selector rules for almost any conceivable location in the tree structure. You experiment with future CSS3 features, including several that are testable now in the Mozilla Firefox browser. You discover ways to do things that would be impossible with CSS alone by adding JavaScript or VBScript to your CSS bag of tricks. Among other techniques, you find out how to actually change your CSS rules, or even add new rules, dynamically while a user is viewing your page in a browser. (You don't even have to be there at the time.) Finally, you delve into the best ways to check your CSS and HTML for errors before you send your baby out into the World (Wide Web, that is).

Chapter 14

Specializing in Selection

*W*hen styles cascade, their effects bump down to lower levels like snow falling down a tree. Unless you specify otherwise, a style cascades down through your document and is applied wherever its targets (the selectors) are located. It's also applied to any descendant elements — elements embedded within the target, such as an italics element embedded within a paragraph.

Is there a way to apply styles to an element only if it's embedded within a particular element, rather than universally? In other words, can you ask for example that italics within headlines be boldface, but not when they're within paragraphs? You bet. Selectors can be designed so they're highly specific. But before looking at special kinds of selectors, it helps to first have a good grasp of how a browser moves down through the structure of a document, deciding how and when to apply CSS styles.

To get a real understanding of selecting, inheritance, specificity, and the cascade, you have to understand the concept of the tree structure that describes the design of a Web page. In this chapter, you see how a tree structure works and also how to use specialized selectors.

Getting Specific with Inheritance

I introduced the concept of specificity in Chapter 2. *Specificity* means that if two styles conflict, the style "nearest" the element wins. Say that a `<p>` style is defined in an external (.css file) style sheet as italic, but `<p>` is defined as normal, non-italic in a document's "embedded" style (inside the `<head> </head>` tags). The embedded style is located closer to the `<p>` elements in the document, so it wins: It's the style that gets applied.

Likewise, in a conflict between styles defined in an embedded style and an "inline" style (a style defined within an HTML element itself such as `<p style="font-style: italic;">`), the inline style is closer. In fact, inline styles are right there inside the element itself, so the inline style is the winner.

Grasping tree structure

Inheritance relates to the tree structure that underlies all Web pages. Imagine a simple document with only two paragraphs. Its tree structure would illustrate how the paragraphs were subordinate (were "child" elements) to the body (the "parent" element of both paragraphs). Put another way, the paragraph tags are *inside* the `<body> </body>` tags, so the `<p>` elements are the children of the parent `<body>`. The tree diagram of this document looks like Figure 14-1:

Figure 14-1:
A simple tree diagram illustrates how these two child `<p>` elements branch off from their common parent `<body>` element.

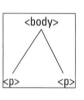

Parents versus ancestors

You'll hear the terms *parent-child* and *ancestor-descendant*. Not all ancestors are parents, although all parents are ancestors. Get it? Probably not. I didn't get it at first. Few people do.

These relationships don't mean exactly the same thing. A parent-child relationship is the closest possible: The parent is precisely one level (in the tree structure) above its child. However, inheritance can flow further than one level, and when it flows down *past* a child (to that child's children or beyond) that relationship is described as an ancestor-descendant relationship.

Still unclear? Well, put down the martini or the cat or "close friend" or whatever it is that's distracting you, and focus.

Consider the structure displayed in Figure 14-2. This tree has more branches than the tree diagram in Figure 14-1 because the first paragraph has a child of its own, the italic element:

```
<body>

<p>I cannot <i>emphasize</i> this point enough!</p>

<p>But in this paragraph, I'm calmer.</p>

</body>
```

Figure 14-2 is a tree diagram of the preceding code:

Figure 14-2:
This
diagram
contains an
ancestor
descendant
relationship
— between
the <body>
and the
<i>.

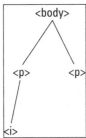

In the diagram in Figure 14-2, the body is the parent of the two paragraphs, but the body is only the *ancestor* of the italics element. The paragraphs are children of the body. The italics element is the child of its parent paragraph, and also the ancestor of the body. Class dismissed.

When a root sits above the tree

Above the <body> is the HTML, the *root* of the structure, as they call it. And the <head> and <body> elements come next in the tree. To help you visualize this, here's a complete Web page. Figure 14-3 is its diagram:

```
<html>
  <head>
    <style>
    </style>
  </head>

  <body>
```

```
<p>I cannot <i>emphasize</i> this point enough!</p>

<p>But in this paragraph, I'm calmer.</p>

</body>
</html>
```

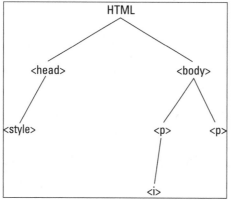

Figure 14-3:
Here's
a com-
plete tree
diagram of
the Web
page code
shown
above.

So, you gaze at Figure 14-3, with its root (html) and branches going down to the body and style and then branching further down to the paragraphs and the paragraph's children.

Wait a minute. Branches *going down from the root*?

The shaky tree

Yep. The "tree" metaphor is a little shaky, to be honest. Perhaps it's quite a bit shaky, given that the tree is upside down if its root is located at the top of the diagram. But don't be picky. Just thank goodness that *those in charge* didn't decide to lay the whole diagram sideways or use an interplanetary metaphor instead.

Back to our attempt to come to grips with this tree structure. Each element on the Web page has its place in the hierarchy, its location within the relationships of parents and children. Each element is either a parent of some other element, or its child, or both. Also, some children are *siblings* (trees so often have siblings). I get to siblings shortly. Anyway, the parent is the bigger branch nearer the root, and the child is the little branch that shoots off from the parent branch. A single parent branch can have several child branches shooting off. And everybody belongs to the PTA in this little town . . . oops, wrong metaphor.

Offspring Inheriting

One reason to try to visualize the tree structure is to grasp how inheritance works. Styles can be applied to some elements, but not to others, based on the structure of the document. Styles wouldn't even know how to work if there weren't a tree structure or something similar.

You can leverage your knowledge of the tree structure to specify various kinds of specialized targets for your styles. What if, for example, you want to underline italics in paragraphs, but never underline them in headlines? You could go through the entire document entering a `border-bottom` property or a `text-decoration: underline` for each italics element in paragraphs, but then you aren't using the efficiency of CSS.

You can create rules that specifically target only those elements with particular ancestors, or certain siblings (related children — as in the two paragraph elements in Figure 14-1, which are children of the same parent body), and other kinds of structural relationships. In this case, I want all italics that are children of paragraphs to be underlined. I don't want underlining for italics in headlines, or lists, tables, or anywhere else. Just paragraphs.

Contextual Selectors

Here's an example that accomplishes just that by using a technique called *contextual selectors*. (Recall that a *selector* is just another name for an HTML element, but it's called a *selector* when it's used to specify a CSS rule.) In the following style, the p and i are both selectors:

```
<style>
p i {border-bottom: 1px solid;}
</style>
```

Contextual selectors is a new kind of style definition not previously discussed in this book. Notice that the p and i are not separated by commas (that kind of style is called *grouping*.)

The code above does not mean that all paragraphs and all italic elements are to be underlined. It means that *only italic elements that are children or other descendants of a paragraph* are to be underlined. So an italics element within a headline is not underlined because that headline is not a descendant of a paragraph. The style only applies to italics descended from paragraphs. It's a contextual selector, not a general selector.

Those in charge of computer programming issues (who *are* they?) have issued a proclamation that henceforth everyone should describe contextual selectors as descendant selectors. But, then, they were the ones who first told us to use contextual. So, rather than wait for their next edict, I think I'll just continue using the term *contextual*.

The result of the following code with its contextual selector is shown in Figure 14-4:

```
<html>
<head>

<style>
p i {border-bottom: 1px solid;}
</style>


</head>

<body>

<h1>This <i>is not</i> underlined</h1>

<p>However, this italics element is a descendant of a
          paragraph, so <i>it does</i> get underlined.</p>


</body>
</html>
```

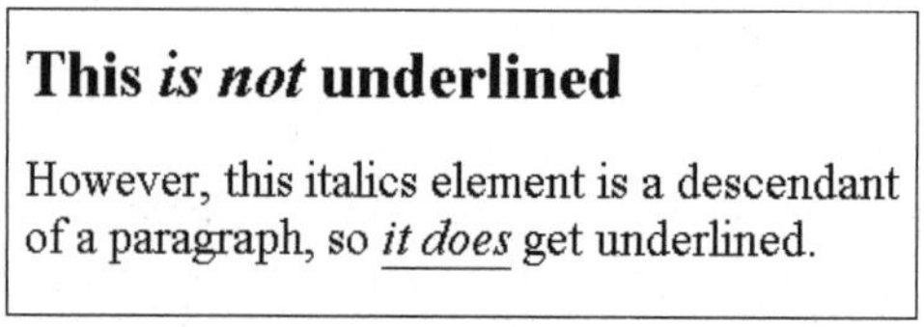

Figure 14-4:
The browser knows you want only paragraph italics underlined, not head-line italics.

> # This *is not* underlined
>
> However, this italics element is a descendant of a paragraph, so *it does* get underlined.

Selecting by context rather than grouping

As you doubtless noticed, and applauded more than once, I've rarely repeated myself in this book. However, because of the similarity between grouping and contextual selectors, I'll repeat myself here. Don't get this contextual selectors technique confused with grouping, where you simultaneously define a style for several selectors. If you want to group p and i so that all paragraphs and all italics are underlined, use commas to create a group style, like this:

```
<style>
p,i {color: blue;}
</style>
```

By adding that one little comma between the p and i selectors, you create a grouping, and both elements are given a border bottom, no matter in what context they appear, as shown in Figure 14-5:

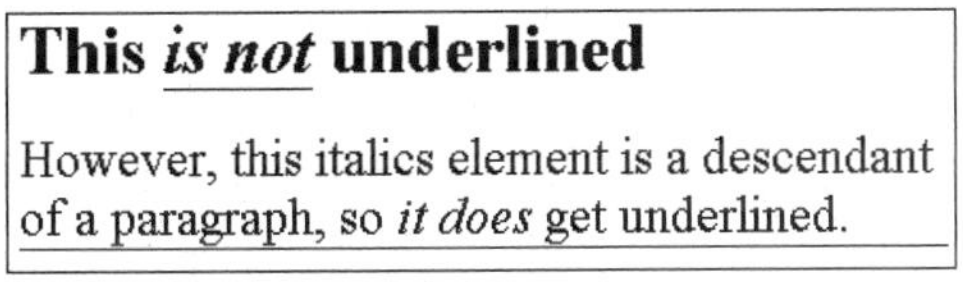

Figure 14-5: Here a grouping causes a border bottom to appear beneath all italics and paragraphs.

This *is not* underlined

However, this italics element is a descendant of a paragraph, so *it does* get underlined.

You can use contextual selectors in a variety of practical ways. For example, you might want to make all text within either a bold or strong element a light red to draw attention to it. That's fine. You can do it with a grouping, like this:

```
b, strong {color: coral;}
```

However, what if you want to specify an additional rule that states that if something needs to be emphasized (with the strong selector) *within* some boldface (b) text (which is coral), the strong text must turn black? This way the viewer can actually see the strong emphasis. Unless you create this style, both the b and strong are indistinguishable — they'll both be coral.

To do this, you create a contextual selector that states that any strong that's a child of (contained within) a b element must be colored black:

```
b strong {color: black;}
```

Here's the complete code that produces the desired result shown in Figure 14-6:

```html
<html>
<head>

<style>

b, strong {color: coral;}

b strong {color: black;}

body {font-size: 24 px;}
</style>


</head>

<body>

<P>
<b>This paragraph is entirely bold, so we <strong>simply had
            to find</strong> a way

to emphasize text within the boldness.</b>


<P>
Here's a paragraph with something <b> just plain bold.</b>

<P>
Here's a paragraph with something <strong> just plain
            strong.</strong>

</body>
</html>
```

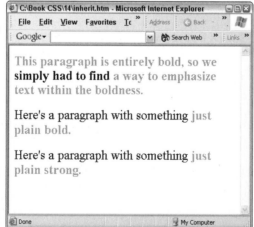

Figure 14-6:
Using a contextual selector, you can emphasize some text within a sentence that itself is already bold.

Descending deeper

Can you go deeper into descendants by adding yet another condition to the previous style? Sure. Say that you sometimes want to add a blue background to a few words inside `strong` text within a bold sentence. You can specify that any `<span>` within a `<strong>` (that itself is within a `<b>`) must have a blue background. This is a three-level contextual selector. It says, "Add a blue background if a `span` is the child of a `strong` and the descendant of a `b`." Here's this style, and the result is shown in Figure 14-7:

```
b strong span {background-color:blue}
```

Figure 14-7:
A three-element contextual selector, darkening the background of a span (but only if it's within a `strong` within a b).

This paragraph is entirely bold, so we simply ███ to find a way to emphasize text within the boldness.

Here's yet another shortcut. What if you want to define multiple contextual selectors using the same style. What if, for example, you wanted `b strong span`'s blue background to also be used when italics appeared with an `h2` headline? You don't have to create a separate style definition, just use a comma to separate the contextual selectors, just as you would when grouping normal selectors:

```
b strong span, h2 i {background-color:blue}
```

After you've described a style for a contextual selector, that style is also inherited by any children of the selector, indeed by any descendant of that selector all the way down the tree. (Or should I say, *up* the tree?)

For instance, if you have a `strong` or `em` or some other child element inside this italics selector, that `strong` or `em` child inherits the green color of its ancestor italics selector:

```
p,i {color: green;}
```

Therefore, the `<strong>` here inherits its parent italic element's green color:

```
<P>
Here's a paragraph with <i>italics, but <strong>also some
          strong inside</strong> the italics</i>.
```

To prevent inheritance from happening all the way down an ancestry line, if it doesn't suit you, see the section titled "Thwarting Descendant Selectors," later in this chapter.

Styling distant descendants

The universal selector makes a change to *every* element. If you want to turn everything on your page red — all headlines, hyperlinks, paragraphs, everything — you can use this rule that employs the universal selector (*):

```
* {color: red;}
```

But can you use the universal selector with a contextual selector? Aren't you the clever kitty! This technique is somewhat confusing, but it can be done. The effect is to apply styles to elements a certain degree of distance from ancestors. For example, if you want only list elements that are great-grandchildren to be red:

```
body * * UL {color: red;}
```

In this next example, only unnumbered list elements that are a grandchild (or further down such as a great-grandchild) of the body become red:

```
body * UL {color: red;}
```

To qualify for this rule, an unnumbered list element must not be a child of the body element; instead, it must be further removed from the body, such as being the child of a list item. (The list item itself is the child of the body.) Only unnumbered list elements that are children of the body are not turned red: All the rest of the descendent unnumbered list elements *do* turn red.

If you think all this is usually more complex than useful, you're an especially cunning kitty. However, should you ever need to create rules for distantly descended elements, combining the universal selector with a contextual selector is the way to go.

Thwarting Descendant Selectors

Warning: At this time, you cannot apply this next selector trick to code used in Internet Explorer — it won't work. What if you only want a child element to be selected, not an entire series of descendants? To do that, you use the > symbol, which means *only if it's a child*. Here's how that looks:

```
p > i {color: blue;}
```

This means, "Color blue any italic that is a child of a paragraph. *But don't go any further if the italic has any children or descendants.*" So, in the following paragraph, the strong element won't inherit the blue color:

```
<P>
Here's a paragraph with <i>italics, but <strong>also some
          strong child inside</strong> the italics</i>.
```

In some cases, you don't want to select an arbitrarily descended element; rather, you want to narrow your range to select an element that is a child of another element. You might, for example, want to select a strong element only if it is a child (as opposed to a descendant) of an H1 element. To do this, you use the child combinator, which is the greater-than symbol (>):

```
h1 > strong {color: red;}
```

This rule makes the strong element shown in the first H1 below red but not in the second:

```
<h1>This is <strong>very</strong> important.</h1>
<h1>This is <em>really <strong>very</strong></em>
          important.</h1>
```

Read right to left, the selector h1 > strong translates as "selects any strong element that is a child of an H1 element." The child combinator is optionally surrounded by white space. Thus, h1 > strong, h1> strong, and h1>strong are all equivalent. You can use or omit white space as you like.

You can also specify a selector in a way that works on adjacent siblings (like two paragraphs that share the same <body> element as their parent). You specify them using the + sign. This, too, however, has not been adopted by Microsoft's Internet Explorer.

Selectors Using Attributes

Warning: This trick also doesn't work in Internet Explorer. Attribute selectors allow you to define a style that applies only to places where a particular HTML attribute exists as part of an element. Here's an illustration. Say you wanted to apply a border around only those paragraphs that had an align-right attribute:

```
<p align="right">
```

Or

```
<p align="right" color="blue">
```

You would then create a style like this, using brackets:

```
p[align='right'] {border: 3px solid gray;}
```

and hope for the best. However, this doesn't work in Internet Explorer, so you can ignore it for now (and perhaps forever). For more on this particular kind of specialized selector, see Chapter 3.

Chapter 15

CSS Moves into the Future

· ·

In This Chapter

▶ Comparing CSS2 and CSS3

▶ Handling pseudo-classes and pseudo-elements

▶ Considering dubious descendants

· ·

*T*echnology marches on. The beavers are busy again, so watch out! Although slow by technology standards (indeed by *any* standards), the committees that define CSS rules and features are still at work, after four years of effort, trying to come up with CSS3. CSS programmers are still governed by the set of specs in CSS2, and most browsers have adopted most of the CSS2 rules. Some browsers — notably Mozilla and Firefox — have gone so far as to adopt some of the more interesting styles and modes of selection in CSS3 drafts.

The CSS committees start out with *drafts*, which are suggestions. After a few years of bickering and mulling things over, CSS committees come out with *recommendations*, which are also like suggested ideas but stronger.

 Nobody actually uses the impolite and, face it, politically incorrect word "rule." Well, I do, but my job doesn't rely on politik jargon or academic doubletalk. I'm supposed to go for clarity, which I generally try to do. (The concept of the "rule" does exist in CSS, but it means styles that you impose on your documents, not rules handed down by The Committee.)

In this chapter, you get to peek under the curtain at some of the more interesting (or in some cases baffling) new regulations being proposed and contemplated for CSS3. You also discover the unique way that some academics use the word *pseudo*. (And you thought it meant *false*.)

Getting to Know CSS3

CSS3 is the name for the next wave of changes and additions to the CSS "core." The core is most of the features described in this book, which are available in Internet Explorer 6 and many of the minor browsers as well.

CSS3 has been in committee for several years. The first few working drafts came out in early 2001. Those involved announced that instead of attempting a sweeping new version, they would roll out "modules" from time to time. Some of the recommendations have begun to be supported in browsers already, and other recommendations are likely to take years to even be formally proposed.

Internet Explorer 6 supports nothing from CSS3. That's why I cover CSS3 features only briefly in this book. No one yet knows what (if any) expansions of CSS will appear in Internet Explorer 7, which will most likely appear in 2006. Considering the market dominance that Internet Explorer enjoys, if IE 7 doesn't support these expansions, what the other browsers do doesn't matter much, unless of course Mozilla Firefox takes over the world in the meantime.

If you want to keep track of the latest recommendations and don't mind reading some white papers that plunge into exceptionally dreary academic writing, you can find the papers on new ideas for CSS at `www.w3.org/Style/CSS/current-work`.

Here are some of the more significant expected changes that fix existing problems, or extend CSS capabilities:

- ✔ Easier downloading of fonts.
- ✔ Greater utility and flexibility in the design of table columns.
- ✔ Greater control for users over color schemes. (This feature seems counter to the idea that a designer should control such issues, in contrast to the next point, which represents something of a contradiction.)
- ✔ Color descriptions so that monitors can more accurately reproduce what the Web page designer intended.
- ✔ More dynamic control over the behaviors of various objects.

Working with Mozilla-supported CSS3 features

Of the minor browsers, Mozilla's Firefox seem to be the most interested in adopting CSS3 features. It permits the use of the new attribute substring selectors (*, $, and ^) to allow matches to parts of words in attributes. For example, say that you want to indicate to viewers that a particular link is to an Active Server Page (Active Server Page filenames end in. asp). Use the $ to indicate that the substring .asp is at the end of your target. This rule makes all links to any page ending in .asp become red:

```
a[href$='.asp']{color: red;}
```

Of course, this approach to specifying substring matches goes against the traditional (back to the early days of DOS) punctuation that used * and ? as the primary symbols. Perhaps even worse, the CSS committee's chosen substitution symbols aren't placed inside the string, but instead are attached to the attribute name (the $ attaches to `href` in this example, not within the string `'.asp'`, where the $ would more effectively convey its meaning). But, in the CSS tradition, don't expect sensible conformity to traditional punctuation when it's so much more adventurous to strike out in new directions and really confuse people.

Mozilla also supports the CSS3 `:not` command. Why they prepended a colon to the traditional and perfectly useful `not` command is anybody's guess. This is a *negation pseudo-class selector* (more about pseudo-classes shortly). Put more simply, if something doesn't pass a test, a certain style is applied. If you want to put a thick border around any paragraph that currently does *not* have a border, for example, here's how to do it:

```
<html>
<head>

<style>


p:not([border]){border: 6px solid red;}

body {font-size: 24 px;}

</style>


</head>

<body>

<P style="border: 3px solid blue">
Here's a paragraph with a border defined in a style. </p>

<P>
Here's a normal paragraph with no border defined, so it gets
         a red border. </p>

</body>
</html>
```

This works as advertised in Mozilla Firefox. The first paragraph has a border style definition, so it's got a blue border. The second paragraph has no border assigned in a style, so it's given a thick red border.

If you're not used to CSS or other computer programming languages (aside from Basic), you may ask: Why did they design this syntax to sound like a two-year-old: *Paragraph not border* is the clumsy syntax of this CSS code. Couldn't they have used ordinary English syntax like *No border on paragraph* and achieved the same result? Sure they could have. It would have been easier to remember, easier to read, and easier to fix mistakes. But committees of academics and professional programmers have agendas other than clarity. So most programming languages sound fairly Martian with their twisted syntactic flow.

Note that for reasons nobody can explain to me, if you apply a style using a class, the :not command doesn't work. In the following example, *both paragraphs* are bordered in red in Firefox:

```
<style>

p.bordr {border: 3px solid blue;}

p:not([border]){border: 6px solid red;}

body {font-size: 24 px;}

</style>


</head>

<body>

<P class="bordr">
Here's a paragraph with a border defined in a style. </p>

<P>
Here's a normal paragraph with no border defined, so it gets
        a red border. </p>

</body>
```

If you remove the square braces, :not works in this example, like this:

```
p:not(border){border: 6px solid red;}
```

Setting opacity

Another new feature that Mozilla has already implemented from CSS3 is *opacity*, the ability to add transparency to an element. Here's how it works in the CSS implementation that Mozilla recognizes and correctly interprets:

```
div.maintext {position: absolute; z-index: 2; opacity: 0.5;
              background-color: darkkhaki; top: 55;left: 100px;
              height: 75%; width: 75%;}
```

Internet Explorer doesn't yet know how to handle the opacity property, but it does have a proprietary opacity filter. To get the same effect in IE, use this code:

```
div.maintext {position: absolute; z-index: 2;
filter:progid:DXImageTransform.Microsoft.Alpha(opacity=50);
              background-color: darkkhaki; top: 55;left: 100px;
              height: 75%; width: 75%;}
```

Notice that IE uses the sensible value 50 for 50 percent (that's the way most people would express the degree of transparency). Unfortunately, the CSS recommendation employs the less intuitive 0.5 value for 50 percent. This isn't to say that Microsoft always makes sensible decisions, but they did in this case.

In general, if you're looking to try out the latest CSS features, you'll find that Mozilla and its relative, Firefox, are the most experimental and *au courant* of the various browsers. Internet Explorer is a bit more conservative, although it has many features that other browsers do not (including proprietary Microsoft extensions such as filters).

Discovering False Pseudo-Classes

I call them *false pseudo* because the double-negative applies. These are *true* classes. They're not fake. They often do a useful job. So, what are these "pseudo" classes?

To understand the idea of pseudo-classes, first review what a CSS class is: It's a way to modify a selector, like an img selector. The class name acts as an adjective. Imagine that you want *some* of the images in your site to be framed in blue. (If you wanted *all* the images thus framed, you could just define a style for the img selector, without having to create a class. That way, all images would get the blue frame.) But you want only some images framed. So you create a class. It's as if you make up a new category of image that you decide to identify as the *framed image*. So the word *framed* is the name of the class. You can use any word to name a class that makes sense to you, but *framed* makes sense to me here.

You can, of course, create any class you want by merely making up a name for your class, like this:

```
<html>
<head>

<style type="text/css">


img.framed {padding-left: 6px; padding-right: 4px; padding-
           top: 6px; border: 12px inset lightblue;}

</style>


</head>

<img  class="framed" src = "texture.jpg">

</body>
</html>
```

In this style, you've created a class you want to call *framed*. Its purpose is to surround any image whose class is specified as *framed* with a nice blue inset border. Any image without the `class="framed"` attribute, or with some other class name attribute, does not get this blue frame. So far so good.

But what is a pseudo-class? Well, folks, it's not a *fake* class, as the term pseudo implies. It's just a built-in style: a class that the CSS specification includes that therefore some browsers support and know how to render. In other words, it's what CSS has been calling a *property*.

Pseudo-classes are designed to provide some useful feature, without creating a new property or adding to the list of HTML elements. It would have probably have made more sense to just create some new properties, as they've done in the past. Confusing as this terminology is, we now have to live with it: CSS now features a small handful of special *pseudo* tricks. Some of them change the color or other style of an element based on context (such as a hyperlink that turns a different color to indicate that the user has already visited that site). Other pseudo tricks are complex ways of selecting based on an element's status within the document tree (such as *select all parents with no child elements*). The job of the CSS programmer is to figure out the handful of pseudo-elements so that we can employ them if needed. Some of them are pretty useful.

Hyperlink formatting with pseudo-classes

Here's an example of a useful CSS pseudo-element. Displaying different kinds of hyperlinks in different colors frequently helps the viewer to navigate your page. So, the good, busy people involved with CSS committees decided to create some built-in (pseudo) classes to handle this very common need.

Here are the four pseudo-classes for the a selector (or element):

```
a:link {color: #FF0000;}      /* an unvisited link */
a:visited {color: #00FF00;}   /* a visited link */
a:hover {color: #FF00FF;}     /* a link with the mouse hovering
            over it */
a:active {color: #0000FF;}    /* the selected link */
```

Notice that the selector (a) is separated from the pseudo-class's name by a colon. Also, you must list these styles *in this order*. Otherwise, the hover and active styles won't work right.

Here's an example to try, to see how convenient this set of built-in behaviors is:

```
<html>
<head>

<style>


a:link {color: blue;}      /* an unvisited link */
a:visited {color: purple;}  /* a visited link */
a:hover {color: red;}      /* a link with the mouse hovering
            over it */
a:active {color: green;}    /* the selected link */

</style>
</head>


<body style="font-size=x-large">

<a href="http://www.cnn.com">Click here for CNN</a>


</body>
</html>
```

Notice that you don't use any code to identify the pseudo-classes (such as class="visited") in the body, in the element itself. Unlike ordinary classes that you write yourself, a built-in (pseudo) class takes effect without you having to add a class= attribute. After all, this set of pseudo-classes work together to modify the behavior (the colors in this case) of the link element a.

If you save this example as an .htm file and load the file into Internet Explorer, you'll notice that the Click here for CNN link does appear blue at first. It then turns red as your mouse goes over it and turns green when you click it. However, if you press F5 and try to "reload" the file to experience these wonderful color changes once again, the link remains green! It's supposed to.

You are now looking at the selected link. It's no longer unvisited. To restart the process, make some change to the code in the .htm file, such as adding a `<p>`. Then resave the .htm file, and reload it into IE. This forces IE to treat this as a new page and reset the behaviors of the pseudo-classes for a.

Hovering with pseudo-classes

You should feel free to experiment by using these pseudo-classes with elements other than the a it was originally designed for. In general, CSS wisely tries to allow you to use most of its features with most HTML elements. Why restrict designers with artificial limitations? Why not let them fool around with the various features and discover new ways to exploit CSS?

Hovering is a particularly interesting feature because in its own cheap way it mimics scripting. (I describe it as *cheap* because you don't have to do any programming to get a Web page to react to the user's mouse.) The user hovers the mouse pointer above something with a hover pseudo-class, and whammo, something happens to the style. At least, that's the theory.

In practice, however, IE doesn't permit hover to be used with any element other than the a, and even the usually generous Mozilla Firefox doesn't seem (in my experiments anyway) to allow all elements to respond to hovering.

You can imagine how this might be useful. With hover, you can achieve a highlighting effect via CSS, rather than the more complex methods of DHTML and scripting. Try viewing this example with Firefox or a browser that supports using the hover pseudo-class for elements other than the a (as I pointed out earlier, IE 6 does *not* support this feature). Here all paragraphs use the pseudo-class hover:

```
p:hover {background: peachpuff; border: 1px solid powderblue}
```

Load this into Firefox and see the interesting effect when you move your mouse pointer over the paragraphs in the browser — try different elements to see which are affected. In theory, they all should be.

You can find loads of examples on the Web showing how to create a hover effect in IE using JavaScript.

Adding your own class name to a pseudo-class

If you want, you can add a personal class name to a pseudo-class. For example, if you want *some* of your links to turn pink when the user's mouse hovers over them, stick your made-up class name between the selector and the pseudo-class name, like this:

```
a.pinklink:hover {color: pink}
```

Then, down in the body, refer to this class in the usual way, with a `class=` attribute:

```
<a class="pinklink" href="http://www.zrsn.ori">Click here for
          a real shock.</a>
```

Selecting first children

A pseudo-class that allows you to select only the *first* child of an element is also available. At the time of this writing, however, it doesn't work in Internet Explorer.

Say that you want to indent only the first paragraph of the body but not the rest of the paragraphs. You can use the first-child pseudo-class, like this:

```
body > p:first-child
{
text-indent:30px;
}
```

Then, later in the body:

```
<p>
This first paragraph is indented, yes?
</p>

<p>
But this second paragraph isn't indented.
</p>
```

Employing Fake Pseudo-Elements

Guess what? The CSS folks have come up with another category of pseudo called the *pseudo-element*. But who cares? I can see no distinction between *pseudo*-classes and *pseudo*-elements, although I've read and researched and pondered. W3.org "explains" the distinction here:

```
www.w3.org/TR/REC-CSS2/selector.html#q15
```

If you have any idea what they're talking about, please email me at richardm52@hotmail.com. Perhaps the wise guys who make up these systems and taxonomies can provide some clarification. But do you really need to know the distinction at all, if in fact there is one? Nope. Just know that these various *pseudo*-whatevers exist in case you ever want to use one of them. It's sort of like a car: You can drive just fine without knowing the genus of all the bugs hitting your window.

Pseudo-elements are used exactly the same way that you use pseudo-styles, with one exception. You can put a pseudo-class name anywhere you want in a selector, but a pseudo-element's name must be listed after the subject of the selector. (*Subject* here means whatever elements in the document that match the selector.) Don't bother with this ultimately pointless distinction either. *Who !@#)!! cares?* Just follow the syntax in the sample code in the next section and you'll be fine.

Creating quick drop caps with first-letter

A quick way to add some elegance to your text is with drop caps: large characters at the beginning of your paragraphs. Sometimes the letter is a different color than the surrounding text as well. Here's a style using the pseudo-element first-letter:

```html
<html>
<head>

<style>

p:first-letter

{color: steelblue;
font-size:44px;}

</style>
</head>


<body style="font-size=x-large">


<p>
This first paragraph has a nice drop cap effect that you can
        see in steel blue.
</p>

<p>
And this second paragraph has a drop cap too.
</p>

</body>
</html>
```

The result is shown in Figure 15-1:

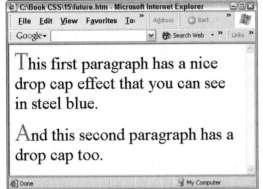

Figure 15-1:
Here's a
quick way
to add drop
caps to your
paragraphs.

You can use the following properties with the `first-letter` pseudo-element: `font` properties, `color`, `background`, `margin`, `padding`, `border`, `text-decoration`, `vertical-align` (if there's no floating in effect), `text-transform`, `line-height`, `float`, and `clear`.

Using the first-line element for special lines of text

You can also provide a special style for the first line of an element, rather than just the first letter. Here in this example that increases the size of the text in the first line of each paragraph:

```
p:first-line {font-size: 45px}
```

You can use the following properties with the `first-line` pseudo-element: `font` properties, `color`, `background`, `word-spacing`, `letter-spacing`, `text-decoration`, `vertical-align`, `text-transform`, `line-height`, and `clear`.

The Future of Pseudo

The CSS committees will likely continue to add pseudo-features to handle various kinds of user interfacing. They may also possibly create some additional dynamic responses that enable the browser window to react without your having to write any scripts (such as the `hover` pseudo-class). Of course, at this time, IE isn't supporting many of the newer pseudo-classes, so you have to essentially avoid these latest pseudo features. Nonetheless, such features as the four pseudo-classes that work with hyperlinks (described earlier in this chapter) are quite useful and work well within IE.

Based on the information in "drafts" floating down from the white towers on the hill where CSS specifications are dreamed up, you can look forward to at least some of the pseudo features in the next two sections making their appearance in CSS in the coming years.

Enabling, disabling

The :enabled and :disabled pseudo-classes allow you to apply the traditional visual cues to such input controls as check boxes, radio buttons, and so on. When elements in Windows are *disabled* (meaning that the user cannot interact with the control), for example, it's a convention to turn the control light gray. This lets people know that the control is inert. One use for such a feature is if the user is filling in a form and clicks the Never Married check box. At this point, you would have your Web page disable the How Long Have You Been Married? check box. There would be no reason to permit the user to enter information about how long he or she had been married, if he or she had never been married, right?

Checking radio buttons and check boxes

The :checked and :indeterminate pseudo-classes provide a style (usually a vibrant color) that indicates the status of a check box. In general, the convention in Windows has been to merely display a check symbol rather than, say, highlight the text associated with a check box or radio button (instead of a check, a selected radio button control gets a dot). Indeterminate works only with the radio button. It has a three-state property: enabled (called *checked* by CSS), disabled, and indeterminate. The checked class works with both radio buttons and check boxes.

I suggest you forget about these button and check box pseudo-classes unless you have some strange requirements for your user input. Just let the controls do their thing automatically: visually cueing the user with dots or checks when the control is clicked. Anything that you add by using a style is probably overkill and violates the visual conventions of Windows. Violating conventions often simply confuses and annoys people who, over the years, have gotten used to the way things work in Windows. Nonetheless, some of the worker bees at Microsoft sometimes decide that they know best and come up with bizarre modifications that confound the rest of us. Try, for example, to find the menus in Windows Media Player version 10. The usual File, Options, Tools, and Help menus at the top left of almost every Windows application for the past decade are really buried in Media Player now. It took me quite a while to locate the Help menu, which I thought was a bit inconsiderate: It's a little like hiding the fire extinguisher. Media Player 10 is an excellent piece of software, and its visual design is, to me, quite elegant. For example, when you hover the mouse pointer over the tabs at the top left, the tabs light up subtly, like wall sconces in an Art Deco theater. But . . . that is where the *menus* should be.

Figuring Out Dubious Descendant Selectors

A set of what are to me dubious "descendant selectors" are coming down from the CSS gurus in CSS3. Some of these selectors may be more confusing than useful, but if you're really into CSS esoterica, grouped patterns could be just the treat you've been looking for.

Descendant selectors specify that a rule applies only to particular children or descendants, such as only the fourth list item in an unnumbered list. You can also use it to apply rules to patterns, such as to every third, or every other, child.

The `:only-child` selector selects only those elements with, you guessed it, no siblings (such as a single paragraph within a `<div>`). A related selector is the `only-of-type` selector, which selects a specific type of element, like an H1 that has no H1 siblings, but *does* have other siblings, such as a group of `<p>` paragraphs. Think of a `<div>` containing four paragraphs but only one headline.

Another descendant selector is called the *nth-child*. To specify a style for only a particular child, say the sixth item in a list, just use the number itself. This is not a repeating pattern. This code sets the background color of one child, the sixth item, to red:

```
ul:nth-child(6){background-color: red;}
```

What if you want to use a *pattern* of styles, such as coloring every other table item's background light blue? This is a fairly common way to help the reader distinguish between the various cells, rows, and columns of a table.

Using the *n*th-child feature, you can specify *groups* of children, thereby creating a pattern. Imagine a list. Inside the `<ul> </ul>` parent element inside are a bunch of child `li` elements, right? What if you want to color *every other child* red in your list? You can use the *n*th-child pseudo-class to create the effect:

```
ul:nth-child(2n+1){background-color: red;}
```

This translates to "Group the children (the li elements within the list in this case) by *twos* (2n). Then apply the style only to the first element in this grouping." To get your head around this brain-twister, it helps to compare that code to another example. The following turns every fourth list item red:

```
ul:nth-child(4n+1){background-color: red;}
```

Instead of specifying a pattern mathematically like the 4n+1 value, you can instead use odd and even as values rather than numbers to affect every other descendant, like this:

```
ul:nth-child(even){background-color: red;}
```

You can count up from the bottom of a group with the nth-last-child selector. You can also create groups when elements are mixed together (they're all siblings, all children of the same parent, but you want to just specify a style for, say, the headlines rather than the paragraphs). For that, use the nth-of-type selector. CSS also offers a combo of the previous two types: nth-last-of-type.

The variety of selectors goes on. The empty selector selects barren elements (elements that have no children). First-of-type (or last-of-type) selectors provide a style for only the first or last child. For example, to italicize the first list item in each list, try this:

```
ul:first-of-type{text-style: italic;}
```

Ever inventive, the CSS governing board also offers a *none* selector: nth-of-none. It selects nothing. (Just kidding about this last one.)

Chapter 16

Programmatic CSS

● ●

In This Chapter

▶ Scripting

▶ Automating CSS features

▶ Changing style and rules on the fly

▶ Playing with timers

▶ Repeating with a metronome timer

● ●

*M*ost ordinary CSS is not dynamic, in the sense that it doesn't respond to the user. One example that does respond is the pseudo-classes for the a element, discussed in the Chapter 15. CSS has a feature called hover, for example, that turns a hyperlink a different color when the user hovers a mouse pointer over the link.

In general, however, CSS puts a pretty face on Web pages, simplifies design across a Web site, and its job is then done. Any interaction with the user thereafter is left up to programming technologies such as ASP.NET or *scripting* (small sections of programming written into an HTML page using the <script> element). However, scripts and other programming can be made to interact with CSS styles, and the result can amplify CSS's usefulness.

Extending CSS with Scripting

Script code is usually written in VBScript or JavaScript. By default, IE uses JavaScript, although you can specify VBScript if you prefer. I prefer.

Some experts warn that VBScript is less universal than JavaScript — all browsers can run JavaScript, but only Internet Explorer recognizes VBScript. However, given that Internet Explorer is the browser of choice for more than 95 out of 100 Internet users, choosing VBScript seems safe enough. If you're concerned, though, go ahead and struggle with JavaScript. It's more likely to be buggy and slow to write, but you may prefer it. What do you do about bugs? More about debugging scripts in Chapter 17.

Writing for users who disable scripts

Script languages were originally designed to be harmless to a computer (dangerous commands like disk formatting have been stripped from script languages). Nonetheless, virus writers, Trojan horse authors, and other social misfits have found ways to use script to spy on people's data, damage files, and so on. However, *you've* written the script examples in this chapter, so you can trust them and test the examples.

But what about using scripts on the Internet? So far, most people using IE seem to be permitting scripts, so you might be safe inserting them into your Web pages. If, however, a browser or user refuses to permit scripts, you should offer an alternative to scripting. You can, if necessary, insert a `<noscript>` element in your code that is executed if your script can't execute because of the user's security settings. Inside this `<noscript>` element, you can include CSS styles, text explaining what the script did, or an `<a>` link they can click for additional information: whatever you think makes your page acceptable comprehensible and aesthetically pleasing if your script fails to run. Here's an example:

```
<noscript>
<p>Sorry, you have configured
    your browser to prohibit
    scripting. If you want to
    allow scripting in Internet
    Explorer, adjust the set-
    tings in the Tools⇨Internet
    Options dialog box. Click
    the Security tab, and then
    click the Custom Level
    button and set the permis-
    sions.
</noscript>
```

Sometimes using the `<noscript>` element isn't necessary because the script is merely doing something visually attractive (like fading a graphic image into the page for decoration). You don't need to provide an alternative for that because *presumably* now that you've read this book, your CSS-designed page is already gorgeous without the added attractions offered by animated scripted design elements. But if the script does something essential, such as making tiny text larger so it can be read or simulating opening a menu, you may want to ensure that those who can't execute scripts can still get this important benefit via a hyperlink that loads another page, or in some other fashion.

Here's an example of scripting, using JavaScript:

```
<html>
<head>

<script type="text/javascript" language="JavaScript">
<!—
function foryou( ) {
    alert("A message for you!");
}
//—>
</script>
```

```
</head>

<body>


<button onclick="foryou()">Click me for a personal
            message.</button>

</body>
</html>
```

If you're sticking to Internet Explorer, you can simplify the code, thus:

```
<script>

function foryou( ) {
    alert("A message for you!");
}

</script>
```

The HTML comment symbols ⟨!-- and --⟩ prevent some browsers from displaying code to the user. (Nothing is commented here — using these symbols just tricks some browsers into ignoring the code.) Comments are never displayed, except to the programmer while writing the code. Worse, the // symbol is a JavaScript comment mark, and you have to stick that in to prevent JavaScript from getting confused by the HTML --⟩ symbol! Talk about workarounds. If I were you, I'd just leave out all these comment symbols and not fret about it. The browsers that don't recognize the ⟨script⟩ element are so old that anyone still using them should be penalized. It may convince them to download a free contemporary browser and join the rest of us.

JavaScript is the default language for IE, so you need not specify it in the script block.

The CSS people want to move away from (deprecate as they call it) the venerable language= attribute in favor of the far less clear type= attribute. (C programmers, and professors of C at universities, are fond of using the word *type.* They apply it here and there to all kinds of things, using it as promiscuously as they use the word *object.* And, as with *object,* the word *type* has lost nearly any meaning it once had — it's applied to variables, custom data structures, arrays, and so on. Now they want to substitute *type* for *language.* Heaven help us.)

Alternatively, you can use more easily understood, more easily programmed VBScript, like this:

```
<script language="VBScript">

function foryou

    msgbox ("A message for you!")

end function

</script>
```

If you want to keep your script out of the HTML and in a separate file, use the src attribute, like this:

```
<script type="text/javascript" src="foryou.js"></script>
```

Ensure that your script file, in ordinary text format like from Notepad, is in the same directory as the .htm file holding the HTML code. The script is imported when the page is loaded, just as images are imported with the <img> element.

Executing Scripts Automatically upon Loading

In the preceding examples, the user must click a button before the script executes. If you want the script to execute when the page first loads, just remove the function. In VBScript, that means removing two lines (function and end function), like this:

```
<script language="VBScript">

    msgbox ("A message for you!")

</script>
```

JavaScript employs braces to indicate the start and end of a procedure, so remove both of the lines containing the braces to make a script execute when the page first loads:

```
<script>

    alert("Hello, HTML world!");

</script>
```

When a Web page with script loads into the latest version of Internet Explorer (Service Pack 2), the script won't immediately execute. Instead, a message appears across the top of the browser window saying, `To protect your security, Internet Explorer has restricted this file from showing active content that could access your computer. Click here for options`. Go ahead and click here. Then choose Allow Blocked Content from the dialog box that appears. Now another warning pops up, just in case you were delirious or roaring drunk when you made your choice. This second warning asks you if you're sure. Go ahead and click Yes. Now, at long last, you can see the effects of your script. Note that once you allow blocked content from one Web page, any other pages you surf to are also permitted to send blocked content. IE only resets itself after you shut it down, and then restart it. After that, the message about blocked content once again appears in response to an attempted script load.

You can include more than one script element in a page, but put them up inside the `<head>` element.

Using the Right Tools for the Job

For small programming jobs, scripting works just fine. Scripting *is* programming, albeit with a somewhat abbreviated language. Scripting is designed to get past firewalls, browser security settings, and other security measures. A script language is quite similar to its parent language (Visual Basic or Java), but some potentially dangerous commands — mainly those that access the hard drive, such as those that delete files — are removed from the script language.

Unfortunately, evil-doers *can* still find ways to make scripting dangerous, but Microsoft has come up with an ingenious solution: Execute your code on the server, compose an ordinary HTML page after the computation has finished, and send *that* HTML back to the user's browser. HTML, like a television show, cannot introduce a virus into your house. It's the difference between seeing a picture of someone with a cold, versus sitting next to somebody on a bus who's hacking and wheezing.

ASP.NET is the name Microsoft gave to this server-side code execution technique. It works quite well, allowing programmers to enjoy the full VBA, VB.NET, or other language rather than simply scripts. For serious, complex Web programming solutions (or what is now often called *enterprise development*), you will find working with the heavy-duty tools available in the Visual Studio .NET suite much more efficient.

But for CSS work, where you want to merely react a bit to user behaviors, make a few changes to the design of a page, or do a little animation, scripting is quite powerful enough.

Modifying CSS Styles through Programming

This next example shows you how to create your own effects — modifying any style of any element (*almost* any style, anyway) in any way. Recall the example from Chapter 15 that used a pseudo-class to change the color of a link (an a element) when the user hovered their mouse over the element?

Now you'll see how to use a bit of trick scripting to make *any* kind of change you want to a style — dynamically, while your page is displayed.

Changing styles

Type this into Notepad or whatever text editor you like, or copy it from this book's Web site:

```
<html>
<head>


<script>

function changestyle(obj,sname,ch) {

var dom = document.getElementById(obj).style;
dom [sname] = ch;


}

</script>

<style>

#pfirst {

font-size: 8px;
width: 400px;

}
```

```
</style>

</head>

<body>

<h1 id="head1" onmouseover=

"changestyle('pfirst','fontSize','24px');

changestyle('head1','color','green');"

>Hover mouse here to expand.
</h1>


<br>

<br>

<p id="pfirst">

For small programming jobs, scripting works just fine.
            Scripting is programming, albeit with a somewhat
            abbreviated language. Scripting is designed to get
            past firewalls, browser security settings, and
            other security measures. A script language is
            quite similar to its parent language (Visual Basic
            or Java), but some potentially dangerous commands
            — mainly hard drive access, such as file deleting
            — are removed from the script language.</p>

</body>
</html>
```

To test this example, follow these steps:

1. **Save this code to a file named scripting.htm on your hard drive, or use another filename if you prefer.**

2. **Double-click that file in Internet Explorer.**

    The page is loaded into Internet Explorer. You see the result shown in Figure 16-1.

3. **Move your mouse pointer over the headline.**

The headline immediately turns green and the paragraph of text expands from a size of 12 pixels to 24 pixels, as you see in Figure 16-2:

Figure 16-1:
The original appearance of the page, with a black headline and small text in the paragraph.

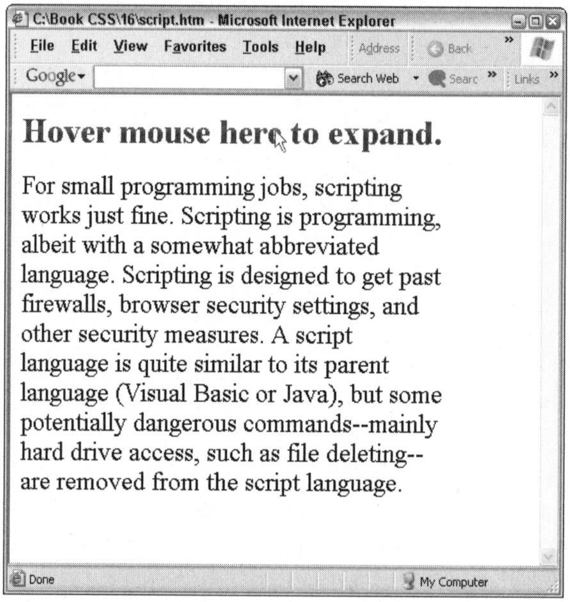

Figure 16-2:
After you hover your mouse over the headline, it changes color and the text increases to a more legible size.

You see the implications. You can use HTML event attributes — such as `onclick`, `onmouseover`, `onchange`, `onkeypress`, `onfocus` and so on — to trigger changes to the CSS styles. You could drop paragraphs or lists (as illustrated in the previous example), manipulate colors, swap paragraphs and other elements' positions, adjust sizes and shapes and positions — whatever you think up.

Pay no attention to the script itself. It works, and you need not know how or why. You don't know how your car's universal joint works, do you? But you drive it nonetheless.

Just plug this script into any Web page where you want to dynamically alter the CSS styles. All you need bother with in this script is what you feed into it and what it then does for you:

```
function changestyle(obj,sname,ch) {

var dom = document.getElementById(obj).style;
dom [sname] = ch;

}
```

To make this work, you must provide three things, called obj, sname, and ch in this code, but the names don't matter. What you actually provide are the ID name you assigned to the element (or *selector* if you prefer), the name of the property you want changed, and the actual value that you want for this change. For example, the first changestyle line changes the paragraph with the id *pfirst,* changes its font-size property, and changes the font-size to 24 pixels:

```
<h1 id="head1" onmouseover=
"changestyle('pfirst','fontSize','24px');
  changestyle('head1','color','green');"
>Hover mouse here to expand.
</h1>
```

Java and JavaScript, like C and similar languages, are quite strict. Their unnecessary punctuation rules, wacky syntax, and spelling restrictions are notorious for causing countless bugs and wasting countless people's time. The script in this example is yet another instance of this sad state of affairs. JavaScript is case-sensitive. It makes a distinction between the words fontsize and fontSize. It won't even permit you to use the correct CSS term font-size for this property. JavaScript allows no hyphens, and what's more, if a word is made of two words, like font-size, you must remove the hyphen and capitalize the first letter of the second word. So fontSize is the *only* way you can send the font-size property to the script. If your scripts aren't working, make sure that the property names you're sending to the script are correctly capitalized.

You can send as many requests for style changes as you wish to the changestyle function. In this example, you made two changes — one to the size of the paragraph's text and one to the color of the headline. But be creative in applying this technique. Consider adding a toggle feature to the script, so that each time the user hovers the mouse, the element is restored to its original status (see Chapter 13 for details about toggling behavior). Or try adding a timer (see the section "Timing Things Right" later in this chapter) to control the speed or timing of a style change.

Changing the rules

In this next example, you modify the `style` area itself. For example, say you have a selector and style definition like this:

```
p {font-size: 8px; color: pink; }
```

When the page loads, your paragraphs are in tiny pink text. What if you want to allow the user to change this style rule? This next line of code changes the p rule when a user's mouse pointer moves over this element so that the text changes to blue and increases to a size of 18 pixels:

```
<h1 onmouseover="newrule('p','font-size: 18px; color:
        blue')">Hover here to drop
```

To accomplish this, first you give a `style` element an id of its own (yes, you can give the `style` element an id). In your script, you use this id to specify which `style` element you're talking about (a page can have more than one `style` element, so this is required):

```
<style id="thestyles">
```

Here's the complete, working example for you to experiment with:

```
<html>
<head>
<script>

function newrule(selector,props) {

document.styleSheets.MyStyles.addRule(selector,props)

}

</script>

<style id="MyStyles">

h1 {font-size: 24pt}
```

```
p {font-size: 8px; color: pink;}

</style>


</head>
<body>

<h1 onmouseover="newrule('p','font-size: 18px; color:
        blue')">Hover here to drop

text</h1>

<p>
For small programming jobs, scripting works just fine.
        Scripting is programming, albeit with a somewhat
        abbreviated language. Scripting is designed to get
        past firewalls, browser security settings, and
        other security measures.
</p>

</body>

</html>
```

In this example, when the user hovers the mouse over the headline, the user triggers this onmouseover event:

```
<h1 onmouseover="newrule('p','font-size: 18px; color:
        blue')">Hover here to drop
```

This causes the newrule function to do its job. The items within the parentheses are sent by the computer to the function. First, the p is sent, identifying the selector you want to change. Then the properties and values are sent to the function as well. You can send as many as you want to send. You don't need to send the same number of properties as are currently in the selector's style definition.

The function then carries out its one job:

```
document.styleSheets.thestyles.addRule(selector,specs)
```

This changes the "rule" (to this selector, changing these properties) in this document's style sheets collection. Use the particular style element with the ID *thestyles*.

Remember, you need not understand programming to use the scripting techniques described in this chapter. Just copy and paste the script element into the `<head>` section, and then follow the examples to pass the correct data to the function (as you just did with the `onmouseover` event in this example). You can easily customize these examples. If you want the p selector's text color to change to green in this example, instead of blue, just make that change in the code:

```
<h1 onmouseover="newrule('p','font-size: 18px; color:
          green')">Hover here to drop
```

Or if you want to change the properties for the `headline` selector rather than the p, just make this change (shown in boldface):

```
<h1 onmouseover="newrule('h1','font-size: 18px; color:
          blue')">Hover here to drop
```

This doesn't work in Firefox.

Timing Things Right

Another interesting use for scripting is to add timers to your Web pages. You can use a timer for two purposes: to do something at a specified time (like setting off an alarm clock at 6 AM) or to repeat something at a particular interval (like a metronome).

Say that you want to turn a green headline blue — as in the previous example — but instead of happening when the user hovers or clicks something, or when the page first loads, you want this event to happen a few seconds or minutes following the page load. To do that, you use a timer.

In this sample HTML page, I switch to VBScript to create, employ, and then destroy a timer:

```
<html>
<head>
<script LANGUAGE="VBScript">

function startTimer()
      timerhandle = setTimeout("changehead",3000)
end function

function stopTimer()
      clearTimeout(timerhandle)
end function
```

```
function changehead()
  h.style.color = "slateblue"
  h.style.fontSize = "36"
end function

</script>

</head>

<body onload="startTimer()" onunload="stopTimer()">

<h1 ID="h">Some headlines can change, all on their
          own...</h1>

</body>
</html>
```

In this example, you first create a script with three functions. The first function, which I named `startTimer`, sets the timer. It runs the function `changehead`: three seconds after this timer is started. The timing can be highly precise if you wish because it's specified in milliseconds (a millisecond is a thousandth of a second, so 3000 milliseconds equals three seconds):

```
function startTimer()
      timerhandle = setTimeout("changehead",3000)
```

This `startTimer` function is triggered when the page is loaded, by this `onload` event in the `<body>` element:

```
<body onload="startTimer()" onunload="stopTimer()">
```

After the page is unloaded, the timer is discarded, usually a good practice because it's no longer needed. The `onunload` event does that cleanup job.

The `changehead` function, when triggered by the timer, modifies the color and font size of the head with an `ID` of `h`:

```
function changehead()
  h.style.color = "slateblue"
  h.style.fontSize = "36"
end function
```

Cool, no? Now you can delay an effect, a filter, a transition or any other feature you want to make happen *some time after* the page loads. You can also delay events for a certain amount of time after the user clicks or some other event occurs.

The important point in this example is the word changehead, which is the name of the script function that you want executed when the timer finishes its countdown.

Changehead (or whatever function name you choose to use) is carried out automatically after the interval is over; three seconds in this example. (To make something happen after a delay of one minute, you would use 60,000 milliseconds.)

Here's what happens, blow by blow, when you load the source code from the previous example into a browser:

1. When the page is loaded (onload), the startTimer function is executed.

2. The startTimer function specifies that after 3000 milliseconds, the changehead function is started: timerhandle = setTimeout ("movep",3000).

3. After the timer counts down three seconds, the changehead function does two things to the style of the H1 object. It changes the color and adjusts the font size:

```
h.style.color = "slateblue"
h.style.fontSize = "36"
```

4. Notice that you can name a paragraph (or a headline or other HTML element) by using the ID attribute, like this: <h1 ID="h">. Then in a function, you can adjust that element's properties by specifying its name: h, or whatever ID you gave the element.

5. Finally, when the page is unloaded (onunload="stopTimer()"), the stopTimer function uses the clearTimeout command to destroy the timer.

TIP

Another use for delays is displaying a splash screen. You may want to show visitors an attractive graphic screen for a few seconds before displaying your Web site's home page. Consider displaying a five-second splash screen to intrigue them. Then display or fade into your real home page automatically (the user doesn't have to click anything — a timer does the work). To show a splash screen, display the graphic page until a timer counts down, and then hide that page and show your home page proper. This code shows you how to display one image (andy.jpg on my computer) for five seconds, and then replace that image with another named colorriot.jpg.

```
<html>
<head>
<script LANGUAGE="VBScript">

function startTimer()
```

```
        timerhandle = setTimeout("jump",5000)
end function

function jump()
document.location = "colorriot.jpg"
end function

function stopTimer()
        clearTimeout(timerhandle)
end function

</script>
</head>

<body onload="startTimer()" onunload="stopTimer()">

<img src="andy.jpg">
</body>
</html>
```

For the `document.location` value, you can provide a second .htm file if you wish. Here's how to load a Web page located on the root directory of c: drive on the same computer as the one on which the first .htm file resides:

```
document.location = "file:///C:/cheese.htm"
```

Grasping countdown timers

A countdown timer (which counts down from a set value, like a kitchen timer) is created by using the `settimeout` command, like this:

```
timerhandle = setTimeout("movep",3000)
```

You can use almost any name instead of `timerhandle` here (except a word already used by VBScript, such as `End` or `Function`). However, `timerhandle` seems like a good name for it. The `timerhandle` is just a name that's given to the timer when it's created by the above line of script (when the page with this script loads into a browser). You can later destroy this timer by using its name, as in this line:

```
clearTimeout(timerhandle)
```

The `clearTimeout` command removes the timer from the computer's memory (destroys it, really). The `clearTimeout` command isn't strictly necessary. Generally, you can count on the computer to destroy timers that are no longer in use. However, explicitly killing off a timer when your program is finished using it is considered good programming practice.

Employing metronome timers

To create a page where something repeats at intervals, you use the same timer object but in a slightly different way. In the previous two timer examples, you used the `setTimout` command to cause a delay, and then activated some behavior. If you want repeating behavior, you need a metronome type of timer. It's created by using the `setInterval` command, like this:

```
timerhandle = setInterval ("movep",200)
```

The difference between `setTimeout` and `setInterval` is that with `setInterval`, the function (`movep`, in this next example) is executed repeatedly instead of executed only once. Here's an example.

```
<html>
<head>

<script LANGUAGE="VBScript">

dim toggle

function startTimer()
      timerhandle = setInterval("movep",100)
end function

function stopTimer()
      clearTimeout(timerhandle)
end function

function movep()

toggle = not toggle

if toggle then
    para.style.color = "slateblue"
else
    para.style.color = "black"
end if

end function

</script>
</head>

<body onload="startTimer()" onunload="stopTimer()">

<p ID="para" style="font-size: 24px;">This text vibrates a
            little bit!</p>
</body>
</html>
```

Here the timer goes off at intervals of 100 milliseconds (ten times a second) because until the page unloads, you don't use the `stopTimer` function — and also because you continually re-execute the `movep` function. This function changes the text's font color from black and blue and back again, creating a subtle, but disturbing, throbbing quality. Don't stare at it too long or you might freak yourself out.

The following list shows the major events that happen as you run the preceding code example:

1. **When a Web page contains a section of** `script`, **any lines of programming that aren't enclosed in a** `Function. . . End Function` **(or** `Sub . . . End function`**) are executed immediately when the page loads.**

   In other words, in the preceding example, the line `dim toggle` is outside any `Function` or `Sub`. Therefore, the variable `toggle` is created when this page first loads into a browser. (The `dim` command creates a variable.)

   The main value of using the `dim` command to create a variable outside of any `Function` or `Sub` is that the variable can then be used by *all* the `Functions` and `Subs` anywhere in the current Web page. (Variables created *within* a `Function` or `Sub` can be used only by other lines of source code *within that single* `Function` or `Sub`.)

   In this example, you wanted to have a variable, `toggle`, that could hold information no matter what function was, or was not, currently executing. Because you create `toggle` outside the `Functions`, it can hold the information you give it as long as this page remains in the browser.

2. **When the** `startTimer` **function is executed (with the** `body onload` **command), the browser is told to execute the** `movep` **function every 80 milliseconds.**

   Note that this execution happens quite often because 1000 milliseconds is one second.

3. **The meat of this program is in the** `movep` **function. The line** `toggle = not toggle` **is like flipping a light switch.**

   If the variable `toggle` was true, it becomes false when you use the `not` command. If it was false, it becomes true.

4. **The variable** `toggle` **is tested. If it's true (**`if toggle then`**), the paragraph is displayed blue. If** `toggle` **is false (**`else`**), the paragraph turns black.**

5. **The** `movep` **function continues to toggle on and off, quite rapidly, until the** `stopTimer` **function is executed when the browser unloads this page, triggering the** `onunload="stopTimer()"` **command.**

You can find lots of scripts ready to copy and paste on the Internet. Consult some of the resources listed in Chapters 18 and 19.

Chapter 17

Testing and Debugging

● ●

In This Chapter

▶ When punctuation goes bad

▶ Handling browser compatibility problems

▶ Debugging CSS

▶ Validating HTML

● ●

Debugging, validating, parsing: Whatever you call it, at one time or another, you'll need to figure out what's going wrong. This chapter shows you techniques and introduces you to free tools that help you fix errors in your CSS and HTML code and double-check your Web page before you put it up on the Internet for all to see.

Checking Punctuation

The single best advice for those times when your CSS code isn't working is to check your punctuation. Unfortunately, CSS was designed to include several punctuations derived from the C-type computer languages. This means that you have to use braces, colons, and semicolons where more sensible punctuation — or no punctuation at all — would have worked just fine.

For example, take a look at the punctuation in this typical CSS style:

```
<html>
<head>

<style>

img {
border: silver outset;
border-width:16px;}
```

```
</style>

</head>
<body>

<img WIDTH=320px HEIGHT=264px src="GrandfatherHouse.jpg">

</body>
</html>
```

Everyone has gotten accustomed to HTML's perfectly serviceable punctuation techniques for years. For a property (such as the width attribute), you use the equals sign (=) to separate the property name (width) from the value that you assign to that property (320px, in the sample code above). If more than one property is present, they're separated by simple spaces, just like words in an ordinary sentence: width height src, and so on. The entire element is enclosed in < > symbols. Everyone is used to this punctuation and knows exactly how it works. It's clear, clean, and effective.

Then along comes CSS with the decision to replace greater-than (>)and less-than (<) symbols with the braces { } as a way of enclosing each style. Why couldn't they have made everyone's life simpler and just stuck to the traditional, well-established <> symbols? By changing the rules, they introduced lots of confusion and bugs. People who write CSS code now have to keep making mental notes and switching between HTML and CSS punctuation when writing the same fundamental grammatical structures of properties and their values. Also, you can no longer simply copy an HTML element with all its attributes, and then paste it into a CSS style rule. That would have been too convenient, too efficient.

What's more, HTML uses an equals sign to separate each property from its value. This is traditional, classic computer programming punctuation that has been in use for decades. Along come the wise ones at CSS and decide to make up some funny, unique trick of their own. Perhaps someone in some meeting said, "Hey, everyone understands and uses the equals sign. Let's stir things up and cause lots of bugs by making them use a colon in CSS code to separate a property from its value (border: silver). That way, two different punctuation styles are used for the same thing. Programmers and designers will keep getting them mixed up and have to waste a lot of time debugging their Web pages!" If I ever meet this joker, I'll have a few choice words for him or her.

Finally, HTML sensibly separated property/value pairs with spaces, like this:

```
width=320px height=264px
```

Note the space separating 320px from height in the preceding code example. Well, the spaces were replaced by the wise CSS designers. With what? With semicolons. The only reason I can think of for this casually malicious and entirely unnecessary complication is that in C-languages such as Java, beloved by academics, logical lines of code are separated by semicolons. Other than that usage (which is a different context completely), I can find no evidence that introducing a new, and bizarre, way of delimiting property/value pairs has any explanation at all. I'd sure like to hear from the comedian who first proposed this terrible idea. Maybe it was the same trickster who decided to separate properties from their values with colons.

To my mind, simply using the same punctuation for CSS styles that everyone was accustomed to from HTML would have made much more sense. That way, designers and programmers wouldn't have to keep switching mentally between the two techniques. A CSS style should be — but alas isn't — punctuated like HTML. It would look like this:

```
<img border=silver outset border-width=16px>
```

If you're concerned that the computer might get confused because outset and border-width don't have a semicolon between them, don't worry about it. The computer is perfectly capable of parsing such code. It has no trouble recognizing the difference between a value and a property name. Or if you're concerned that this line is less readable by us humans, just break the line into two lines, like this, in your code (the computer won't care):

```
<img border=silver outset
     border-width=16px>
```

Problem solved. *Or so it would seem.* Actually, in the real world, everyone has to accept that the CSS committee people decided to employ two punctuation systems operating side-by-side on the same information. One system only works in a CSS style, and other in HTML code. The more you work with CSS, the more often you'll find that your bugs result from simple punctuation mistakes that are hard to see. The real mystery is why this harebrained state of affairs was decided upon in the first place.

I cover this punctuation issue in depth here for two reasons. First, if I don't talk about it, I might go barking mad from sheer frustration. Second, demonstrating all the ways that CSS punctuation differs from HTML punctuation alerts you to the various traps you can fall into when writing a CSS rule. You now know all the differences in the punctuation where to look most of the time when your CSS styles don't work as you expect.

Of rebates and punctuation insanity

Yes, the punctuation madness is baffling, but I sometimes wonder if it isn't meant to be that way, like one of life's other little inefficiencies, rebates. Somebody is making a buck off the confusion. You buy because the price is low but then forget to send in the rebate card. Experts say that more than $500 million in rebates are unclaimed every year.

You can see why companies deliberately introduce all kinds of hassles into the rebate process: due dates in fine print (rebate ended last year), you left out one of the required items, you bought *two* and the rebate only works for one (fine print again), you accidentally damaged the bar code, and so on.

I suspect that at least some of the annoying and inefficient aspects of computer programming languages fall into this same category: deliberate confusion is designed into the "code" diction, punctuation, and syntax to preserve the jobs of people who program or teach programming. After all, if programming were straightforward, they couldn't sell their services. Everybody could tell computers how to behave, not just the elite.

Like it or not, designers and programmers must wrestle with the reality that CSS is less clear and efficient than it could have been. What you're faced with when writing CSS is the need to always stay on your toes. And — given the general lack of effective HTML and CSS code debugging messages — when your Web page doesn't work as expected after you load it into Internet Explorer, you should first check the punctuation. Punctuation gone awry is the source of most errors in CSS. Ensure that your open and close braces are in place, that you have semicolons and colons in the right places, and that you've not left off something else such as a close tag (such as using <script> but forgetting to insert the closing </script>, for instance).

Also, some experts suggest that you always write your styles the same way, so you get into the habit of including everything. One approach is to start each rule by first typing in the opening and closing braces { }. Then type each property and its ending semicolon. Finally, fill in the value for each property. This approach works for some people, cutting down on some errors. But common sources of errors, such as last-minute tweaking, aren't prevented by this technique.

Validating Your Work

Ensuring that your CSS or HTML code has no problems is called *validating*. This process can assist you in locating actual bugs and can also provide other useful information. For example, validation can warn you that you're using "nonstandard" HTML tags or other features that work in Internet Explorer but might not always be supported in future versions or that may not work in other browsers such as Netscape.

Ignoring Fringe Browsers

As I've mentioned elsewhere in this book, to me, Netscape and the other fringe browsers are of negligible impact on my programming because so few people use them. Internet Explorer is the standard — it won the browser wars. So I'm a bit puzzled why other books on CSS and HTML spend 30 percent of their time worrying about how to ensure compatibility with, for example, Netscape 4 (which probably nobody still uses) or Opera and the rest. You should see some of the multiple if . . . else complexity in some scripts — attempting to accommodate every last possible browser variation. Rather than spend lots of time on these minor compatibility issues, I've instead used the space saved to explore and demonstrate additional CSS features and capabilities.

Going back in time

You'll even find books including elaborate lists showing whether each CSS element, property, and value works with every browser, *along with every version* of every browser.

Who wants to go for the lowest common denominator? Why bother with browsers that are years old and whom nobody in their right mind is still using?

If you take compatibility issues to extreme, you have to avoid using CSS itself! For example, if you want to be sure that your Web page works on every possible device from PDAs to refrigerator doors with Internet LCDs, you must entirely avoid CSS. You have to use HTML version 3.2, and it doesn't include style sheets at all.

Most browsers are free for the download. So if somebody is still using an ancient version, they've got many more computing problems to wrestle with than seeing text in the wrong place on your Web page. My advice: Write and test your Web pages for Internet Explorer and you'll be just fine.

What if you must consider compatibility?

I do, however, realize that some designers must, for various reasons, take into account alternative browsers and older versions. If that describes you, I think you'll find most all the information on CSS in this book is still of use to you. It's merely that after designing your Web page, you have an extra step to take: Run the page through a validator, or, better yet, load it into Firefox, or Netscape 4, or whatever browsers you're worried about. You'll immediately see what, if anything, needs to be adjusted or worked around.

Only one version of IE at a time can be installed on a Windows computer.

Checking compatibility charts

You can find online compatibility lists and charts detailing browser compatibility for all CSS properties and other features. Here are some resources:

```
www.corecss.com/properties/full-chart.php
www.westciv.com/style_master/academy/browser_support/basic_
        concepts.html
www.quirksmode.org/css/contents.html
css.nu/faq/ciwas-mFAQ.html
```

To test how your Web page looks in a browser that doesn't support your CSS formatting styles, follow these steps

1. **Choose Tools⇨Internet Options in Internet Explorer.**

   The Internet Options dialog box opens.

2. **Click the Accessibility button.**

   The Accessibility dialog box opens.

3. **Check the various checkboxes under Formatting, particularly the Font Styles box.**

4. **Click OK twice.**

   The dialog boxes close and you see your Web pages without the deselected CSS formatting.

Sniffing browsers

Browsers are divided into two primary categories: uplevel and downlevel. Downlevel means that they support HTML 3.2 (no scripts, no CSS). Uplevel browsers support HTML 4.0 and later, and consequently they can also handle JavaScript 1.2 and CSS.

Experts suggest several solutions to handling browser incompatibilities, none of them entirely successful. You can provide a splash screen or special page that you show users *before* you show them your home page. On this page are links to alternative home pages that, for example, don't rely on CSS if the user's browser doesn't support it. However, who wants to put Internet Explorer users, who make up 95 out of the 100 visitors to your site, through this little quiz? Also, nothing's to stop other sites or search engines from providing links to your actual home page and just bypassing the quiz page.

A better solution is to automate the process. Have your page execute a little script when the user loads the page to test which browser and which version the user has. Then your page can make either dynamic adjustments to the styles (described in Chapter 16), display a warning to the user, or redirect their browser automatically to your non-CSS, or otherwise lower-grade, pages.

Such scripts are called *browser sniffers*. As with all scripts, they work only if the user hasn't disabled scripting in their browser security settings. If you want to experiment with sniffers, start here where you'll find additional details and working sniffers:

```
www.webreference.com/tools/browser/
```

Forcing users to upgrade

If you want to severely discipline any wayward visitors to your site using weak or outdated browsers, you can use what's called a DOM (document object model) sniffer. If they are using a browser that's not up to your standards (in other words, if your page won't look the way you like in their bad browser), tell them to upgrade. You redirect them to this location:

```
www.webstandards.org/upgrade/
```

There they are told why they should, if possible, upgrade, and to which browsers and versions. The site contains links to allow the user to download browser versions that are CSS-compliant, including IE v6 (v5 for Mac users), Netscape v7, Firefox, Galeon, Opera v7, Safari, and Konqueror.

If you want to take this approach and redirect the user, insert this script into the <head> section of your Web page:

```
<script>

<!-- //

if (!document.getElementById) {
    window.location = "http://www.webstandards.org/upgrade/"
}

    // -->
</script>
```

By using the window.location = command, you force the user's browser to the Internet page specified in quotation marks. The user doesn't click a link; the browser just automatically avoids displaying your Web page and instead displays, in this example, the Web Standards Project's page.

Trying Out the W3C Validator

W3C — the World Wide Web Consortium (*W* times 3, get it?) — offers a way to test your Web pages' HTML and CSS code. However, the W3C offers debugging utilities (they call them *validators*) that are so strict and exacting that you might want to consider alternative utilities.

Before you even resort to a professional utility, I suggest you first try to locate errors in your code by yourself. Not only do you find the problem fairly often, but this approach helps your to remember what to watch out for (what your personal boo-boos often are). Also, a validator tends to give you more information than you want. It might tell you not just what doesn't work, but also what doesn't work in some obscure browser, or what might not work in the future. It also makes quite a few "recommendations," like telling you that you should provide a generic font family just in case somebody doesn't have the one you're expecting.

To look at the validator, go to the main W3C page:

```
www.w3.org/
```

and click the <u>Validators</u> hyperlink. Alternatively, go directly here (this address was correct at the time of this writing, but may change):

```
http://jigsaw.w3.org/css-validator/
```

You can test your page three ways:

- ✔ Provide the validator with the URI (address) of the Web page or pure CSS external style file.
- ✔ Upload the code file (this is only for CSS files).
- ✔ Copy and paste the CSS code directly into the W3C Web page.

You're probably familiar with the term URL (Uniform Resource Locator), but the good folks at W3C call it instead a URI (Uniform Resource Identifier). They have their technical reasons for doing this.

Try the second validation approach (specifying a .css file on your hard drive to be uploaded for validation) by following these steps:

1. **From this book's Web site, copy this code:**

```
p
{
color: green;
text-align: center;
font-family: arial!Important;
```

```
font-size:18.0pt!Important
}

h1, h2
{
font-family: ravie!Important;
font-style: normal!Important
text-align: center;
}
```

2. **Paste the code into Notepad.**

3. **Choose File⇨Save As in Notepad.**

   The Save dialog box opens.

4. **Click the down arrow symbol to change the Save As Type list box from Text Documents (*.txt) to All Files.**

5. **Type in** myfirst.css **as the file name.**

6. **Click the down arrow symbol in the Save in list box at the top of the dialog box.**

   A list is displayed, showing various locations in your hard drive.

7. **Navigate through the list to locate the c: drive (the main root directory of c:)**

8. **Click the c:.**

   Your save now puts this file on c:.

9. **Click the Save button.**

   The file myfirst.css is now located on c:.

To test this CSS code, all you have to do now is to follow these steps:

1. **Open this CSS test page at**

   ```
   http://jigsaw.w3.org/css-validator/
   ```

2. **Find the section on that Web page titled Validate by Upload.**

3. **Click the Browse button on the Web page.**

   A Choose File dialog box opens.

4. **Navigate to locate your file at c:\myfirst.css.**

5. **Double-click c:\myfirst.css in the dialog box.**

   The dialog box closes and your file's address is now displayed in the Local CSS File text box on the Web page.

6. Click the Check button on the Web page.

You then see a report on the errors and the overall compliance of your CSS code. As an example, I got these results from the validator:

```
W3C CSS Validator Results for file://localhost/C:\MyFirst.css
To work as intended, your CSS style sheet needs a correct
            document parse tree. This means you should use
            valid HTML.
Errors
URI : file://localhost/C:\MyFirst.css
Line: 13 Context : h1 , h2
Parse Error - text-align: center;
Line: 14 Context : h1 , h2
Parse error - Unrecognized : }

Warnings
URI : file://localhost/C:\MyFirst.css

Line : 5 font-family: You are encouraged to offer a generic
            family as a last alternative
Line : 11 font-family: You are encouraged to offer a generic
            family as a last alternative
Valid CSS information

p {
color : blue;
text-align : center;
font-family : arial !important;
font-size : 18pt !important;
}
```

Whew!

Do you see why the validator claims to have found an error in the h1, h2 selector rule? The rule *does* contain an error, but the validator can't be specific about what the error is or even precisely where. Here's the validator's error message:

```
Line: 13 Context : h1 , h2
Parse Error - text-align: center;

Line: 14 Context : h1 , h2
Parse error - Unrecognized : }
```

The validator appears to have a problem with text-align: center;, but that code actually works just fine — it's not an error at all. Likewise, the validator says it doesn't recognize the colon and brace, whatever that means.

Hoping for helpful error messages

A really helpful error message would say specifically what the error is and where it's located. Finding the location of the error is often the biggest problem when debugging code.

At least the parser is correctly informing you that an error exists in either line 13, line 14, or both. That's useful information, but actually the error is not in either of these lines — just *near* them. The validator should be able to report the precise location, specify the error itself, and provide a suggested cure. That would be a truly helpful debugging utility.

The error in this code is common in languages like C and Java, and, thanks to the CSS committees, it's now unnecessarily common in CSS. A good error message would be specific, like this:

```
Line 12 is missing an ending semicolon:

font-style: normal!Important

To fix this error, add a semicolon to the end of this line,
        like this:

font-style: normal!Important;
```

Perhaps there's hope that one day that the validator (debugger) and the debuggers for other languages can actually be precise about a problem and offer a suggested cure. (JavaScript is pretty weak in this area too, and most languages have vague error messages and often point to the wrong location in the code.)

In any case, if you add the semicolon to the line in the .css file and then rerun the validation, you get this result (no error section this time):

```
W3C CSS Validator Results for file://localhost/C:\MyFirst.css
To work as intended, your CSS style sheet needs a correct
        document parse tree. This means you should use
        valid HTML.

Warnings
URI : file://localhost/C:\MyFirst.css

Line : 5 font-family: You are encouraged to offer a generic
        family as a last alternative
Line : 11 font-family: You are encouraged to offer a generic
        family as a last alternative
```

```
Valid CSS information

p {
color : green;
text-align : center;
font-family : arial !important;
font-size : 18pt !important;
}


h1 , h2 {
font-family : ravie !important;
font-style : normal !important;
text-align : center;
}
```

This time through the validator, the H1, H2 section has been moved down from the *error* zone into the *valid* zone (meaning the code now passes their tests).

When the validator issues a warning, that's less severe than an error. A warning just means that your code might not work universally on all past and future devices, including browsers from 1995 or Internet screens built into refrigerator doors. A warning means, well, your code does *work* in Internet Explorer, but you really should give a default font family, just in case Arial ever gets replaced by something else and you want to ensure that the font remains sans serif. Big freakin' deal.

Did that comment about a "correct document" send chills down your spine? The validator always displays the comment To work as intended, your CSS style sheet needs a correct document parse tree. This means you should use valid HTML. Actually, you can just ignore it. It's always there as a scold to hector you. Your HTML may well not have anything wrong with it — they're just telling you to check it. For more on that, see the section later in this chapter titled "Validating HTML."

Identifying property value problems

What kind of error message do you get if you try to use a value that can't work with a particular property — such as assigning 12px to the color property?

If you feed this CSS code to the validator:

```
p
{
color: 12px;
text-align: center;
}
```

You get this excellent answer — both specific and accurate about the location:

```
Line: 3 Context : p
Invalid number : color 12px is not a color value : 12px
```

So you see, the validator can come through when it really wants to. And, certainly, validating your CSS code is most useful in two situations:

✔ **When you've tried reading through the code to debug it, but cannot find the reason why your Web page is misbehaving or a style isn't working.** (The default black headline style appears, even though you're trying to turn it green, for example.)

✔ **Just before you're ready to publish your Web page on the Internet for all to see.** You want to find out whether any errors have slipped through.

Run your code through an HTML parser to ensure that you don't have an nasty surprises in that part of your Web page code either.

Sometimes, in the warning section, you'll find a valuable suggestion. Consider this possibility: You neglected to specify a background color for one of your paragraphs of text. You did specify that the foreground (the text characters themselves) should be dark green, and you assumed that the background would remain the default white. But what about those people who've got their own user style sheets turned on or are otherwise customizing their browser's behaviors and display characteristics? What if one of them has set the background to a color that makes your dark green text pretty much unreadable? The warning section of the validation report makes suggestions about this kind of problem, and even if you ignore many of those suggestions, at least you're able to consider them and make an informed decision.

Validating HTML

HTML errors can sometimes cause CSS errors. And, of course, your Web page is made up of both CSS and HTML, so you do need to test both types of code. Fortunately, many HTML parsers (utilities that read through code to see if tag pairs are matched, and so on) are available. *Parser, validator,* and *debugger* are just synonyms for the same idea: letting you know whether your code contains problems, potential (warnings) or real (errors).

I suggest you find a parser that's a bit less — shall I say, *authoritarian* — than the one offered by W3C. It criticizes lots of HTML code that works perfectly well in Internet Explorer. However, if you want to get the full rigorous treatment, here's how to get a reading from W3C's HTML debugger.

Just as CSS has had several versions, so too has HTML. To use the W3C valida-tor, you must specify at the top of an HTML document which version you're using before validating it. That way, the validator knows how to analyze your code. Declare your documents as HTML-4 compliant. (HTML 3 doesn't allow span, ID, style, or class attributes, among other shortcomings.) You'd really cramp your CSS styles if these attributes are missing, right? And if you've got them in your code, the HTML validator lists them as errors unless you specify HTML-4.

Go to this address for the HTML validator:

```
http://validator.w3.org/
```

If your Web page is already on the Internet, you can validate it by giving its URL (or URI, as the W3C calls it) address. The information that appears in the Address field of Internet Explorer when you visit a Web page is its URL.

If you're still working on your page and haven't published it yet, you can browse to an .htm file on your hard drive, just as you browsed to a .css file in the example earlier in this chapter of CSS validation.

Meeting some requirements

The HTML validator wants to know two things about your document: which version of HTML are you using (4 is the right answer) and which *flavor* (strict, transitional, or frameset). *Strict* means you aren't using any questionable or recently deprecated HTML code (code that's frowned-upon or intended for eventual replacement). *Transitional* means you're using some of the deprecated tags. If you want to include *framesets*, you have to specify that flavor. I suggest you use the loose transitional or frameset flavor. Here's what you should insert at the *top* of your .htm file (above the <html> tag):

```
<!DOCTYPE HTML PUBLIC "-//W3C//DTD HTML 4.01
          Transitional//EN"
          "http://www.w3.org/TR/html4/loose.dtd">
```

As you know after trying the various examples in this book, the browser doesn't care about the doctype "declaration" info. Some validators, though, do.

For a way to use !DOCTYPE to force IE (or other browsers) to be CSS standards-compliant, see Chapter 11, or take a look at this online discussion:

```
http://msdn.microsoft.com/library/default.asp?url=/library/en
          -us/dnie60/html/cssenhancements.asp
```

Test the W3C HTML validation now by following these steps:

1. **From this book's Web page, copy this code:**

```
<!DOCTYPE HTML PUBLIC "-//W3C//DTD HTML 4.01
        Transitional//EN"

"http://www.w3.org/TR/html4/loose.dtd">

<html>

<head>

<style>

body { margin-top: 20px; color: lightgray;}

</style>

</head>

<body>

<P>This is paragraph one.</P>


</body>
</html>
```

2. **Paste the code into Notepad.**

3. **Choose File⇨Save As in Notepad.**

   A Save dialog box opens.

4. **Click the down arrow symbol to change the Save As Type list box from Text Documents (*.txt) to All Files.**

5. **Type in** myfirst.htm **as the filename.**

6. **Click the down arrow symbol next to the Save in list box.**

   A list displays various locations on your hard drive.

7. **Navigate through the list to locate the c: drive (the main root directory of c:).**

8. **Click the c:.**

   Your save now puts this file on the c: drive.

9. **Click the Save button.**

   The file myfirst.htm is now located on c:.

Now follow these steps to validate this HTML code:

1. **Open this HTML validation page at**

   ```
   http://validator.w3.org/
   ```

2. **Find the section on that Web page titled Validate by File Upload.**

3. **Click the Browse button on the Web page.**

   A Choose File dialog box opens.

4. **Navigate to locate your file at c:\myfirst.htm.**

5. **Double-click c:\myfirst.htm in the dialog box.**

   The dialog box closes. Your file's address is now displayed in the Local File text box on the Web page.

6. **Click the Check button on the Web page.**

   You then see a report on the errors in, and warnings about, your HTML code.

The debugger might complain that you're sending ordinary text (text/plain) and it doesn't support plain text. Whatever. If you're determined to use this debugger, you can fiddle around with IIS or IE to try to specify a text/html MIME Content-Type value. Getting into all this is beyond the scope of this book. I tried using IE in a different computer and the W3C site accepted that .html file and parsed it.

Here's a shortcut: Try downloading Mozilla Firefox. It's free and the W3C debugger seems to find it more congenial. So if you experience problems using IE to send files to the validator, try Firefox.

Using Firefox, I managed to get a report from the debugger. It said that character encoding was missing (it almost always seems to say that) and that my page was not valid HTML 4.01 transitional (it almost always seems to say that, too).

As for errors in my code, the validator said that line 7 (`<style>`) needed a `type` to be specified (the `type` attribute is required, it said). It also complained about a missing end tag in line 13 for the `head` element, even though a `</head>` end tag *is* present. I assume that this is likely to be a side-effect because of the problem it sees with the `<style>` element. Browsers seem to have no problems with this simple HTML page, but the validator did. I tried providing the `type` attribute that it requested:

```
<style type="text/css">
```

Then I ran the page through the validator again (using Firefox). This time, it didn't find fault with the `style` element, but it still complained about that "missing" `</head>` end tag. Not willing to let this validator get the best of me, I then ran an .html file that I knew to be "fully compliant" through it and sure enough, it passed. This other file got this blessing from the validator: `The uploaded file was tentatively found to be valid.` A victory! Well, not a complete victory because it's just *tentatively* valid.

So I tried deleting various elements near the `<head>` element to see if removing something would trigger the same error message about the `<head>` end tag. Eureka! It's this:

```
<title>My Title</title>
```

If you omit the title element (optional, I always thought, because *browsers* don't care about it), the validator tells you that you're missing a head element. Well, that's not what's missing, but at least after some experimentation, I was able to satisfy the validator and get its tentative approval with the following change to the code:

```
<!DOCTYPE HTML PUBLIC "-//W3C//DTD HTML 4.01
          Transitional//EN"

"http://www.w3.org/TR/html4/loose.dtd">

<html>
<head>

<title>Some Supposedly Optional Title</title>

<style type="text/css">

body { margin-top: 25px; margin-bottom: 25px; margin-left:
          25px; margin-right: 25px; }

</style>

</head>

<body>

<P>This is paragraph one.</P>


</body>
</html>
```

Firefox offers some excellent developer extensions. You can easily download them by selecting Tools⇨Extensions, and then clicking the <u>Get More Extensions</u> link. You're taken to this page:

```
https://addons.update.mozilla.org/extensions/?application={ec
            8030f7-c20a-464f-9b0e-13a3a9e97384}
```

One very popular extension is Web Developer, which adds a menu and a tool-bar that offer the Web designer and programmer lots of useful extra features for both designing and debugging. One word of caution though about down-loading extensions: These are executables, so they can easily contain viruses or other damaging code. To me, the safe approach is to avoid downloading the latest, newest extensions (which by definition haven't yet been proven safe because few people have tried them out). On the other hand, popular, classic extensions like Web Developer are pretty much guaranteed safe. If an extension such as Web Developer posed a problem, you would hear about it pretty quickly in the computer press.

Finding a better bug trap

Some people like the strictness of the "official" validator, with its stern insis-tence on the most meticulous code. It's just not me (nor is it Microsoft, thank goodness). I got tired of that kind of infinite attention to inconsequential detail in graduate school. The further I went up the academic ladder, the nar-rower the focus. Some people thrive in this environment (take a look at any academic journal to see the kind of writing it produces — sometimes there are more footnotes than article text).

If you're like me, you may find this validator more trouble than it's worth. Happily, others are available. You can use the facilities built into Microsoft's Visual Studio, or try the Web Design Group's (WDG) CSS and HTML valida-tors. I've found them to be more flexible and friendly that the W3C utilities. Go here for the WDG HTML validation:

```
http://www.htmlhelp.com/tools/validator/upload.html
```

Or simply Google for *CSS validator* or *HTML validator* to find other good debugging utilities.

Debugging Script

Debugging programming is quite a bit more complex than debugging HTML or CSS code. In script, the possible side effects and complex interactions between program elements are much more extensive than between elements and attributes in markup languages like CSS and HTML.

Explaining how to debug programming code is quite beyond the scope of this book, not to mention rather off the topic. However, I do give you a few pointers in Chapter 18.

Part V
The Part of Tens

The 5th Wave   By Rich Tennant

"Sometimes I feel behind the times. I asked my 11-year old to build a web site for my business, and he said he would, only after he finishes the one he's building for his ant farm."

In this part . . .

This part is called The Part of Tens, after a mystic ritual performed once every 89 years on the island of Samnos, involving three large fish, green ribbons, and a goat. You really don't want to know. Actually, Part V is called The Part of Tens because both chapters in this part have ten items in them. Get it?

Anyway, Chapter 18 gives you some of the most important tips that a CSS designer needs to know: Things like watching out for invisible borders, taking care to prevent color clash, debugging scripts, how to braise carrots, and other hot tips. (Actually, this chapter has eleven tips because the carrot recipe is a tad off-topic.)

Chapter 19 is a catch-all of items that I wanted to tell you about, but couldn't find a good place for in the rest of the book. Some of the topics covered in this chapter include layering, visiting the official CSS site, upgrading HTML to CSS, and several good online resources, in the unlikely event that you come up with a question not answered in this book.

Chapter 18

Ten Great CSS Tips and Tricks

● ●

● ●

*L*otsa tips are scattered throughout this book. But, what the heck! Here are some more.

Letting Users Control Font Size

Try to avoid specifying the body font size. Don't do this, for example:

```
body {font-size: 24px;}
```

I used this code in Chapter 15 and similar code elsewhere throughout this book. I'm changing the body font size from whatever is set as the default in the browser to 24 pixels. *Don't do it.* People have set their browser's options to a text size that's readable for them. You don't know whether they've got a pixel resolution of 1680x1050 or 800x600 pixels. It makes a difference. The user should be the one to decide this issue, not you. Why did I do it in this book? Because it is a book. At default font sizes, screen shots used for the figures in this book wouldn't be readable, so I sometimes boosted the body text size to make it possible for the readers to see what I'm talking about.

Making Sure Your Borders Show Up

Here's a common head CSS programming head-scratcher:

```
p {border: 12px;}
```

In spite of this rule that you wrote, no border shows up around the paragraphs. You'd logically think that by specifying a border size, you'd see a border. Not so. Unless you also specify a border *style*, you don't get a border. The default style is *none*, so change it to include a style:

```
p {border: solid 12px;}
```

Watching Out for Color Clash

What if you specify a text color, but fail to specify a background color? Sounds harmless, but it can be a problem. Some users employ personal style sheets, including their favorite colors. What happens if a user specifies brown for their backgrounds and white for their text? Say that you specify brown for your text:

```
BODY {color: brown;}
```

The user won't see your text at all because their background color and your foreground (text) color are identical. The solution? *Always* specify a background if you're going to color the text. Then you have control over how the text looks against that background:

```
BODY {color: brown; background-color: yellow;}
```

Centering for Everyone

Centering elements on a Web page still isn't quite solved. It's a common enough task — you want some things centered on the page, such as certain kinds of titles and headlines. But how to do it?

One method is to put an element inside a div, and then center the div (this works in Netscape or Mozilla or Firefox and so on, but *not* in Internet Explorer). Setting a div's margin to zero and auto, you effectively center it in all browsers except IE:

```
<div style="width: 400px; background-color: lightblue;
        padding: 4px; margin: 0px auto;">
```

To center something in IE, you can use `text-align=center` (which is frowned upon by non-IE types):

```
<div style="text-align:center;">
```

The solution? Make everybody happy by wrapping a `div` with the `0px auto` inside another `div` with `text-align` set to `center`, like this:

```
<html>
<head>

<style>
</style>

</head>
<body>

<div style="text-align:center;">

<div style="background-color: lightblue; width: 400px;
padding: 4px; margin: 0px auto;">

<p>HERE I am...

</div></div>

</body>
</html>
```

Timing Blurring and Other Effects

Combine timers, scripting, and filters to create lots of dynamic visual effects. Try this cool effect in Internet Explorer:

```
<html>
<head>
<script LANGUAGE="VBScript">

dim counter

function startTimer()
        timerhandle = setInterval("sizeit",130)
end function
```

```
function stopTimer()
        clearTimeout(timerhandle)
end function

function sizeit()
counter = counter + 1
if counter > 49 then counter = 1
n = "blur(add=1, direction=125, strength=" & counter & ")"
divider.style.filter= n
end function
</script>

<style>

div {position: absolute; filter: blur(add=1, direction=15,
        strength=90";}

</style>

</head>

<body onload="startTimer()" onunload="stopTimer()">

<div id="divider">
<h1>This is a blur effect over time.</h1>
</div>
</body>
</html>
```

See an example of this effect in Figure 18-1. For more details on how to create these various effects, see Chapter 16.

Figure 18-1:
Imagine this effect moving, as if the shadow were slowly growing.

This is a blur effect over time.

Try varying the speed of the filter by adjusting the value 130 in this line:

```
timerhandle = setInterval("sizeit",130)
```

Debugging Script

Script and code-behind programming such as ASP.NET are such an important aspect of Web programming that you may want to know how to set breakpoints and otherwise debug scripts. Your best bet for IE work is to download the Microsoft script debugger from this location:

```
http://msdn.microsoft.com/library/default.asp?url=/downloads/
            list/webdev.asp
```

After you've installed it, you can turn it on while in Internet Explorer by choosing View ⇨ Script Debugger ⇨ Open. You then see the debugger (it works with both VBScript and JScript), as shown in Figure 18-2:

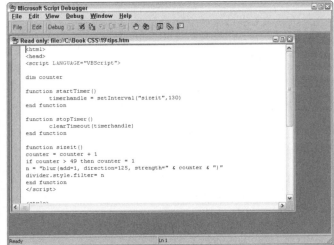

Figure 18-2:
Use this
debugger to
get your
scripts
working
right.

To ensure that the debugger works, follow these steps:

1. **In Internet Explorer, choose Tools⇨Internet Options.**

    The Internet Options dialog box opens.

2. **Click the Advanced tab.**

3. **Scroll down the Settings list box until you locate the Browsing section.**

4. **Uncheck the following two boxes: Disable Script Debugging (Internet Explorer) and Disable Script Debugging (Other).**

5. **Check the Display a Notification About Every Script Error Entry (this is optional).**

Go here for instructions on setting breakpoints, stepping through code (both often very useful techniques), looking at variables, editing variables (a command window), and other features:

```
http://msdn.microsoft.com/library/default.asp?url=/library/en
        -us/sdbug/Html/sdbug_1.asp
```

Finding a List Apart (Get It?)

One source for excellent ideas, samples, and articles — submitted by some of the most talented Web designers around — is to be found here:

```
www.alistapart.com/topics/css/
```

You can find some really cutting-edge CSS tricks and techniques described here. And who knows? Maybe someday you'll send in a cool idea or two of your own.

Using Your Own Bullets in Lists

With CSS, designing custom bullets in a graphics program and then assigning them to list items is easy. The following code produces the result shown in Figure 18-3:

```
<HTML>
<HEAD>
<style>

ul { list-style-image: url("mybullet.jpg"); font: 32px; }

</style>
</HEAD>
<body>

<ul>
<li>first
<li>second
<li>third
</ul>

</body>
</html>
```

Figure 18-3:
Add custom-designed bullets to your lists the easy CSS way.

◆ first
◆ second
◆ third

When you cut your custom bullet down to size by cropping it in the graphics program, leave some white space on the right size so that the bullet won't butt right up against the text items. Another tip: Be sure to put the .jpg or .gif graphic file in the same folder as the .htm file that contains the code above. Otherwise, the browser won't know how to find the graphic file. (Also see the next section on specifying locations for graphics.)

Specifying Graphics Locations

If you store a graphics file in the same folder as your .htm or .html file, the HTML code needs only the name of the graphics file, like this:

```
list-style-image: url("mybullet.jpg")
```

However, if the file is in another location, you must provide the path to that location, and do some bizarre punctuating as well — adding a ///, for some reason. This next example finds this file in the root directory of the c: drive:

```
list-style-image: url("file:///C:\mause.jpg")
```

Here's a file located in the \photos subdirectory of the f: drive:

```
list-style-image: url("file:///F:\Photos\mause.jpg")
```

Here's the additional bizarre punctuation (///\\) you must add for a local net-work location:

```
list-style-image: url("file:///\\Hp\servr\PHOTOS\mause.jpg")
```

If you keep your graphic files on an Internet site, provide the URL address.

Lastly, if your graphic file is stored on the space shuttle, use this punctuation:

```
"file:///\\\\\\\/^^^\\outerspace\servr\PHOTOS\mause.jpg"
```

The same punctuation and conventions are used when specifying the `src=` attribute to load a graphic into an HTML `<img >`element.

You might not see some of your graphics when you move your Web pages from your local computer to a server to post them on the Internet. If that happens, check file paths to ensure that the graphics files are located where your code says they are. The simplest tactic is to just keep all dependency files (such as graphics files) in the same directory as your .htm and .css files. That way, you can use *relative* paths, meaning you don't specify any path at all in your code, just the filename. The browser understands it should look for your graphics in the same path that it found the HTML file.

Combining Classes

You can save yourself some time and trouble by defining classes that are later combined, like adjectives combine with nouns. Say that you want some of your paragraphs framed in green, some in blue, and others in pink. You could create a separate class for each kind of paragraph, *or* you could be clever and create a general border style class, and three additional classes for the coloring. Here's how it works. First, you create four styles, and then you combine the class names in the HTML elements when you use the `class=` attribute:

```
<HTML>
<HEAD>

<style>

.framed {
          border: solid 3px red;
          padding: 6px;}

.pink { background-color: pink; }
.blue { background-color: blue; }
.green { background-color: green; }


</style>
</HEAD>
<body>
```

```
<p class="framed green">
You can save yourself some time and trouble by defining
          classes that are later combined, like adjectives
          combine with nouns.
</p>

<p class="framed blue">
You can save yourself some time and trouble by defining
          classes that are later combined, like adjectives
          combine with nouns.
</p>

<p class="framed pink">
You can save yourself some time and trouble by defining
          classes that are later combined, like adjectives
          combine with nouns.
</p>

</body>
</html>
```

Aunt Mildred's Glazed Carrots

Here's a prize-winning recipe for braised carrots.

1. **Cook peeled carrots in a half cup of water and two tablespoons of butter.**

2. **Sprinkle on a teaspoon of brown sugar and a pinch of tarragon.**

3. **Simmer until water disappears (a few minutes), and then gently simmer in butter until carrots are just tender.**

   This will take a few more minutes; keep testing with a fork.

4. **Now turn the fish (assuming you're also cooking a fish).**

Mr. and Mrs. Ratlick — who both look like Elton John — were the vegetable judges at the 1992 State Fair in Seeping Bog, La. and they awarded my Aunt Mildred second prize for this recipe. Is this the wrong book for a recipe? In any case, you didn't get cheated because this is the eleventh tip in this chapter; the other ten are about CSS. Try the carrots. They should have won first prize.

Chapter 19

Ten Topics That Don't Fit Elsewhere in the Book (But Are Important)

. . . .

In This Chapter

▶ Visiting the official site: Be afraid

▶ Upgrading HTML to CSS

▶ Reading good tutorials and reference information

▶ Nailing down inheritance

▶ Getting explanations about complicated rules

▶ Offering alternatives

▶ Allowing the user to decide

▶ Considering Visual Studio

▶ Playing with columns

▶ Layering

. . . .

Don't take the title of this chapter as a confession of my disorganization and confusion when I planned this book. No, it merely represents some ideas and resources I think you should know about, even though they don't comfortably fit within other chapters. Take a look at all the other chapters and you'll see that the book is not chaotic or, as your grandmother might say, higgledy-piggledy. It's a model of method and logic. Really.

So, at least please glance at the headings in this chapter and see if some of these subjects interest you. I think you'll find a few topics here worthy of your inspection.

Keeping Current via the Internet

The most thorough descriptions of the latest proposals, drafts, and recommendations can be found at the official site for CSS:

```
www.w3.org/Style/CSS/
```

At this site, you find tutorials, news, reviews of utilities, actual utilities (such as the various "validators" that check your HTML or CSS code for errors described in Chapter 17), and other information. Although heavily slanted toward the academic community — where theory and minutia so often triumph over efficiency and common sense — you can also find practical advice at this site too. True, you must ferret out the practical info because it's surrounded by smoke and mist. Let me be plain: I suggest you first try some of the other sources of CSS information described later in this chapter. (However, if you have any suggestions about future CSS features, you can send them to the official committees via this site, so keep that in mind.)

Upgrading HTML Web Pages to CSS

Many designers find CSS so efficient that they decide to translate their existing HTML-based Web pages into CSS-based pages. This involves more than simply replacing <font> tags, but you'll likely find the payoff well worth the effort. You can find an excellent, step-by-step tutorial on migrating a site from HTML to CSS here:

```
www.websitetips.com/info/css/intro1/
```

Finding Good Tutorials and Reference Information

Besides this book (and I say this in all humility), one of the best places to find solid, useful advice and tutorial lessons about CSS (and related technologies as well) is the w3Schools site. It's good for looking up details about CSS features, finding code examples, or just reading some well-done descriptions of how and why CSS works. Take a look here:

```
www.w3schools.com/css/default.asp
```

In addition to CSS information, this site explores many other topics related to Internet programming: scripting, XML (and its many flavors), DHTML, ASP.NET, SOAP (Simple Object Access Protocol, a light, flexible communications protocol built on XML), DOM (the Document Object Model, a standardized model of the structure of an XML object), and so on.

Also take a look at these sites for valuable, advanced CSS information:

```
www.nypl.org/styleguide
www.quirksmode.org/
```

Remembering Inheritance

One problem that many CSS authors, including *moi,* face is confusion about why some styles are inherited and others are not. For example, say that you specify that the text in a paragraph should be green, but somehow the entire text is not green after all. Consider this example:

```
<p style="color: green;">This paragraph includes
        <strong>boldface</strong> and also a link <a
        href="http://www.ebay.com/">eBay</A> to a Web
        page.
</p>
```

You specified green in your style, yet the hyperlink text (eBay here) isn't green. It's blue or whatever color the user's browser specifies for hyperlinks. A browser rule wins over your style. But because the browser has no rule for `<strong>`, *that* element turns green (inherits the color from the parent paragraph element). So if you find yourself perplexed about why some style isn't being inherited, chances are you're dealing with this issue. If you really, really want to turn the link text green, you must override the browser style by adding a style to that link, like this:

```
<p style="color: green;">This paragraph includes
        <strong>boldface</strong> and also a link <a
        style="color: green;"
        href="http://www.ebay.com/">eBay</A> to a Web
        page.
</p>
```

The SelectORacle: Getting Explanations About Complicated Rules

Do you have a CSS style so complex that you're not sure even you, the author, understand it? Or did you come across an interesting Web page and look at the source, only to discover a line of CSS code that you simply can't visualize, like this one:

```
body > h2:not(:first-of-type):not(:last-of-type);
```

What does that CSS code mean? What does it select in the body? Some H2 headlines, but *which ones*?

To find a well-explained answer, a translation of the meaning of the rule, and also get a list of any possible errors, go to this site:

```
http://gallery.theopalgroup.com/selectoracle/
```

You'll be glad you did. Explanations in English or Spanish are available. What does the SelectORacle say about that H2 rule? Here's his/her/its answer:

"Selects any h2 element that is not a first child of its type and that is not a last child of its type, that is a child of a body element."

For an automated translation, this oracle does a pretty fine job. It can be especially helpful in clarifying complicated relationships.

Providing Alternatives

For space conservation and other reasons, I've avoided using the alt attribute with the img element in this book. In plain English, when I displayed a graphic, I didn't simultaneously supply a text explanation of that graphic. The text is supposed to fill in the gap left if, for example, the user has a slow Internet connection (or a device that has a very small screen like that of a cell phone or PDA) and, consequently, a graphic cannot be displayed. Another scenario: The blind often listen to audio versions of Web pages. They appreciate hearing a text description of the graphics that they can't see. These are all valid reasons for using alt.

```
<IMG SRC="seashore.jpg" ALT="This is a pleasant, if clichèd,
          photo of a typical, deserted Aussie beach.">
```

"So, why didn't you use alt?" I can hear someone saying. "What's *wrong* with you?"

My defense is straightforward. Many computer books include long code examples that go on and on, sometimes for pages. I think that's bad practice. Sample code should make its point as simply and clearly as possible. I don't want the reader struggling through lots of code that's not related to the topic being illustrated. So I leave out as much as I can (for example, it's desirable to use the `<title>` element in your Web pages, but you won't find that in this book).

Another alternative technique, although perhaps less important than `alt`, is providing a default font family. You do this on the assumption that not everyone has, for example, Microsoft's famous sans serif font Arial. Yet you want even those viewers to see a sans font (not a serif font, like Times Roman). This isn't essential, but it's nice. Even some validators that check CSS code suggest that you do this, if they catch you specifying a particular font family, like this:

```
p
{
font-family: arial
}
```

The suggestion is that you specify the font you really want first, and then you can add any additional fonts that you want to use as substitutes. Finally, if *none* of your substitutes are available (where *are* these people with zero fonts?), you end your wish list with a generic font, of which CSS has five: Serif, Sans Serif, Monospace, Cursive, and Fantasy. I suggest that you stick with the first three, unless you design wedding invitations (Cursive) or work for a clown school (Fantasy). Here's how to add a generic font family:

```
p
{
font-family: arial, sans-serif
}
```

Letting the User Decide

How about providing some alternative style sheets, rather than just enforcing one look on your Web documents? Who gets to select between these alternatives? Your audience, the viewers of your Web pages, the welcome guests. I'm not suggesting that you become as superhumanly accommodating and polite as some societies. I understand that in some countries, hurricanes are respectfully described as "guest winds." I'm not prepared to go that far. But civility is always welcome, and users usually appreciate having some say in how things look.

Netscape 6 lists any alternative styles in its View⇨Use Stylesheet menu. Internet Explorer doesn't offer this feature, but users can adjust their color preferences, for instance, by following these steps:

1. **Choose Tools⇨Internet Options in Internet Explorer.**

   The Internet Options dialog box opens.

2. **Click the General tab.**

3. **Click the Colors button.**

   Make changes in the Colors dialog box that opens and click OK.

Similarly, from the General tab, you can click the Fonts button to modify those.

Don't follow Netscape's example (it's not convenient for users to check a menu each time they visit a new Web page, just to see if alternative styles are available). Instead, describe alternative styles right on your Web page and provide links for users to click to shift to a new style. Perhaps you have a style for fewer graphics or larger text (for people with vision problems). You could also vary the styles based on the user's favorite color or personal hobbies. It's simply always nice to ask a guest if they want something to drink, and if so, *what would they prefer*. Even a guest wind appreciates consideration.

If you want to have alternative style sheets for Netscape menus, just add extra `link` elements in your `head` section, like this (the *title* appears in the menu):

```
<link type="text/css" rel="stylesheet" title="Oldstyle"
href="MyDefault.css">

<link type="text/css" rel="alternate stylesheet"
          title="Conservative" href="MyDefault.css">

<link type="text/css" rel="alternate stylesheet"
title="Out There" href="MyDefault.css">
```

To provide alternatives for most of the world (Internet Explorer users), you could insert `<a>` elements in the body of your document that can simply send the user to a different page, or an alternative site altogether. This isn't a CSS solution, though. So if you want to switch styles via CSS external style sheets (as the Netscape solution does), you have to write a script for IE. For examples, go here:

```
http://www.alistapart.com/
```

Exploring Visual Studio

Several years ago, starting in 1997 with Visual Interdev, Microsoft managed to merge all of its programming languages and programming tools into a single suite of tools, now called Visual Studio. You'll find lots of ways to create Web sites, attach databases to them, build modules in several languages (that can work together), and otherwise simplify life for programmers and people creating Web sites. CSS was not omitted from this suite.

Although many Web developers and programmers in other fields are rather unhappy with Microsoft, the company remains difficult to ignore. For good or ill, Microsoft sets the standards and will continue to do so for the foreseeable future. Developers and programmers who refuse to use Microsoft products are a bit like drivers who refuse to use highways. It's possible to do but inconvenient.

If you haven't looked it over, you might want give Visual Studio a try. Inexpensive versions are available on eBay. Sure, other CSS editors are out there, but none offers the huge number of features built into Visual Studio. None comes remotely close. We're talking advanced debugging, macro facilities, direct connection to databases, and hundreds of tools, wizards, controls, add-ins, and other features that make the journey from idea to finished Web site much easier and faster. If you prefer the back roads, more power to you (and I mean that literally). If you want the highway, no other programming suite is even worth considering.

Some may say that this book is too Microsoft-centric, but my only response is to look at the marketplace. The huge majority of *users* (as opposed to some computer professionals for whom Microsoft can do nothing right) are overwhelmingly Microsoft-centric too.

Figure 19-1 provides a look at some of the features in the CSS design area of Visual Studio.

 During 2005, Microsoft is rolling out a set of programming products it calls Express versions. Microsoft touts these technologies — including Visual Web Dev 2005 Express (ASP.NET) — as products that expand the Visual Studio line to include easy-to-use tools for hobbyists and novices who want to build dynamic Windows applications and Web sites. All the same, these are powerful products. For example, the Visual Basic Express version is actually capable of doing what the "professional" version can do. The primary difference is that the Express version has a friendlier user interface (fewer options are immediately visible, so you don't get overwhelmed) and a less technical slant (so beginners can get acquainted without feeling threatened). Give these products a try. The beta versions are free for the download now at

`http://lab.msdn.microsoft.com/express/`

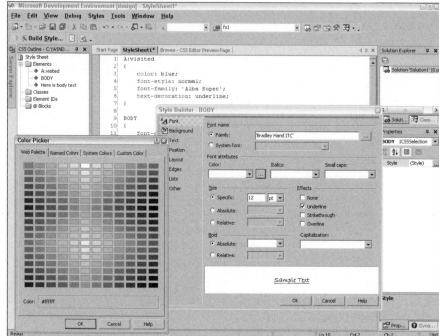

Figure 19-1:
If you plan to do any serious Web site development — no matter what kind — give Visual Studio a try.

Rediscovering Columns

Lots of sites (like those for newspapers and magazines) cry out for columnar layouts. Web pages often look best when the text is divided into easily-scanned widths, perhaps two or three columns per page. Maybe you remember from Chapter 12 the exploration of various ways to use columns in your Web pages that you can do with pure CSS, without resorting to tables.

However, there are additional techniques involving columns you might want to experiment with. If this topic is of further interest to you, try visiting this Web site, which specializes in CSS column design and has excellent information and resource lists for other aspects of CSS as well:

```
http://glish.com/css/
```

Playing with Positions

Setting the CSS `position` property to `absolute` enables you to superimpose elements to your heart's content. The following sample code paints text on top of text. This is also one way of adding simple shadows (merely offset the absolute positions by a small amount, as in this example). Also notice that the order in which you place these divisions matters: They're painted on the browser window in the order in which they're listed. So, in this example, the last `div`, colored hot pink, is *on top of* the other two. Its characters are superimposed on the other text, as shown in Figure 19-2.

```
<HTML>

<HEAD>
</HEAD>

<BODY">

<DIV style="position: absolute;
top: 35px;
left: 150px;
color:lightgreen;
font-size: 90pt ">
SUPER
</DIV>

<DIV style="position: absolute;
top: 98px;
left: 181px;
font-size: 40pt;
font-style: italic;
letter-spacing: .9cm;
color: gray;">imposition
</DIV>

<DIV style="position: absolute;
top: 95px;
left: 179px;
font-size: 40pt;
font-style: italic;
letter-spacing: .9cm;
color: hotpink;">imposition
</DIV>

</BODY>
</HTML>
```

Figure 19-2:
Experiment
with super-
imposing
elements
on top of
each other
by using
absolute
positioning.

Index

translucence
  Mozilla Firefox browser features,
    268–269
  with stacking, 82–84
trapped white space, 163
tree structure, inheritance
  branches, 255–256
  parents and children, 254–255
tutorials, 330–331
typefaces
  capitalization, 104–105
  drop shadow, 105–106
  font family, 62
  image and, 85
  line height, adjusting, 101–103
  monospace, avoiding, 90–91
  Optima, 89
  points specifying size and position, 107
  Roman, 92–94
  serif versus sans serif, 87–88
  simple style, 96–97
  sizes, 97–99
  small caps, 96
  synonymous, 90
  system styles, 91–92
  text, 87–92
  underline and strikethrough, 103–104
  variants, 94–95
  weight, specifying, 95

• U •

ultra kerning, 131–133
underline
  paragraphs, 171
  words, 103–104
Uniform Resource Locator. *See* URL
universal selector, 49
unnumbered list, 262
unusual positioning, tables and, 217–221
upgrading
  browsers, forcing visitors to, 303
  HTML pages to CSS, 330

uplevel browsers, 302–303
uppercase
  enlarged overlapping at start of
    paragraph, 160–162
  headlines, 88
  kerning, 131
  specifying all, 104–105
uppercase letters, smaller (drop caps)
  design rules, 160–162
  false pseudo-element (first-letter),
    274–275
  left float, 193
upper-roman numbered lists, 209
URL (Uniform Resource Locator)
  case-sensitivity, 41
  link formatting, 49, 270–272
  validating Web page at, 310
user interface
  buttons, 121, 276–277
  image-exchange script, 244–246
  text, considering, 85–86
users
  alternative style sheets, providing,
    333–334
  redirecting to browser upgrade
    site, 303
  who disable scripts, programming for,
    280–282

• V •

validating work
  HTML, 309–314
  importance, 300
  W3C tool, 304–309
value
  attribute selector matching, 52
  color, validating, 308–309
  defined, 34–35
  language, matching, 53
  semicolon, leaving out, 62

INESS, CAREERS & PERSONAL FINANCE

0-7645-5307-0

0-7645-5331-3 *†

Also available:

- Accounting For Dummies †
  0-7645-5314-3
- Business Plans Kit For Dummies †
  0-7645-5365-8
- Cover Letters For Dummies
  0-7645-5224-4
- Frugal Living For Dummies
  0-7645-5403-4
- Leadership For Dummies
  0-7645-5176-0
- Managing For Dummies
  0-7645-1771-6

- Marketing For Dummies
  0-7645-5600-2
- Personal Finance For Dummies *
  0-7645-2590-5
- Project Management For Dummies
  0-7645-5283-X
- Resumes For Dummies †
  0-7645-5471-9
- Selling For Dummies
  0-7645-5363-1
- Small Business Kit For Dummies *†
  0-7645-5093-4

ME & BUSINESS COMPUTER BASICS

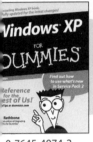

0-7645-4074-2

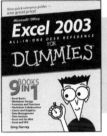

0-7645-3758-X

Also available:

- ACT! 6 For Dummies
  0-7645-2645-6
- iLife '04 All-in-One Desk Reference
  For Dummies
  0-7645-7347-0
- iPAQ For Dummies
  0-7645-6769-1
- Mac OS X Panther Timesaving
  Techniques For Dummies
  0-7645-5812-9
- Macs For Dummies
  0-7645-5656-8

- Microsoft Money 2004 For Dummies
  0-7645-4195-1
- Office 2003 All-in-One Desk Reference
  For Dummies
  0-7645-3883-7
- Outlook 2003 For Dummies
  0-7645-3759-8
- PCs For Dummies
  0-7645-4074-2
- TiVo For Dummies
  0-7645-6923-6
- Upgrading and Fixing PCs For Dummies
  0-7645-1665-5
- Windows XP Timesaving Techniques
  For Dummies
  0-7645-3748-2

D, HOME, GARDEN, HOBBIES, MUSIC & PETS

0-7645-5295-3

0-7645-5232-5

Also available:

- Bass Guitar For Dummies
  0-7645-2487-9
- Diabetes Cookbook For Dummies
  0-7645-5230-9
- Gardening For Dummies *
  0-7645-5130-2
- Guitar For Dummies
  0-7645-5106-X
- Holiday Decorating For Dummies
  0-7645-2570-0
- Home Improvement All-in-One
  For Dummies
  0-7645-5680-0

- Knitting For Dummies
  0-7645-5395-X
- Piano For Dummies
  0-7645-5105-1
- Puppies For Dummies
  0-7645-5255-4
- Scrapbooking For Dummies
  0-7645-7208-3
- Senior Dogs For Dummies
  0-7645-5818-8
- Singing For Dummies
  0-7645-2475-5
- 30-Minute Meals For Dummies
  0-7645-2589-1

ERNET & DIGITAL MEDIA

0-7645-1664-7

0-7645-6924-4

Also available:

- 2005 Online Shopping Directory
  For Dummies
  0-7645-7495-7
- CD & DVD Recording For Dummies
  0-7645-5956-7
- eBay For Dummies
  0-7645-5654-1
- Fighting Spam For Dummies
  0-7645-5965-6
- Genealogy Online For Dummies
  0-7645-5964-8
- Google For Dummies
  0-7645-4420-9

- Home Recording For Musicians
  For Dummies
  0-7645-1634-5
- The Internet For Dummies
  0-7645-4173-0
- iPod & iTunes For Dummies
  0-7645-7772-7
- Preventing Identity Theft For Dummies
  0-7645-7336-5
- Pro Tools All-in-One Desk Reference
  For Dummies
  0-7645-5714-9
- Roxio Easy Media Creator For Dummies
  0-7645-7131-1

SPORTS, FITNESS, PARENTING, RELIGION & SPIRITUALITY

0-7645-5146-9

0-7645-5418-2

Also available:

✓Adoption For Dummies
0-7645-5488-3

✓Basketball For Dummies
0-7645-5248-1

✓The Bible For Dummies
0-7645-5296-1

✓Buddhism For Dummies
0-7645-5359-3

✓Catholicism For Dummies
0-7645-5391-7

✓Hockey For Dummies
0-7645-5228-7

✓Judaism For Dummies
0-7645-5299-6

✓Martial Arts For Dummies
0-7645-5358-5

✓Pilates For Dummies
0-7645-5397-6

✓Religion For Dummies
0-7645-5264-3

✓Teaching Kids to Read For Dummi
0-7645-4043-2

✓Weight Training For Dummies
0-7645-5168-X

✓Yoga For Dummies
0-7645-5117-5

TRAVEL

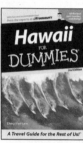

0-7645-5438-7

0-7645-5453-0

Also available:

✓Alaska For Dummies
0-7645-1761-9

✓Arizona For Dummies
0-7645-6938-4

✓Cancún and the Yucatán For Dummies
0-7645-2437-2

✓Cruise Vacations For Dummies
0-7645-6941-4

✓Europe For Dummies
0-7645-5456-5

✓Ireland For Dummies
0-7645-5455-7

✓Las Vegas For Dummies
0-7645-5448-4

✓London For Dummies
0-7645-4277-X

✓New York City For Dummies
0-7645-6945-7

✓Paris For Dummies
0-7645-5494-8

✓RV Vacations For Dummies
0-7645-5443-3

✓Walt Disney World & Orlando For Dum
0-7645-6943-0

GRAPHICS, DESIGN & WEB DEVELOPMENT

0-7645-4345-8

0-7645-5589-8

Also available:

✓Adobe Acrobat 6 PDF For Dummies
0-7645-3760-1

✓Building a Web Site For Dummies
0-7645-7144-3

✓Dreamweaver MX 2004 For Dummies
0-7645-4342-3

✓FrontPage 2003 For Dummies
0-7645-3882-9

✓HTML 4 For Dummies
0-7645-1995-6

✓Illustrator CS For Dummies
0-7645-4084-X

✓Macromedia Flash MX 2004 For Dum
0-7645-4358-X

✓Photoshop 7 All-in-One Desk
Reference For Dummies
0-7645-1667-1

✓Photoshop CS Timesaving Techniq
For Dummies
0-7645-6782-9

✓PHP 5 For Dummies
0-7645-4166-8

✓PowerPoint 2003 For Dummies
0-7645-3908-6

✓QuarkXPress 6 For Dummies
0-7645-2593-X

NETWORKING, SECURITY, PROGRAMMING & DATABASES

0-7645-6852-3

0-7645-5784-X

Also available:

✓A+ Certification For Dummies
0-7645-4187-0

✓Access 2003 All-in-One Desk
Reference For Dummies
0-7645-3988-4

✓Beginning Programming For Dummies
0-7645-4997-9

✓C For Dummies
0-7645-7068-4

✓Firewalls For Dummies
0-7645-4048-3

✓Home Networking For Dummies
0-7645-42796

✓Network Security For Dummies
0-7645-1679-5

✓Networking For Dummies
0-7645-1677-9

✓TCP/IP For Dummies
0-7645-1760-0

✓VBA For Dummies
0-7645-3989-2

✓Wireless All In-One Desk Referenc
For Dummies
0-7645-7496-5

✓Wireless Home Networking For Dum
0-7645-3910-8

TH & SELF-HELP

645-6820-5 *†

0-7645-2566-2

Also available:

- Alzheimer's For Dummies
  0-7645-3899-3
- Asthma For Dummies
  0-7645-4233-8
- Controlling Cholesterol For Dummies
  0-7645-5440-9
- Depression For Dummies
  0-7645-3900-0
- Dieting For Dummies
  0-7645-4149-8
- Fertility For Dummies
  0-7645-2549-2

- Fibromyalgia For Dummies
  0-7645-5441-7
- Improving Your Memory For Dummies
  0-7645-5435-2
- Pregnancy For Dummies †
  0-7645-4483-7
- Quitting Smoking For Dummies
  0-7645-2629-4
- Relationships For Dummies
  0-7645-5384-4
- Thyroid For Dummies
  0-7645-5385-2

ATION, HISTORY, REFERENCE & TEST PREPARATION

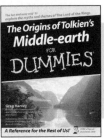

-7645-5194-9

0-7645-4186-2

Also available:

- Algebra For Dummies
  0-7645-5325-9
- British History For Dummies
  0-7645-7021-8
- Calculus For Dummies
  0-7645-2498-4
- English Grammar For Dummies
  0-7645-5322-4
- Forensics For Dummies
  0-7645-5580-4
- The GMAT For Dummies
  0-7645-5251-1
- Inglés Para Dummies
  0-7645-5427-1

- Italian For Dummies
  0-7645-5196-5
- Latin For Dummies
  0-7645-5431-X
- Lewis & Clark For Dummies
  0-7645-2545-X
- Research Papers For Dummies
  0-7645-5426-3
- The SAT I For Dummies
  0-7645-7193-1
- Science Fair Projects For Dummies
  0-7645-5460-3
- U.S. History For Dummies
  0-7645-5249-X

Get smart @ dummies.com®

- **Find a full list of Dummies titles**
- **Look into loads of FREE on-site articles**
- **Sign up for FREE eTips e-mailed to you weekly**
- **See what other products carry the Dummies name**
- **Shop directly from the Dummies bookstore**
- **Enter to win new prizes every month!**

CSS Web Design For Dummies®

Cheat Sheet

Common CSS Properties and Values

Units of Measure

px	pixels
em	M-width
pt	point
in	inches
mm	millimeter
cm	centimeter
pc	picas
ex	x-height

The Font Properties

font
font-family
font-size
font-style
font-variant
font-weight

The Text Properties

letter-spacing
word-spacing
line-height
vertical-align
text-align
text-decoration
text-indent
text-transform

The Border Properties

border-top-color
border-right-color
border-left-color
border-bottom-color
border-top-style
border-right-style
border-left-style
border-bottom-style

The Positioning Properties

position
top
bottom
right
display
clear
z-index

The Parts of a CSS Rule

A CSS rule is made up of a selector (p.alert in this example), and a declaration (the items inside the braces):

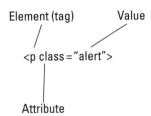

Selector   Property

p.alert {color: red}

Class name   Value

A matching element in an HTML document

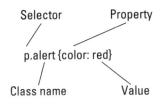

Element (tag)   Value

<p class = "alert">

Attribute

This figure shows the parts of a CSS *rule*. This rule says, "Display in red the text of any paragraph <p> in the document with a class name attribute alert."

You can make up any name for the class name (I chose *alert* here), but the name in the CSS rule must match the name later used in the HTML attribute.

For Dummies: Bestselling Book Series for Beginners

CSS Web Design For Dummies®

Cheat Sheet

Internet Explorer Colors

You can specify any of these colors as values for such properties as `background-color` or `color` (text color) for Internet Explorer:

AliceBlue, AntiqueWhite, Aqua, Aquamarine, Azure, Beige, Bisque, Black, BlanchedAlmond, Blue, BlueViolet, Brown, BurlyWood, CadetBlue, Chartreuse, Chocolate, Coral, CornflowerBlue, Cornsilk, Crimson, Cyan, DarkBlue, DarkCyan, DarkGoldenrod, DarkGray, DarkGreen, DarkKhaki, DarkMagenta, DarkOliveGreen, DarkOrange, DarkOrchid, DarkRed, DarkSalmon, DarkSeaGreen, DarkSlateBlue, DarkSlateGray, DarkTurquoise, DarkViolet, DeepPink, DeepSkyBlue, DimGray, DodgerBlue, FireBrick, FloralWhite, ForestGreen, Fuchsia, Gainsboro, GhostWhite, Gold, Goldenrod, Gray, Green, GreenYellow, Honeydew, HotPink, IndianRed, Indigo, Ivory, Khaki, Lavender, LavenderBlush, LawnGreen, LemonChiffon, LightBlue, LightCoral, LightCyan, LightGoldenrodYellow, LightGreen, LightGrey, LightPink, LightSalmon, LightSeaGreen, LightSkyBlue, LightSlateGray, LightSteelBlue, LightYellow, Lime, LimeGreen, Linen, Magenta, Maroon, MediumAquamarine, MediumBlue, MediumOrchid, MediumPurple, MediumSeaGreen, MediumSlateBlue, MediumSpringGreen, MediumTurquoise, MediumVioletRed, MidnightBlue, MintCream, MistyRose, Moccasin, NavajoWhite, Navy, OldLace, Olive, OliveDrab, Orange, OrangeRed, Orchid, PaleGoldenrod, PaleGreen, PaleTurquoise, PaleVioletRed, PapayaWhip, PeachPuff, Peru, Pink, Plum, PowderBlue, Purple, Red, RosyBrown, RoyalBlue, SaddleBrown, Salmon, SandyBrown, SeaGreen, Seashell, Sienna, Silver, SkyBlue, SlateBlue, SlateGray, Snow, SpringGreen, SteelBlue, Tan, Teal, Thistle, Tomato, Turquoise, Violet, Wheat, White, WhiteSmoke, Yellow, YellowGreen

For Dummies: Bestselling Book Series for Beginners